Tasks for Language Teachers

A resource book for training and development

Martin Parrott

CAMBRIDGE
UNIVERSITY PRESS

Published by the Press Syndicate of the University of Cambridge
The Pitt Building, Trumpington Street, Cambridge CB2 1RP
40 West 20th Street, New York, NY 10011–4211, USA
10 Stamford Road, Oakleigh, Melbourne 3166, Australia

© Cambridge University Press 1993

First published 1993
Third printing 1995

Printed in Great Britain
by Bell & Bain Ltd, Glasgow

Library of Congress cataloguing in publication data

Parrott, Martin.
  Tasks for language teachers: a resource book for training and
  development / Martin Parrott.
  p.   cm. – (Cambridge teacher training and development)
  ISBN 0-521-41648-5. – ISBN 0-521-42666-9 (pbk.)
  1. Language teachers – Training of. I. Title. II. Series.
  P53.85.P37 1993   92–34467
  418'.007–dc20   CIP

A catalogue record for this book is available from the British Library

ISBN 0 521 41648 5   hardback
ISBN 0 521 42666 9   paperback

WD

Tasks for Language Teachers

CAMBRIDGE TEACHER TRAINING AND DEVELOPMENT

Series Editors: Ruth Gairns and Marion Williams

This series is designed for all those involved in language teacher training and development: teachers in training, trainers, directors of studies, advisers, teachers of in-service courses and seminars. Its aim is to provide a comprehensive, organised and authoritative resource for language teacher training and development.

Teach English – A training course for teachers
by Adrian Doff
Trainer's Handbook
Teacher's Workbook

Models and Metaphors in Language Teacher Training – Loop input and other strategies
by Tessa Woodward

Training Foreign Language Teachers – A reflective approach
by Michael J. Wallace

Literature and Language Teaching – A guide for teachers and trainers
by Gillian Lazar

Classroom Observation Tasks – A resource book for language teachers and trainers
by Ruth Wajnryb

Tasks for Language Teachers – A resource book for training and development
by Martin Parrott

English for the Teacher – A language development course
by Mary Spratt

Teaching Children English – A training course for teachers of English to children
by David Vale with Anne Feinstein

Contents

List of Tasks in Part B

Thanks

I have worked in International House for many years and could not have written this book without the support and help of colleagues during this time, and without the ideas I have gained from participants on courses for teachers run in International House and elsewhere. I regret that the individuals to whom I am indebted are too numerous to name.

I should also like to express my particular gratitude to my colleague, Benita Cruickshank, and to Andrew Scales of Pitman School of English for piloting draft materials from this book and for giving me invaluable feedback, and to my colleague Richard Acklam for reading an early draft of this book and restoring my confidence and enthusiasm when they were waning.

Finally, I should like to thank my series editor, Marion Williams, who has given me support and constructive criticism since the idea for this book was first mooted and Alison Silver for her inestimable help in the final stages of preparing the manuscript and for her unfailing patience and good humour.

Acknowledgements

The author and publishers are grateful to the authors, publishers and others who have given permission for the use of copyright material.

Thomas Nelson and Sons Ltd for the extract on p. 182 from *Counterpoint Coursebook – Beginners* by Mark Ellis and Printha Ellis; Oxford University Press for the extract on pp. 300–1 from *Streamline English: Departures* by Bernard Hartley and Peter Viney; Gail Ellis and Barbara Sinclair for the extract on pp. 303–5 from *Learning to Learn English*, published by Cambridge University Press; Michael Swan and Catherine Walter for the extract on pp. 306–7 from *The New Cambridge English Course* and for the extract on pp. 308–9 from *The New Cambridge English Course Teacher's Book*, published by Cambridge University Press; *The Observer* for 'Small scale schools' by Helen Pickles included in the extract on pp. 310–11 from *Fast Forward 3* by Marion Geddes, published by Oxford University Press; Cambridge University Press for the illustrations on pp. 312–13 from *Discussions that Work* by Penny Ur; Longman Group UK Ltd for the extract on pp. 314–17 from *Building Strategies* by Brian Abbs and Ingrid Freebairn.

Introduction

Principles behind this book

Any materials designed for teaching a language necessarily embody assumptions about the nature of language, the nature and objectives of learning a language, and what teaching a language involves. Similarly, materials designed for use in the training and professional development of language teachers embody assumptions about the nature of teaching and what is involved in helping teachers to become more effective in their work. The aim of this section is to make the assumptions embodied in this book explicit.

It is assumed in this book that while teachers and prospective teachers can constantly improve their awareness, knowledge and skills, this is not achieved by subscribing to any particular method, approach or set of precepts. It is assumed that there is no general 'right way' to teach. Teachers need to take account of the ways in which their students are predisposed to learn and to recognise the range of different predispositions which may be found in most groups of learners. These differences may be cultural, relating to local educational and intellectual traditions, or may be individual, relating to personality factors or to the effects of specific prior experience of learning. Teachers also need to take account of the fact that the skills and knowledge learners need or want to acquire will depend on the purposes for which they are learning.

Just as teachers need to take account of these factors as they relate to the specific learners in any group, they equally need to recognise and take account of their own individual preferences and predispositions as teachers. They must also recognise both the possibilities afforded by the educational traditions and systems in which they work and the constraints that are imposed by these.

In part, thus, developing professional competence involves teachers in investigating the ways in which their students are disposed to learn and the purposes for which they are learning. It involves teachers in exploring their own dispositions on the one hand and more external factors in their working environments on the other. Developing professional competence also involves, however, teachers identifying their own assumptions about the nature of language and of learning and teaching. It involves them in examining and developing their 'experiential knowledge' (their opinions and beliefs about learning and teaching based on their own experience of language classrooms), and extending their 'received knowledge' (for example, their knowledge of theories of language, of the psychology of language learning, and of opinions, beliefs and practices which are different from their own). (See Wallace, 1991, pp. 14–15 for a fuller discussion of 'experiential' and 'received knowledge'.)

The aim of this book is in part to help teachers to increase their awareness and knowledge in these various fields. However, the Tasks in this book also aim to encourage them to question and evaluate their assumptions, their awareness and their knowledge, and ultimately to modify these. Teachers are constantly required to use their experience to test out theory, and to use theory to test out their assumptions.

The place of task-based activities in language teacher training and development

This book aims to provide a resource pool of Tasks which groups of teachers will work on collaboratively. This is not to suggest that all teacher training should be task-based and indeed, in most training circumstances task-based activities will be used in conjunction with a range of alternative activities such as lectures, seminars, demonstrations, observation of teaching and 'loop input'. (Refer to Ellis, 1986 for a discussion of a full range of teacher training activities and refer to Woodward, 1991 for a discussion of 'loop input'.)

The use of tasks in language teacher training and development, however, is particularly appropriate where participants are encouraged to value their own experience, beliefs, opinions and knowledge, and to reflect on these and evaluate them in the light of new input. Collaboration in carrying out tasks means that this input comes not only from the tasks and from the materials which accompany them, but also from a sharing of diverse experience, opinions, beliefs and knowledge.

The Tasks in this book encourage participants to make explicit and to analyse a wide range of factors relating to their own experience of learning and teaching languages, and to investigate the experience and opinions of their students and colleagues. Input is provided in many of the Tasks, but participants are asked to evaluate this according to their own experience, and to 'test it out' in the context of small-scale classroom-based research projects. The book, thus, subscribes to what Michael Wallace calls a 'Reflective' model of teacher education in which 'trainees' engage both 'received knowledge' and 'experiential knowledge' in a process which Wallace calls the 'reflective cycle'. (See Wallace, 1991, pp. 6–15 for a discussion of 'Reflective', 'Craft' and 'Applied Science' models of teacher education.)

A further advantage of task-based activities in teacher training is that the process the participants/teachers engage in resembles the process that the learners themselves engage in in any classroom where they collaborate together. The teachers are thus learning something about the experience of their students, or are at least re-familiarising themselves with the experience. These Tasks may also be seen as a 'mirror' of the learning activities teachers may initiate in the classroom in that they pre-suppose both that participants bring their own experience and knowledge to the process of learning, and that this experience and knowledge are to be valued and that they form the basis for further learning.

This task-based approach ensures that the participants are actively involved, and that (in many of the Tasks) they are taking the kinds of decisions that they need to take in the classroom. For example, some of the Tasks ask them to think about the content of lessons and the sequencing of activities. In doing this they are not only exposed to alternative approaches (from other group members as well as from the material itself) but, in discussing the choices available to them, they are obliged to examine the assumptions which underlie their 'normal' practice.

Who this book is for

PARTICIPANTS

The Tasks in this book may be used by teachers working alone or, preferably, in small groups. Although they are suitable for use by teachers working in a wide range of circumstances, and both for teachers who are and are not native speakers of the language, most of the Tasks pre-suppose that the teachers already have some classroom experience. In the case of potential or 'pre-service' teachers, lack of teaching experience may to some extent be compensated for through observation of classes, through 'teaching practice', and even through activating the experience of having been language learners themselves. Most of the Tasks are suitable for teachers of learners of any age or level of attainment, and they may be used both by groups of teachers with similar experience of learning and teaching, and by those whose experience is diverse.

The Tasks vary in the amount of experience and knowledge they assume. Where it is felt that knowledge of a specific subject is important for participants to gain maximum benefit from a Task, reading is recommended in the notes which accompany that Task.

The Tasks in this book will be of interest to all teachers who wish to extend their professional competence, and in particular to those who feel the need for input to stimulate and motivate them in their work. It will be of interest to those who feel that their teaching has become routine, and that they are in some sense 'in a rut'. The Tasks aim, primarily, to develop the sensitivity and awareness of teachers so that they feel confident to initiate informed change in their teaching, and so that they have a sense of direction to follow in initiating such change. Many of the Tasks, moreover, refer explicitly to classroom activities, in some cases describe them, and frequently ask participants to compare their practical experience. Participants who feel that there is a lack of variety in their teaching will thus find that working with these materials also introduces them to new ideas for classroom activities even where this is not a primary aim of the material.

Although this material has been prepared with institutional programmes of training and development in mind (i.e. programmes not necessarily leading to a formal qualification), many of the Tasks in this book are suitable for use in courses leading to state teaching qualifications or to qualifications such as the RSA/Cambridge COTE, DOTE and DTEFLA, or Diplomas in TESOL awarded by universities.

Teachers intending to follow a course in English Language Teaching or Applied Linguistics at Masters level will also find many of the Tasks particularly useful as an introduction to and preparation for issues which are dealt with more fully at this level. In particular, the book introduces a certain amount of basic terminology, making clear both the terms themselves and the concepts to which they refer.

Most of the Tasks in the book are of relevance to teachers of any foreign language. Where examples of language or language-learning activities and materials are given in the Tasks, however, reference is made specifically to English. These references can be adapted so that the Tasks address the needs of teachers of other languages.

TRAINERS

This book is intended not only for use by professional teacher trainers, but also for directors of studies, senior teachers and, indeed, anyone who has the responsibility for organising sessions in a programme of teacher education or development. The book can be used as a course in itself, but it also provides a resource for trainers to select from in supplementing their courses. It will be of particular use to trainers who have little familiarity with a task-based approach to teacher training and who may value guidance in using this approach. It will also be of particular use to trainers who are familiar with this approach but who would like some input to their work in the form of new ideas.

The notes which accompany each of the Tasks are intended to provide guidance to trainers who feel that they may benefit from support and direction in selecting and using the Tasks. Experienced trainers may sometimes prefer to use and adapt the Tasks with little reference to these notes.

Choice of topics

A number of general topic areas are specified, and these have been chosen with an eye to the kinds of interests expressed by practising teachers who have the opportunity to attend courses of professional development or teachers' groups. Within each topic area some Tasks focus on background issues while others focus on aspects of classroom methodology. This 'focus' is always made clear in the title and expressed aim of the Task, and in the accompanying notes.

Certain topics lend themselves to a more theoretical orientation than others. Thus, for example, many of the Tasks in Part B Chapter 4 *The learners* have a more generally theoretical emphasis than many of those in Chapter 7 *Teaching: Developing skills*.

In addition to the *Contents* page and the *List of Tasks in Part B*, which list these major topic areas, there is a more detailed index at the back of the book. This enables materials which are relevant to a particular topic to be located, even where this topic is not its primary focus.

Each chapter provides a range of Tasks on a general topic and normally the trainer or the participants themselves will select the Tasks of most relevance and interest to them. Although there is no sense in which a chapter should necessarily be 'worked through' systematically, there is minimal overlap between the different Tasks and participants can also use all the material in each chapter in this way if time permits. Most of the Discussion Tasks are divided into a number of sections. Groups of participants may work on different sections simultaneously, and in any session a combination of sections from different Tasks may be used in order to achieve a particular emphasis or balance.

How the book is organised

Part A of the book comprises three chapters.

Chapter 1 *Using the Tasks* deals with general methodological issues related to the use of these materials. Although it will be of interest to participants, it is intended primarily for the trainer, and sets out basic procedures which are recommended for exploiting the materials, and looks at some of the problems which may arise and at ways in which these problems may be approached (specific details on how to use each Task can be found in the notes that accompany that Task).

This chapter also includes a short section for teachers using this book without a trainer.

Chapter 2 *Carrying out small-scale research in the classroom* provides both trainers and participants with some guidelines for conducting classroom-based research. The Classroom-based Tasks in this book involve participants carrying out small experiments or surveys, and this part of the book offers general advice, suggestions and warnings to help them in this work. It also offers a more extended rationale for the inclusion of Classroom-based Tasks, both in the book and, more generally, in any programme of professional training or development for teachers.

Chapter 3 *Devising and evaluating Tasks* aims to help the trainer to look at the material in the book analytically. It also aims to give guidance to trainers in devising their own tasks on topics which are not dealt with in the book, and for adapting or supplementing the Tasks in the book for use in particular circumstances.

Part B contains five chapters, each focussing on a particular topic. The Tasks in each chapter aim not only to highlight issues of general relevance or of particular interest within the field, but also to illustrate some of the different kinds of Task which may be used in teacher training and development.

Each chapter is prefaced by an *Introduction to the chapter*. This includes a list of the *Contents*, provides further information relevant to the topic (*General discussion of issues*) and reviews some of the relevant background literature (*Reading*). These sections may be used by the trainer in preparation for the sessions, by the participants in following up the work they have done in the sessions and by teachers who are working with the Tasks on their own.

The chapter is further divided into *Discussion Tasks* and *Classroom-based Tasks*, and each Task is accompanied by supporting notes, which provide trainers with detailed guidance to help them in preparing and running sessions, and to participants should they want to follow up their discussion.

These supporting notes are divided into *Suggestions for procedure* and *General discussion and possible outcomes*.

Part C, the *Resources bank*, contains the different materials that the Tasks refer to. It is divided into three sections:
Section 1 *Compositions written by learners of English*
Section 2 *Schemes of work and lesson plans*
Section 3 *Extracts from published materials*

Types of task

Within each topic area there is a range of kinds of task. Although they all involve some degree of discussion of issues, some Discussion Tasks contain a small amount of informational input for this, while others aim more to encourage evaluation and reflection on the experience that the teachers already have. Many Discussion Tasks also include both.

Classroom-based Tasks require participants to try out particular ideas in the classroom and to evaluate their effectiveness or to conduct some informal research into the attitudes and learning of their students.

There are very rarely 'correct' answers to the Tasks – in most cases the exchange of ideas and thinking-through of issues are the justification for the activity. The emphasis is thus primarily on process rather than on the transmission of a certain set of precepts.

It is recognised, however, that participants may sometimes want some kind of product in the form of a set of possible guidelines, procedures or principles. Although the Tasks encourage participants to arrive at these themselves, the notes which accompany each Task also suggest possible outcomes. It is important that these are not perceived to be doctrines or 'final answers'.

These issues are dealt with at length in Part A Chapter 1 *Using the Tasks*.

A note on language used in this book

Throughout this book the terms 'trainer' and 'participant' are used. This is for the sake of convenience – the 'trainers' are not necessarily assumed to be professional teachers of teachers, although this will sometimes be the case. They might equally well be volunteers or appointed members of informal teacher development groups who have assumed the responsibility for 'leading' particular sessions. The term 'participant' is used to describe the teachers or prospective teachers (the 'students of teaching') who are the users of the Tasks.

Both 'he' and 'she' are used in the book to refer to individual learners and teachers. In an attempt to be fair to everyone I have used 'she' in the odd-numbered chapters and Tasks and 'he' in the even-numbered ones.

Photocopying

In cases where it is not possible for each participant to have a copy of the book, the trainer may photocopy relevant pages of the Tasks for use by the participants. Pages which may be photocopied are clearly marked '© Cambridge University Press 1993'. The participants should file these photocopied Tasks under the relevant chapter heading, in numerical order, for future reference.

1 Using the Tasks

1.1 Introduction

As stated in the Introduction, very few of the Discussion Tasks are intended to lead to a 'correct' answer. They provide a framework in which to reflect on and analyse beliefs, assumptions and experience. The Tasks are intended to lead the users to increased awareness of the processes involved in language learning, and of the range of options available to the teacher. The role of the trainer is thus very much one of facilitator, and only rarely one of provider. It is assumed that she will be responsible for selecting Tasks (often in conjunction with the course participants themselves), for setting them up and for 'chairing' subsequent plenary discussion or for coordinating the presentation of results of experiments and research. It is important that these expectations and the rationale behind them are discussed with the participants so that they are not looking for 'right' answers' where this is inappropriate.

1.2 Setting up and managing Discussion Tasks

Most of the Discussion Tasks envisage that participants work together in groups of three or four, brainstorming ideas, answering questions, discussing statements or carrying out a variety of other activities which similarly involve the sharing and comparison of ideas and experience. Where this is not the case, this is made clear in the accompanying *Suggestions for procedure.*

The most practical way of dividing a large group into these smaller groups may often be simply according to where people are sitting in the room. However, for some of the Tasks there will be a distinct and obvious advantage in the small groups being either diverse or homogeneous in terms of the experience of their members. In this case the trainer can prepare a list of the names of the participants, already 'grouped' in advance, or make clear the principle on which the groups should form, and leave it to the participants to ensure that their small groups include an appropriate balance. If the participants do not know each other well, some minutes can initially be devoted to their exchanging personal information so that they create a more comfortable working relationship.

The small groups may feel more secure in carrying out the Task if they are clear about the amount of time they have. The trainer may like to advise them of this or discuss it with them before beginning the activity, and often it may be constructive to find out how much longer they feel they need some time before this provisional 'deadline' is reached by stopping the activity and asking for a show of hands. In the case of longer Tasks, trainers may wish to discuss and determine the allocation of time in this way section by section.

During the small-group discussion, the trainer will probably move from group to group simply monitoring the discussion, but may also either become involved in that discussion herself or keep completely apart from the small groups. The role of the trainer during small-group discussion may depend on how she is perceived by the participants (if she is perceived as an equal it may be easier for her to become involved in the discussion, whereas if she is in any way perceived as threatening, she may prefer to keep apart).

Depending on the amount of time available during a session, only selected sections of a Discussion Task may be used or, indeed, a combination of sections from different Tasks. These may follow consecutively, or different Tasks or sections of Tasks may be assigned to different small groups to work on simultaneously, who will then 'present' the Task as well as their conclusions to the whole group in a plenary mode. Where more than one section of a Task is used in one session, the interest of participants may be sustained most effectively by organising plenary presentations and discussions after each section, rather than at the very end of the session. On occasions the trainer may also want to integrate some plenary discussion after just one or two items in a section of a Task have been discussed in small groups. This may be particularly appropriate where clarification of terminology or concepts is involved. Where it is thought to be advisable, reference is made to this in the accompanying *Suggestions for procedure*.

1.3   Preparation for Discussion Tasks

A projected 'timing' is provided for each Task and each section of each Task. The precise time any activity takes, however, will depend on the extent to which participants are interested in the topic and on how much they know about it. It will also depend on the size of the groups and on whether all the sections of the Task are used, and on whether they are used consecutively or simultaneously. This projected 'timing', thus, is given only as a guide, to be used flexibly in differing circumstances.

Very few of the Discussion Tasks require specific preparation by participants in advance. However, there are two ways in particular that discussion in small groups can be facilitated.

Participants can be asked to look at the Task in advance and to make provisional notes on their own response, so that the process of initial reflection has been carried out when the collaborative work begins. Although this saves time, where this is not feasible (because the group does not meet on a regular basis or because participants have very little free time) the Tasks can still be used successfully.

The second kind of preparation is reading. Some of the Tasks (particularly in Chapter 4) are greatly facilitated by some particular 'received knowledge' among members of the group. In cases where it is felt that this may be lacking, participants can be asked to acquaint themselves with the relevant texts in advance of the session. The collaborative nature of the Tasks means that not all the participants need to have read all the texts. It may be sufficient for each of the members of the small group to have read different parts of a text or different texts, or it may be sufficient for only one member of each small group to have read the text. Where it is felt that an element of 'received knowledge' is essential, the notes which accompany the Task make this clear and provide specific references. The notes accompanying many of the Tasks also make reference to optional reading. If some of the participants have already looked at the texts, this is an advantage although it is not essential.

1.4   Setting up and managing Classroom-based Tasks

The first stage of this process is likely to take place at the end of a session which has been devoted to a Discussion Task on a topic related to that of the Classroom-based Task.

Participants can be asked to look at the Classroom-based Task, and in pairs or small groups to brainstorm ways in which it might be carried out. Where the Task involves preparation of a questionnaire, this often requires work in pairs or small groups followed by a more general discussion of the issues and, possibly, a finalisation of the form and content of the questionnaire. A substantial amount of time may need to be devoted to this during a session, and provision for this needs to be made in the overall planning of the allocation of time during that session.

In most cases it is recommended that a small number of participants actually carry out the research. Where this is the case, a meeting between them may need to be planned at which they will compare their results and decide how to present these to the rest of the group at a subsequent session. The time of the final session may need to be agreed in advance both in this case and in cases where all participants are involved in carrying out the Task. Where the trainer anticipates that problems of either logistics or motivation may arise in the carrying out of the Task, she may also want to organise some system of monitoring and coordination of the participants concerned, although it may be another participant rather than herself who takes on this responsibility.

Organisation of the session in which feedback on the Classroom-based Tasks is presented and discussed may resemble that of the Discussion Task sessions (see 1.2) where all participants have been involved in the Task. Where selected participants have been involved, feedback may be given in a written format (if this has been pooled and collated at a previous meeting between the participants), or in the form of brief lecture-style presentations. In either case this will normally be followed by plenary questions and discussion. Much of the following section (1.5) is relevant to the organisation of this.

1.5   Reporting back

The Discussion Tasks invariably pre-suppose that the 'core' of the thinking and learning takes place in small groups of three or four participants. Sometimes this will be enough, and on occasions the accompanying *Suggestions for procedure* recommend that the activity is left at this point. However, more frequently it may be desirable to follow small-group discussion with some form of plenary presentation and discussion. This is particularly the case where the small groups have been working on different sections of a Task or on different Tasks, or where the small groups have been constituted in such a way that each or some of them represent groupings of people with a particular kind of experience. Moreover, participants may well be curious about the conclusions of the other groups, or while monitoring discussion in the groups, the trainer may have identified particular divergences of opinion, or particular points of interest which she feels are valuable for everyone to hear, or points of confusion which she feels need to be aired and cleared up.

This section suggests some ways of organising the reporting back and group discussion ensuing from the small-group collaboration on the Discussion Tasks or from the Classroom-based Tasks. Choice of mode will depend on the equipment and resources available (e.g. use of OHP) as well as on the nature of the Task (this is dealt with below). The allocation of time to this part of the session will depend on the degree of interest of the participants. It is important that plenary discussion does not simply 'drag on' with the regurgitation of points already made by other groups, or with discussion monopolised by one or two voluble participants. It is also important that clear instructions are given to the group – whether to summarise the discussion, itemise the main points or, perhaps, simply to pick out one or two points of particular interest or contention.

1 **Group spokesperson** A 'group secretary/spokesperson' can be appointed in each small group. They will make notes during the discussion and then present the points to the re-constituted large group orally or by using the board or OHP. It is important that subsequent spokespeople are clear as to whether or not they should simply skip over points already made by previous representatives of other small groups.

This format is particularly suitable where discussion has been wide-ranging and the aim of the 'reporting back' is not so much to summarise this as to draw attention to points which may be of particular interest to other participants.

2 **Posters** Groups can design a poster jointly in a format which represents their views/feelings, or a secretary can be appointed in each small group. They can make notes on a sheet of paper which will then be 'posted' on the wall sufficiently far apart from those of the other groups for participants to wander around and read the conclusions reached by the different groups. This may be followed by a plenary session in which participants comment on points made in the other groups.

3 **Overhead projector** Where there is access to an OHP, the secretary can record points on an OHP transparency and then simply show these to the large group, who may ask for clarification or question any of the points.

This format is particularly suited to reporting back on an activity in which points have been classified or ranked in some way.

4 **Re-constituting groups** Each member of each small group can record points on a piece of paper. The groups are then re-constituted so that the new groups comprise one member of each of the previous ones, who then share their conclusions. One straightforward way of organising this is to number the members of each group (1–?). All the number 1s then form a new group as do all the number 2s, 3s, etc.

5 **'Plenary circle'** The group can also be re-constituted to form a circle. Comments are made to the whole group by individual participants (frequently after an initial silence).

This format is particularly valuable where the discussion has involved reflection on personal experience and the comments are to some extent 'from the heart'. The role of the trainer is firstly to encourage and confirm, and secondly to indicate an order for speaking if several people want to speak at the same time. If the trainer wishes to add comments, these may also be 'from the heart'.

1.6 'Round-up' by the trainer

On the whole this material assumes that the comments made by the participants in the activities are valid in their own right. Trainers may be tempted to add to the discussion what they see to be 'key points' that the group has missed. However, trainers are advised to be very circumspect in doing this as the points which seem crucial or even obvious to the trainer may well not be appropriate to the participants at their particular stage in thinking through the issues. The assumption which underlies most of the material in this book is that the crucial learning takes place in the process of carrying out the Tasks rather than in conclusions presented to participants subsequently.

There will, nevertheless, be occasions when the trainer feels that it is useful to tie ends together and crystallise points which have been raised by the participants. This may particularly be the case where the Task involves dealing with terminology which is only partially familiar to some of the group, and there will also be occasions where the trainer feels that there is a psychological need in the group for confirmation and expansion of their conclusions. Participants may also get a sense of security from the points they have made being organised into some form of systematic framework and reported back to them.

The notes which accompany each task include *Possible outcomes* to the discussion, and these may be useful to the trainer in deciding what points, if any, to add.

Here are some of the approaches the trainer may choose to adopt where she has decided that she does need to make points for one of these purposes:

1 Points can be written up on the board as they are elicited from the small groups. The trainer can comment on them/add to them and structure/organise them as she goes along.

   This technique is widely practised but puts considerable pressure on a trainer in terms of having to think quickly.

2 The trainer can elicit all the points and then make her own.

3 The trainer can elicit all the points and then present the group with a pre-prepared list of her own (using an OHP or photocopied handouts where these facilities are available). She might draw attention to those points which were not mentioned by representatives of the small groups and to any particular structure she has used in organising her own points. Alternatively, she may simply ask for comment on any differences that participants perceive between the points they have made and those of the trainer.

1.7 Procedural problems which may arise and measures for dealing with them

To some extent the skills of managing groups of teachers are little different from those of managing groups of learners. Nonetheless, it is also the case that less experienced teacher trainers or 'group leaders' working with a team of colleagues may feel inhibited about operating a 'teacher-like' degree of control in training circumstances. The following hints are offered with this in mind.

Problem 1.   Discussion in the small groups seems unfocussed and is 'off the point'.

When this happens it may be worthwhile for the trainer to gain the attention of the whole group and to draw attention explicitly to what she perceives the problem to be. Participants themselves will often offer solutions, perhaps involving a modification in the activity.

It is also possible that the precise aim of the section of the Task is insufficiently clear. This aim can be made explicit, and the trainer can give examples of the kinds of points she would expect to be made.

Sometimes it may emerge at this stage that the Task itself is insufficiently related to the interests and experience of the participants. In this case it may be worthwhile bringing the activity to a premature close. Another Task from the same chapter may be more appropriate and can be used in its place.

Alternatively, it may sometimes also be the case that the discussion which is perceived as being 'off the point' has simply shifted to accommodate the participants' real preoccupations. Before addressing ways of 'bringing the discussion round to the point', the trainer may want to listen and ask questions to ascertain whether this is the case, and may decide to take advantage of the shift in topic and to encourage rather than curtail the discussion which is under way.

Problem 2.   The discussion in small groups is dominated by one individual.

This problem is familiar to most teachers but can be more difficult to deal with if the group comprises colleagues. Such problems are often better noted silently. If there is to be a series of sessions with the same group, it may be helpful to discuss the problem with the dominant person privately before the next session.

Alternatively, dominant people may be given a special responsibility within the small group. For example, they may be asked to chair the discussion and to ensure that everyone gets the opportunity to contribute, or to act as spokesperson for the group and to note down points made by other participants.

Problem 3.   Some groups work much faster than others.

In any discussion activity it can be helpful for the trainer to estimate the time required and to tell the participants in advance how long she thinks the activity will last. Halfway through this period she can check with each group how much more time they feel they would like to have, and continue checking periodically. It also helps, sometimes, to point out to unusually slow or fast groups how quickly they are carrying out the Tasks in relation to the others.

Since the emphasis in most of these Tasks is on process rather than product, it is rarely essential to cover a particular quantity of ground, and it is often advisable to stop the activity when the first group begins to feel that they have exhausted the Task.

Problem 4.   In the plenary discussion, the small-group discussion is rehashed and representatives of the small groups repeat points already made.

When this happens it may be advisable for the trainer to gain everyone's attention, to point out what is happening and to state very clearly that she only wants points to be made which are additional to those which have already been presented.

Problem 5.   The course participants seem reluctant to value their own experience and judgements, and are eager for the trainer to provide a 'correct' answer.

This problem requires considerable skill on the part of the trainer as a fine balance has to be achieved between providing a sufficient degree of the psychological security sought on the one hand, and not 'hijacking' the discussion and stifling the participants' thinking and confidence in the value of their own observations on the other.

Where this problem arises, it is advisable for trainers to 'come clean' about their own point of view and to negotiate this balance with the group, subsequently monitoring and checking with the participants the extent to which an appropriate balance is being achieved. With some groups of teachers who really do not value their own experience and judgement, a process of 'weaning' can take place over several sessions.

It is also important that the rationale for the Tasks and the trainer's approach are discussed (and to some extent 'negotiated' with participants) before the Tasks are used.

1.8   Using the Tasks without a trainer

The preceding discussion has assumed the involvement of a teacher trainer or designated 'session leader'. Groups of teachers working together may also use this material without anyone necessarily leading or organising the activity. In such cases it may be desirable for everyone involved to read this chapter and to begin each session by agreeing on the Task(s) to be used as well as on a procedure and a provisional allocation of time for the Task(s).

2 Carrying out small-scale research in the classroom

2.1 Introduction

Each of the chapters in Part B includes at least one Classroom-based Task, and it is the aim of this chapter to provide a general introduction to the topic, and to offer some practical advice in the form of hints and warnings. There is a considerable literature which deals with classroom-based research and any reader wanting to explore the area further will find the following of particular interest:

Nunan, D. (1989), *Understanding Language Classrooms*, Prentice Hall.
Brumfit, C. & Mitchell, R. (1989), *ELT Documents 133: The Language Classroom as a Focus for Research*, Modern English Publications in association with the British Council.
Allwright, R. & Bailey, K. (1991), *Focus on the Language Classroom*, Cambridge University Press.

2.2 Research as a tool in teacher training

The Discussion Tasks in this book aim to help participants to expand their awareness of factors which affect their students' learning, and which affect choices made about the organisation of activities in the classroom and the use of techniques and materials. They aim to encourage an attitude of ongoing exploration and enquiry.

The Classroom-based Tasks are intended to complement these. They provide a systematic framework in which to carry out this 'exploration and enquiry'. They aim to provide participants with means of obtaining data about the extent to which certain ideas about teaching and learning appear to be confirmed (or otherwise) in the particular circumstances in which they work. They also aim to develop in participants a general willingness to question and explore assumptions, and to use the classroom as a basis for testing these out.

The Classroom-based Tasks suggest particular areas for enquiry, but it is intended that teachers develop the practice of using a similar methodology to enquire into areas which their experience or reading may have led them to wonder about, and to use the results of this enquiry both to help them to refine their beliefs and assumptions and to formulate new questions to pose and to stimulate further research.

Research of this kind may also be of particular value where teachers are offered points of view which appear unacceptable to them. In such instances there may be a temptation to dismiss the point of view ('It wouldn't work with a class of fifty!' or 'My kids would never be prepared to do that in front of everyone else!'). In such cases, a small-scale research project may help teachers to discover the extent to which this point of view really is or is not 'acceptable' in the particular circumstances in which they work. One of the processes of teacher development or training which this book espouses, thus, is a cycle of reflection → action → reflection → action, etc., in which research tasks provide the primary tool for 'action'.

The very term 'research' can sometimes seem daunting, conjuring up visions of years of devising tests and surveys, and further years of statistically analysing the data. While large-scale research projects of this kind have their place, the view of research which is presented in this book is far more modest. The scale of the research projects suggested here is deliberately small. The results of these projects are not in any way assumed to be definitive, but should generally be regarded as provisional and tentative, to be subjected to ongoing testing and evaluation. The basic assumption is that even provisional and tentative evidence is better than unsupported 'hunches' or no evidence at all.

The Classroom-based Tasks provide a 'taster' for research. It is beyond the aims and scope of this book to introduce participants to the complexities of extensive research methodology. Participants who find particular interest and enjoyment in carrying out these Classroom-based Tasks, and who would like to develop their skills in this field, may be motivated to attend an academic course which deals with research more extensively and systematically.

2.3   Research techniques

There are many models and techniques of classroom-based research (comprehensively discussed and illustrated in Nunan, 1989). The Tasks in this book, however, require only a small number of techniques to be used, and the following list outlines some of the features both of these techniques and of other 'simple' techniques which participants and trainers may wish to employ in extending these Tasks or in devising complementary Classroom-based Tasks of their own.

1 Observation schedules
  These enable teachers to develop a more objective understanding of what is happening in their classes.

2 Tests
   These help teachers to learn more about their learners' needs and progress and about the effectiveness of their teaching.

3 Questionnaires, diaries and interviews
   These techniques enable teachers to learn more about their learners' perceptions or attitudes towards their own learning and the approaches, methods and materials used by the teacher.

The value of tests and questionnaires often rests in the repetition of their use. This may involve a 'before and after' situation where the test or questionnaire is administered twice, once before a change is initiated in the classroom, and once after. Alternatively, 'repetition' may involve the administration of the test or questionnaire to two groups whose experience of the subject being examined is in some way qualitatively different. (For example, the teacher explains all new vocabulary to Group 1 but obliges Group 2 to rely on dictionaries. Both groups might then take the same vocabulary test or complete a questionnaire focussing on how they like the teacher to deal with vocabulary.)

2.4   Observation schedules

The use of observation tasks or schedules is dealt with very fully in Wajnryb (1992). For the purposes of this book, an 'observation schedule' is considered to be a framework for directing the attention of an observer of a lesson, and for recording the results of this observation in a systematic way. The data provided by this experience is used for further analysis and reflection, not for any subjective judgement or criticism.

The ideal context for this observation is for a colleague to attend the lesson of a participant or, depending on the objectives of the task, for the participant to attend the lesson of a colleague. In either case, the presence of the observer should be discreet and, if either the class or the teacher finds the observation unsettling initially, the observation may need to be carried out after a number of 'visits' during which the presence of the observer comes to be taken more for granted. Where this is not feasible much can also be achieved through the use of video (or even audio) recordings of lessons.

It is intended that observation schedules suggested in this book or prompted by it should be simple and descriptive.

Example
The observer draws a 'map' of the classroom, showing where each student sits. Each time there is any interaction in the classroom he draws a line between the two interlocutors to show who is involved. The figure overleaf provides a completed example of such a schedule.

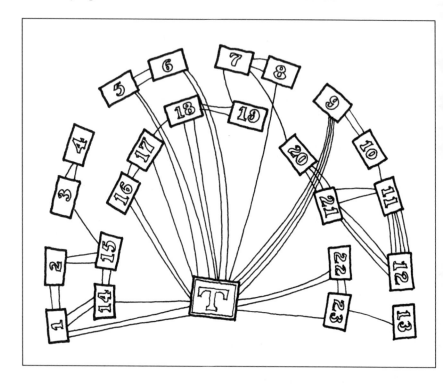

This task provides the teacher with an objective record of the amount of attention he gave to individual students in the lesson, about the balance between different focusses of interaction in the lesson (Teacher → Student, Student ↔ Student, etc.), or about the extent to which different students participated actively. Where this evidence differs from the teacher's subjective impressions, it may serve to develop the teacher's insight and sensitivity with regard to these factors in subsequent lessons.

Descriptive tasks of this kind provide concrete data about the nature of activity in the classroom. Where this differs from the teacher's subjective impressions about the activity, this provides a rich source for reflection and consequent learning. One advantage of their being purely descriptive is that they avoid the potential embarrassment of one colleague criticising another. The clarity of the implications of the results will depend on the nature of the schedule and of the results themselves, and these implications may often become clearer when a group of teachers compare the results of the same task carried out in their different classrooms. A completed 'map' of the classroom (as above) which reveals that the interaction is very largely between the teacher and a small number of individual students clearly raises questions about the involvement of the other students in the lesson, and the lack of interaction between students themselves.

2.5 Tests

These do not need to be complicated to be useful. A test can be as simple as a dictation of six monosyllabic words to test the ability to discriminate between two phonemes (e.g. /i/ /iː/ – fill; cheap; weak; chip; wick; feel), or it might be a brainstorming exercise in which two classes are each asked to write down as many words as they know on a particular topic. The number of different relevant words contributed jointly by the members of each class would then be compared.

It is beyond the scope of this book to deal with the complexities of the construction and piloting of tests. Tests used in small-scale research are not intended to provide definitive results, but simply to provide teachers with some form of feedback to set against impressionistic judgements about the effectiveness or otherwise of particular materials, techniques or approaches and to help them in making future decisions about using these.

2.6 Questionnaires, diaries and interviews

Many of the Classroom-based Tasks in this book involve the construction and administration of questionnaires. These are used to provide data about the general characteristics and preferences of learners, as well as to elicit the response of learners to specific factors in their learning experience. In each case detailed guidance is given to participants in the Task itself.

Diaries kept by learners and written up at the end of lessons or after them, also enable teachers to learn more about their learners' perceptions, responses and attitudes towards their experience of learning. Whole classes can be encouraged to keep diaries, or certain students may like to volunteer. Whether or not the teacher responds to the entries when he collects the diaries in (and the ways in which he responds) can be discussed and agreed between the teacher and the students in advance.

Although data from diaries is more difficult to quantify and process than the results of questionnaires, there is less danger of the responses being influenced by the specific questions asked. Teachers are also able to compare responses to specific lessons or parts of lessons without drawing attention to the fact that these have been, in some way, 'experimental'.

Teachers may also keep diaries and compare their own perceptions of how particular students have responded to particular events in the classroom with the learners' own perceptions.

Interviews with students, either individually or in groups, can constitute a compromise between the very tightly controlled responses to questionnaires and the very general, sometimes 'hit or miss', evidence from diaries. They may also be used to probe further into comments made in diaries and responses in questionnaires.

Where the 'interviewer' wishes the interviews to lead to general discussions of issues, it may be helpful for students to be interviewed in groups rather than individually.

As in the case of tests, the objectives of using these techniques are modest. They are intended to provide information to set against impressionistic judgements and to inform thinking and discussion. There is no sense in which participants are encouraged to act on the findings as though they were definitive.

2.7   Scale and simplicity

It is sometimes assumed that the wider and more complex the observation schedule, test or questionnaire is, the more reliable and illuminating the data gained will be. However, as many teachers who have been involved in classroom-based research have learnt through the experience of distributing ambitious tests or questionnaires to classes, this can result in accumulating data which is ultimately too complex or too weighty to analyse and interpret.

The Classroom-based Tasks in this book are intended to be simple and practical. Any claims as to the generalisability or reliability of their results are correspondingly modest – it is important that teachers are not tempted to generalise about other groups of students or groups in other circumstances on the basis of small, localised findings.

Where a large group of teachers is collaborating or participating in a programme of professional development using Tasks in this book, it makes sense for only a small number of them to agree to carry out a particular Classroom-based Task before comparing their results and reporting back to the larger group.

The following guidelines are generally applicable for teachers wanting to use research in a modest way in their classrooms:

1 Observation schedules
   Focus on only one factor of the teaching/learning context in one lesson (for example, patterns of interaction as in 2.4 above).

2 Tests
   – Include very few items.
   – Try to obtain data which is quantifiable. It helps if tests are constructed either so that answers can be judged clearly as right or wrong, or can be counted up so that the teacher has a figure or figures for comparison with a parallel figure or set of figures.
   – Use a very small sample. For example, if a test is administered to a

whole class, six students can be pre-selected whose results will be analysed.

3 Questionnaires, diaries and interviews
   The guidelines which relate to tests are equally applicable to questionnaires.
   – Although 'ranking' activities and open questions provide interesting data, this is often difficult to process. It may be more practical if answers are either yes/no or if they can be numerically recorded, e.g.
     1 I don't like this.
     2 I like this.
     3 I like this very much.
   – Again, very small samples may be used. (For example, if the aim of the investigation is to compare the responses of students who appear to learn with facility with the responses of those who have particular difficulty, two or three students in each category may be chosen for comparison.)

With regard to diaries and interviews, teachers may again prefer to look at the data provided by only certain pre-selected students. According to the circumstances in which they work and the amount of time available, participants will make decisions about whether or not to interview a whole class or ask a whole class to keep diaries. In this event they can then choose only to make use of the data from the selected students. Alternatively, they may be able to ask only the 'selected' students to keep the diary or take part in the interview.

2.8   Networking

'Networking' is desirable precisely because of the need to be modest about the scope of conclusions from individual research tasks of this nature. The more networking which takes place, the broader the picture teachers are able to establish.

On the smallest of scales, networking involves a group of teachers carrying out similar research tasks and simply pooling and exchanging the lessons they have learnt, noting similarities and arguing through possible causes of dissimilarity. This is the basic model of networking encompassed in this book. In the case of Tasks involving research of some kind, it is envisaged that a session is arranged for a specific time in the future, when the participants will come back having carried out their experiments to share and communicate their experience and conclusions.

Networking, however, can also take place on a considerably larger scale. Teachers on courses or development programmes, or involved in

B

local professional associations, can also exchange and compare their conclusions from classroom-based research tasks either through informal contacts or, more formally, through the exchange of news-letters or by submitting articles to journals.

3 Devising and evaluating Tasks

3.1 These Tasks as a model for creating new ones

Many teacher trainers or groups of teachers using these Tasks will probably find that they adapt them, leaving out some sections, adding components and changing others. There is no sense in which a collection of materials such as this could attempt or claim to be comprehensive. Inevitably, there will be topics missing or topics which are dealt with here at an inappropriate level or from an angle which is inappropriate for the needs of the particular group of participants.

It is thus intended that these Tasks will form the basis for trainers to devise new ones to fill the gaps as they are perceived in any particular circumstances. This chapter encourages the trainer to look at the Tasks in this book analytically, and provides some guidance for designing further Tasks.

3.2 Analysis of Tasks in this book

Each of the Tasks in this book can be classified and defined in relation to three variables:

a) Aim
b) Focus
c) Activity

Aim refers to the aim of the Task in general terms. Although in any Task certain aims will have particular prominence, there is a sense in which the aims are interdependent. In any programme of seminars, whether or not these constitute part of a formal training course, a wide range of these aims is likely to be covered.

Focus refers to the input which provides a stimulus for the activity (for example, in the form of a text which is used in the Task). The choice of **Focus** also determines, to some extent, the **Activity**.

The **Activity** refers to the manner of the participants' interaction with the stimulus provided in the Task, how the participants are exposed to the stimulus and the mechanics of what they do with it. For example, on a mechanical level a Task may involve *reading, numbering* and *ranking.*

The following taxonomies aim to list examples of the factors present in each of these categories. Although any such model inevitably simplifies the data and involves a degree of overlap and duplication, it is intended to provide a basis for describing the Tasks, and will help to generate further examples. The lists aim to be wide-ranging, but cannot claim to be comprehensive. Trainers and participants may well find that further items occur to them which could usefully be included here. One Task may, of course, include more than one **Aim, Focus** and **Activity.**

a)   Aim

Each Task is prefaced with a statement of what it aims to achieve. These aims are very specifically related to the topic of the Task and are expressed differently from the aims in the following taxonomy, which are intended to have a more general, topic-independent application.

The aims of the Tasks all involve an element of reflection, 'finding out', analysis and evaluation. However, these may be defined in greater detail.

1 Exploring experiential knowledge. Identifying and exploring assumptions: making the implicit explicit in order to test it against personal and external theory.
2 Exploring unrecognised complexity in issues which may appear to be superficially and misleadingly straightforward, e.g.
   – factors involved in learning.
3 Developing received knowledge, e.g.
   – of principles underlying materials and procedures;
   – of alternatives in classroom practice;
   – of historical context.
4 Developing awareness, e.g.
   – of own skills as a teacher.
5 Increasing the range of options available to the teacher in classroom practice, e.g.
   – through exposure to alternative approaches.
6 Developing sensitivity to learners, e.g.
   – the ways in which individuals respond to different kinds of activity in class;
   – their preferred learning styles and strategies.
7 Developing the skills of evaluating materials and procedures according to rationale.
8 Developing the skills of evaluating theory according to practice.

9 Developing pedagogic skills, e.g.
 – lesson planning.
10 Developing the ability to evaluate practice.

NOTE ON TERMINOLOGY

The terms *'received'* and *'experiential' knowledge* are considered in the Introduction (see pages 1–2).

Skills is used to refer both to cognitive skills (e.g. evaluating materials) and classroom skills (e.g. giving clear instructions).

Theory is used to refer to models of language and learning. For example, Krashen's distinction between language acquisition and language learning (frequently cited in Krashen's publications and possibly most accessible to teachers in Krashen & Terrell, 1983, pp. 26–7), and his proposition that language is acquired through exposure to and inter-action with comprehensible input would constitute an 'external' theory. A 'personal' theory is one which the teacher may have formulated through experience, and may not be conscious of. A teacher who automatically corrects learners' mistakes of grammar might thus be subscribing to a 'personal theory' which holds that controlled, correct language use facilitates learning.

Principles is used to refer to the discrete components of a theory. A principle related to the 'external' theory described above would be that teachers should provide learners with comprehensible input, and one which related to the 'personal' theory described above would be that mistakes of grammar should be corrected.

b) Focus

Some examples are:

1 Comments made by learners (from a series of brief statements to a diary study).
2 Comments made by teachers (from a series of brief statements to a diary study).
3 Comments made by writers ('recognised experts' or, in some cases, the designer of the Task) about learning and teaching.
4 Lesson plans (own and others').
5 Schemes of work (own and others').
6 Course materials.
7 Samples of students' output (written, or recorded on video or audio cassette).
8 Questionnaires and their results.
9 Explanatory written text.

10 Lists of terms.
11 Video or audio recordings of lessons or parts of lessons.
12 Transcripts of lessons.
13 Recordings or transcripts of discussion between teachers and/or learners.
14 Questions about the participants' beliefs or experience.

c) Activity

Participants may engage in some of the following activities:

1 Reading, e.g.
   - texts about teaching;
   - course materials;
   - statements made by learners.
2 Listening to, e.g.
   - tapes of lessons;
   - opinions of learners;
   - descriptions of the experience of colleagues or co-participants on the course.
3 Watching, e.g.
   - the activity and involvement of teachers and learners (either by being present in a lesson or watching a video).
4 Speaking, e.g.
   - collaborative brainstorming (pooling, exchanging and comparing opinions, ideas, knowledge, beliefs, assumptions and experience with co-participants in the Task);
   - asking questions of learners, etc.
5 Writing, e.g.
   - brainstorming ideas;
   - describing lessons;
   - preparing questionnaires;
   - summarising the results of research.
6 Drawing, e.g.
   - diagrams to represent the interaction in a class;
   - diagrams to represent the sequence of time in a graphic illustration of an aspect of the tense system.
7 Ticking, e.g.
   - to indicate agreement with statements;
   - to show approval of materials.
8 Numbering, e.g.
   - to show an approved order for items;
   - to rank ideas or statements.
9 Teaching, e.g.
   - to experiment with an unfamiliar approach;
   - to demonstrate an approach or technique.

10 Matching, e.g.
   - a procedure to a theoretical tenet;
   - the role a teacher is likely to be performing to an activity within a lesson.
11 Comparing, e.g.
   - personal opinions and experience with those of co-participants;
   - two or more lesson plans;
   - two or more mistakes made by a learner in a written text.
12 Ordering, e.g.
   - the stages in a particular lesson.
13 Ranking, e.g.
   - statements made about language learning according to the extent to which they reflect the participants' own beliefs.
14 Classifying, e.g.
   - grouping a series of statements about learning or teaching according to the theoretical assumptions underlying them.
15 Selecting, e.g.
   - materials which would be appropriate to a particular group of learners.
16 Recalling, e.g.
   - types of materials used in the classroom;
   - learning styles of students taught.
17 Producing, e.g.
   - materials for classroom use;
   - lesson plans and schemes of work;
   - questionnaires for eliciting opinions from learners.
18 Recording, e.g.
   - interviews with learners (audio);
   - lessons (own or colleagues' – audio, video or written).
19 Gathering data, e.g.
   - asking questions to colleagues or learners (informally or more systematically using a questionnaire).
20 Putting forward arguments, e.g.
   - justifying points of view with which the participant may or may not agree.
21 Adding, e.g.
   - personal examples to extend a given list of criteria for making decisions, characteristics of learners, etc.

3.3 Tasks: 'Level' of difficulty

The activities in the above list are in no particular order. However, it is clear that certain kinds of activity are logistically or cognitively more difficult than others. In selecting, adapting or devising Tasks, it is useful to bear this in mind in relation to factors such as the time available and the motivation and degree of experience of the participants.

Logistically, activities which involve ticking, numbering or ordering statements are clearly easier than those which involve producing materials, recording interviews or gathering data through questionnaires. However, even ticking, numbering or ordering statements can involve significant cognitive involvement on the part of participants, depending on the content of the statements. Where these relate to theories of learning and give rise to an evaluation of 'external' theories in relation to experiential knowledge, for example, the cognitive process is a complex one. The process may be still more demanding where participants are required not to comment in some way on data which is presented to them in the material, but instead are asked to brainstorm and pool their own ideas. Recording interviews may be a great deal simpler on this level.

3.4   Exercise to demonstrate the application of this taxonomy

The following is part of Discussion Task 8 (see page 94). It can be analysed using this three-part system of classification and each of these factors can be looked at in more detail.

Section A   *Roles and functions*

Look at the following 'role definitions' and the list of some of a teacher's functions.

For each of these functions, decide which role is most appropriate (in some cases more than one 'role' may be involved):

Roles
a) DIAGNOSTICIAN
b) PLANNER
c) MANAGER
d) PROVIDER

Functions
i)   To find out (as far and as consistently as possible) the needs, interests, language difficulties and preferred learning styles of the students.
ii)   To cater for these (as far as group exigencies allow).
iii) To foster a group feeling (cooperation, liking, common aims, mutual confidence, etc.).

iv) To ensure that learners have clear short and long-term learning objectives.

v) To assess the progress of individuals and of the class as a whole.

vi) To ensure that learners are aware of this progress.

vii) To encourage students to take responsibility for their learning.

viii) To vary patterns of interaction within the lesson according to the precise aims and the nature/feeling of the group.

ix) To ensure that the students find their involvement sufficiently challenging.

x) To analyse and present realistic 'chunks' of the target language for students to process.

xi) To select and introduce activities and materials for language work.

xii) To help students develop positive, individual strategies for learning.

Example *Function (i) – Role (a):* The teacher is clearly acting as a diagnostician in performing this function, although the results of this diagnosis will subsequently form the basis for the teacher to act as a planner (b).

a) Aim

Developing experiential knowledge; identifying and exploring assumptions

Many teachers have adopted a certain amount of ritual behaviour, and will perform certain roles in the classroom in a routine way. This Task aims to make teachers aware of these personal routines. (See Maingay, 1988 for a more extended discussion of ritual behaviour.)

Exploring unrecognised complexity in issues

These routines are often unconscious and, indeed, in the classroom teachers may be unaware of the roles they are performing. By focussing the participants' attention explicitly on the roles they perform, they are encouraged to consider the complexity of the range of choices available to them.

Increasing the range of options available to the teacher in classroom practice

By presenting a selection of the teachers' 'functions' and asking the participants to match these with 'roles', the Task begs the question of the procedures the teacher adopts to fulfil these functions. Different individuals will have different routine ways of doing this, and the discussion in groups should encourage the participants to consider alternatives to their own practice.

b)   *Focus*

Comments made by writers
In this case the material includes twelve descriptions of possible functions of a teacher. The 'writer' here is the designer of the Task.

Lists of terms
Four possible roles of a teacher are listed.

c)   *Activity*

Reading
Participants read the list of roles and the description of teachers' functions.

Speaking
As with all the Tasks in this book, participants are intended to share and compare their ideas, and to work towards a consensus. The discussion involved is intended to stimulate fresh thinking.

Matching
In this case roles are matched to functions.

Classifying
In this case functions are classified according to the role of the teacher.

3.5   Optional exercise on analysing Tasks

Choose any other Task from the book, preferably one with which you have practical familiarity.

Using this three-part taxonomy, specify the **aims, focus** and **activities** involved in carrying out the Task. If possible, work on this in partnership with a colleague and compare the results of your analysis.

3.6   Devising further tasks

The primary aim of elaborating this taxonomy is to provide examples of the wide range of choices available to the task designer, and also to provide a checklist that the trainer may find useful to consult before and during the process of task design.

Exactly how a trainer uses this will depend on the circumstances in which she is working, the topic and objectives of the seminar, and the nature and interests of the course participants and of their students. The following two examples, however, are intended to illustrate how this taxonomy might be used in preparing tasks. The topic of the seminar (and of the task) is in both cases: *Use of the learners' first language (L1) in the classroom.*

Example 1

You have been asked to organise a seminar on this topic for a group of teachers who are very diverse in terms of previous teacher training, teaching experience and assumptions about what is and is not appropriate classroom practice. You suspect that some of the teachers make extensive use of the learners' language and have not really considered the alternatives. Conversely, you suspect that the group also contains teachers who have internalised an erstwhile prohibition on the use of the learners' first language.

In this case the group appears to contain conflicting routine assumptions and practices, and this conflict itself is a great resource.

Your final **aim** will probably be to *increase the range of options available to the teacher in classroom practice* so that the teachers use a wider repertoire of skills – those who avoid use of the L1 may consider using it, and those who use it excessively may explore alternative approaches.

In order to achieve this aim, however, your starting point may well be to make the teachers aware of the unconscious assumptions underlying what they do: *Exploring experiential knowledge: identifying and exploring assumptions, making the implicit explicit in order to test it against personal and external theory.*

The participants would be *finding out* what their colleagues do in the classroom and what they believe, they would be *analysing* their own practice, and *evaluating* the use of L1 against the aims of different teaching/learning activities, the characteristics of their own students and their own abilities (e.g. knowledge of the learners' L1) and preferences.

To achieve these aims, the opportunity and stimulus need to be created for them to exchange descriptions of their own practice, assumptions and beliefs. The most important **activity** will thus probably be *speaking* (to each other), and if at all possible, *teaching* to experiment with 'alternative teaching behaviours' (for example, teachers who normally avoid use of L1 would deliberately use it at every opportunity in order to evaluate its effectiveness in different kinds of lesson and to achieve different objectives) and/or *watching* each other teach – using or not using the learners' L1.

The **activity** might also involve *matching* or *classifying*. In both these cases the participants would be exploring things a teacher does in order to decide whether use of the L1 would or would not be possible, appropriate or advisable. They might also be involved in *putting forward arguments* – justifying their own practice or, possibly, arguing contrary to their beliefs.

There is a wide choice of **focus** which could be used in this task – the choice ultimately might be determined by availability, observed preferences in the group, or by the wish for variety.

Comments made by learners, teachers or writers could provide the stimulus, as could *lessons* in the form of recordings or written plans. *Questionnaires* could be prepared to elicit the reactions of learners to the use/non-use of L1.

Example 2

You are aware that this particular group of teachers makes extensive use of the learners' first language in class as a part of their routine teaching behaviour.

In this case the **aims** would be similar to those in Example 1, except that the *finding out* would rely on resources outside the experience and beliefs in the group itself.

It is not possible for the **focus** in this case to rely on an exchange of views, and more input is probably required. This could be provided in the form of *explanatory written text* arguing against the use of L1 and describing alternatives to its use, or a (video) *recording of a lesson* which demonstrates some of these alternatives.

The **activities** might be similar to those in Example 1.

3.7   Optional exercise on devising tasks

Choose either Example 1 or Example 2 above and produce the task itself. If possible, work on this in partnership with a colleague and either design the task together, or work separately but compare the finished results.

To see exactly how the topic of *Use of the learners' first language* has been treated in this book, refer to Discussion Task 10 (see page 106) and Classroom-based Task 5 (see page 112). These two Tasks have been devised for use in a wide range of circumstances. The task you produce will probably differ from these because it will reflect both your own preoccupations and preferences on the one hand, and on the other because it will take account of the precise circumstances described in the Example you have chosen.

3.8   Evaluating tasks

Evaluation of any material is ideally an ongoing process – problems arise as it is used, and writers/task designers will usually wish to carry out modifications to the materials as they evaluate them on the basis of feedback from the users, their own observation of how they work, and the extent to which the materials fulfil their aims in devising them. This section concerns the evaluation of tasks in very general terms, and more specifically refers to the evaluation of tasks that trainers have devised themselves.

The starting point for evaluating any tasks will normally be a definition of the aims. To some extent it is possible to observe how far the aims are achieved, but it is also helpful to engage the assistance of the users in this. They can simply be asked what they understand the aim of the activity to have been or, more informally, what they feel they have learned or gained from the activity. Alternatively, they can be told the aim and asked to what extent they think this has been achieved.

Where the aim has been achieved, it is still useful to explore whether it was achieved in the most efficient of ways. Again the reactions of the users are helpful in this respect. They may be able to suggest modifications with regard to the choice and quantity of material in the task, and with regard to the choice of activities. In evaluating this it is useful to refer to the taxonomy (3.2, on pages 26–9) as a checklist of possibilities, and this can be made available to the users where it is thought to be appropriate.

One of the joys of devising and using any materials is the unexpected pay-offs – the users may well feel that they have learnt or developed their awareness in areas that the designer of the materials did not anticipate. Even where the original aims have not been realised, it is important to canvass from the users what they feel they have gained from the activity. There are cases where this feedback leads not to a revision of the tasks themselves, but rather to a revision of the purposes to which they are put.

PART B   Tasks and accompanying notes

4   The learners

Introduction to the chapter

1   Contents

Discussion Task 1   Learners: Personality, styles and characteristics
Discussion Task 2   Autonomy and learning
Discussion Task 3   Motivation and learning
Discussion Task 4   Learning strategies
Discussion Task 5   Learners' roles
Discussion Task 6   Learners' language

Classroom-based Task 1   Materials designed to develop learning skills
Classroom-based Task 2   Learning styles and strategies
Classroom-based Task 3   Learners' awareness of errors and mistakes
                         and attitudes towards these

2   General discussion of issues

The Discussion Tasks in this chapter focus on a variety of factors which contribute to and affect learning. Reference is made to theory, and in some cases (for example, in Discussion Task 1) this involves addressing technical descriptive terminology. At the same time, however, participants are encouraged to apply this discussion of theory by reflecting on their own experience and by observing and investigating the learning processes of their own students. The Classroom-based Tasks formalise and extend this application.

3   Reading

Dickinson, L. (1987). *Self-instruction in Language Learning*. Cambridge University Press.
Edge, J. (1989). *Mistakes and Correction*. Longman.
Ellis, G. & Sinclair, B. (1989). *Learning to Learn English*. Cambridge University Press.
Ellis, R. (1985). *Understanding Second Language Acquisition*. Oxford University Press.

Gower, R. & Walters, S. (1983). *A Teaching Practice Handbook.* Heinemann.

Harmer, J. (1991). *The Practice of English Language Teaching.* Longman.

Littlewood, W. (1984). *Foreign and Second Language Learning.* Cambridge University Press.

McLaughlin, B. (1987). *Theories of Second Language Learning.* Edward Arnold.

Norrish, J. (1983). *Language Learners and their Errors.* Macmillan.

Nunan, D. (1989). *Designing Tasks for the Communicative Classroom.* Cambridge University Press.

Richards, J. C. & Rodgers, T. S. (1986). *Approaches and Methods in Language Teaching.* Cambridge University Press.

Skehan, P. (1989). *Individual Differences in Second Language Learning.* Edward Arnold.

Wenden, A. & Rubin, J. (eds.). (1987). *Learner Strategies in Language Learning.* Prentice Hall.

For both the trainer and the participants, Littlewood probably provides the most straightforward introduction to the topic of this chapter. Even though this is not a recent publication, the book is short and very accessible. It is equally suitable for preparatory reading and as a follow-up to the Tasks.

Ellis is similarly general, but is considerably longer and is recommended for participants who want to extend their reading in this area further. Dickinson considers issues which are a great deal more general than the title suggests.

Both Norrish and Edge provide excellent, short introductions to the topic of learners' errors. The topic is also dealt with in Gower & Walters, and in Harmer, and specific reference is made to the relevant sections of these two books in the notes which accompany Discussion Task 6.

McLaughlin, Skehan, and Wenden & Rubin deal with research and are all, in a sense, books which review the 'state of the art'. Participants may be motivated to use the index in each of these books to explore areas of specific interest to them.

Nunan (pp. 79–84) contains a useful discussion of learners' roles. Although these are viewed from a perspective which is different from that of Discussion Task 5, it provides relevant and interesting background to the topic. Richards & Rodgers (pp. 23, 38, 56, 76–7, 93, 106, 121–2, 136–7, 149) explore the roles of learners in relation to different approaches and methods.

Although participants will find that it is valuable to read before using the Tasks and to follow up issues raised in them, the only Task for which specific reading may be necessary is Discussion Task 1. Reference is made to the appropriate sections of Dickinson and Skehan in the notes which accompany this Task.

The material used in Classroom-based Task 1 comes from a book intended for classroom use (Ellis & Sinclair). The accompanying Teacher's Book also merits study, providing a very practical view of many of the issues considered in this chapter.

Discussion Task 1

Learners: Personality, styles and characteristics

Aim   This Task sensitises you to individual differences in approaches to learning languages. Although Section B deals with the topic in a somewhat academic way, you are still asked to relate this to your own experience, and to 'test' the technical distinctions against your practical awareness.

TASK

Section A   *General sensitisation*

Look at the following statements made by learners of English.

a) I want my teacher to correct all my mistakes.
b) I want to be in an easier class so that I can understand everything on the tapes.
c) I don't want to study grammar in class. I can do that at home.
d) I like my teacher because she lets me ask questions about things I want to know.
e) I like being in a pair with a student who is better than me.
f) I had a frustrating weekend because I ran out of simplified readers.
g) I didn't buy anything because I didn't know how to ask for it.
h) I know the rule but I forget it when I'm speaking.

1   Speculate about the personalities of the learners who made these statements.
   Example *Statement (a):* The student who made this comment may be preoccupied with correctness and afraid of making mistakes. She may be reluctant to express herself because of this. She may also want any feedback on her performance to come from the teacher rather than from other students.

2   Do you think it is likely that any of these statements were made by the same learners?
   Example *Statements (a), (b) and (g):* These might have been made by the same learner as they all seem to suggest a learner

who is very concerned with accuracy, and seems reluctant to challenge herself in communication.

3   Do any of these characteristics seem to you to reflect either positive or negative approaches to learning? (Where your judgement on this issue would depend on the circumstances, specify in which circumstances the statement might reflect either a positive or a negative approach.)

Example *Statement (f):* This learner would appear to be motivated to read English outside the class, a very important element in successful learning. However, if the learner is able to read unsimplified texts and has access to them, her unwillingness to tackle them might reflect a reluctance to stretch herself, a wish to 'play safe'.

4   Do any of these statements remind you of students you know or reflect your own experience of learning foreign languages?

Section B   *Ways of characterising individual approaches to learning*

A learning *style* is an individual predisposition to learn in a particular way. The term is used to describe broad, general characteristics of approach to learning, and it is likely that the preferred learning styles of any one learner will be manifest in all aspects of learning, not just in relation to learning foreign languages. There is clearly an area of overlap between learning styles and general personality characteristics.

The following are some of the terms which are used to characterise the preferred styles of learners, aspects of their personality relevant to learning and other relevant characteristics:

Tolerant of ambiguity   –   Intolerant of ambiguity
Visual   –   Aural   –   Kinaesthetic
Holist   –   Serialist
Field-dependent   –   Field-independent
Syllabus-bound   –   Syllabus-free
Introvert   –   Extrovert

1   Discuss these terms and ensure that you are clear about the features they describe.
Example *Tolerance of ambiguity* is one of the components which may constitute an overall 'style'. Learners who are *tolerant of ambiguity* may be content to accept something

Task

which is partially understood without needing to clarify it completely. In the context of language learning, this tolerance may be exemplified with regard to a learner's understanding the informational content of texts, and also to the understanding of the meaning of specific items of language.

Learners who are *intolerant of ambiguity*, on the other hand, may have difficulty in accepting the feeling that they have understood something only incompletely. They may feel frustrated until they have been able to satisfy their need to define and categorise what they are learning, and to relate this to what they already know, in English and perhaps in their own languages.

2 Look at the following profiles of learners and specify which of these terms might be used to describe their learning styles. More than one of these terms may describe each of the learners.

a) She is eager to use everything she learns in class and is uninhibited about 'trying out' new language in interaction with other students as well as outside the class. She is impatient with regard to detail and tends to make minor mistakes, but she remembers the general features of what she learns easily. She 'picks up' expressions she hears, and enjoys using them herself, tending to over-use them while they are still new to her.

b) She likes to write everything down and revises all her lessons very systematically and carefully. She enjoys reading, and keeps a record of the new vocabulary she comes across. She enjoys using new language most of all in compositions. If she knows she will have to speak in English in class or outside, she likes to prepare for this so that she can use correct and appropriate grammar and vocabulary.

c) She has a fascination for the systems of language, and reads about the grammar and phonology of English in her own language. She gets pleasure from discovering the underlying grammar in some expressions she uses, and this helps her to remember it. An example of this is invitations. She learned to ask '*Would you like . . . ?*', but only really felt she knew this when she realised that it was conditional, and that the implied 'if I invited you' was a kind of escape clause.

Example Learner (a) is clearly *extrovert*.

3   Think of your own experience of learning languages. Is it possible to characterise your own preferred learning styles and characteristics using any of these terms?

4   Think of students you have taught and try to identify two or three students who seemed to learn with particular facility and two or three who seemed to learn with particular difficulty.

Attempt to identify their preferred styles and characteristics.

Does it seem that certain styles or characteristics favour greater success in learning? (For example, it is sometimes argued that being extrovert is an advantage in language learning.)

5   To what extent and in what ways can the teacher accommodate the variety of learning styles which may be present among members of a class?

Discussion Task 1

Learners: Personality, styles and characteristics

Notes

Timing   Section A   c. 30 minutes
Section B   c. 45 minutes
Total   c. 75 minutes

Although this Task is intended to be suitable for all teachers, participants who prefer to avoid dealing with technical terms and concepts may prefer to omit Section B. In this case, a suitable alternative might be provided by Discussion Task 5, which deals with learners' roles.

Classroom-based Task 2 involves practical research into issues dealt with in this Discussion Task.

Suggestions for procedure

Section A   *General sensitisation*

These questions can be discussed in small groups. A secretary in each group can note down any points of contention or particular interest which arise in this discussion. Some of these can subsequently be reported back to the whole group and comments can be invited from other participants.

Section B   *Ways of characterising individual approaches to learning*

There may be a case for a brief plenary discussion after participants have discussed the first question in small groups. The aim of this would be for the trainer to clarify the terminology if necessary.

The rest of this section of the Task can be discussed in small groups. Only the final question (5) necessarily requires some kind of plenary feedback. One group can be asked to prepare a 'poster' or OHP transparency listing ways the teacher can accommodate different learning styles. Other groups can add points to this.

Notes

Participants who are unfamiliar with this topic may like to prepare for this part of the Task by reading before the session. Many of the terms are described in Dickinson (1987) pp. 20–3 or Skehan (1989) pp. 100–6, 111–15.

General discussion and possible outcomes

Section A of this Task encourages participants to reflect on characteristics of learners and to relate this to their own experience as learners and teachers of language.

Section B is more technical than most of the materials in this book, and deals with theory more explicitly. Some participants may find it 'difficult' and it may not be suitable for all groups of teachers.

Part of this 'difficulty' involves grasping the concepts implicit in the terms. However, there is a further difficulty in applying them in the description of specific learners. This difficulty is inherent and inescapable. The terms describe tentative models for categorising and explaining individual differences, rather than watertight descriptions of objective reality.

Section A   *General sensitisation*

Question 1
Participants are asked to *speculate* and there are no 'right' or 'wrong' answers.

Question 2
Further likely 'groupings' might include (c) and (d) (a learner who appears to be willing to take initiatives in learning). Statement (e) might also have been made by the same learner if the statement reflects a willingness to be challenged. The statement might, however, reflect the converse – a wish to 'coast' with a 'better' learner.

Question 3
It is likely that participants will see (d) as positive and (a) and (g) as negative. However, the opposite could also be argued depending on the circumstances. The aim of this question, indeed, is primarily to encourage participants to explore ways in which the value of these attitudes and opinions may depend on

the characteristics of the learners and the circumstances in which they are learning.

Participants may be able to advance arguments that the following are either positive or negative, depending on the circumstances they specify: (b), (c), (e), (f), (h).

Question 4
Responses will depend on the individual experience and characteristics of the participants.

Section B *Ways of characterising individual approaches to learning*

Question 1 (briefly)
Visual/aural/kinaesthetic   Terms used in Neurolinguistic programming to describe personality orientations – a visual person learns more easily if data is presented through the visual channel, etc.
Holist/serialist   Holist learners are believed to be predisposed to learn through global exposure whereas serialist learners tend to learn through analysing elements sequentially.
Field-dependent/independent   Field-independent learners are believed to be able to perceive systems in larger structures whereas field-dependent learners see only the general structure.
Syllabus-bound/free   Syllabus-free learners are believed to learn from elements in the general learning context and outside it whereas syllabus-bound learners require the 'packaging' and presentation of data which the teacher provides.
Introvert/extrovert   Introverts tend to learn analytically in a planned and organised way. Extroverts are people-orientated, and their learning is believed to be more intuitive and to depend more on interaction with others.

Extroverts are likely to be holist and syllabus-free, but the interface between these different systems for categorising personality or learning types is blurred and it is difficult to translate the concepts from one system to another.

Question 2
The following are probable, but other answers could be argued:
a) extrovert/holist/syllabus-free/aural
b) introvert/intolerant of ambiguity
c) serialist/field-independent

Notes

Note that these profiles describe somewhat extreme cases of particular styles and characteristics. In reality it is often more difficult to apply the terms to describe individuals.

Questions 3 & 4
Responses will depend on the individual experience of participants.

Question 5
One point which can be made is that teachers can try to find out about this systematically (see Classroom-based Task 2). Teachers can raise the awareness of their learners with regard to the range of ways in which different individuals approach learning, and encourage them to identify their own preferred styles and characteristics. This may involve reading and discussion (possibly in the learners' first language), and guided self-observation (for example, by keeping diaries in which they record how they approach different tasks and activities, and try to identify the factors which lead to their feeling satisfied or, perhaps, frustrated in their learning).

See Ellis & Sinclair (1989) for examples of materials which might be used.

Teachers can also deliberately vary their approach in order to:
1   Make provision for learners with different preferred styles.
2   Encourage learners to develop alternative styles.

Discussion Task 2

Autonomy and learning

Aim This Task draws your attention to the extent to which
different kinds of activity encourage (or do not
encourage) the learners' development of autonomous
learning skills. It also encourages you to explore and
evaluate the desirability and appropriateness of these
skills with reference to your own experience of learning
and teaching languages.

TASK

It is often argued that among the attributes of a 'good' language
learner is the ability and willingness to take responsibility for
learning, to initiate and to take risks – the 'good' learner is one
who:
– takes decisions with regard to:
  • areas of language to focus on
  • activities to facilitate learning
  • strategies to apply in learning, and
– actively seeks:
  • information
  • opportunities for practice
  • assistance from proficient language users and general
    resources (dictionaries, reference grammars, etc.)

1   To what extent does your own experience of learning and
    teaching validate this argument? (For example, can you find
    examples of successful learning by teacher-dependent learners
    who resist taking responsibility for their learning?)

2   To what extent do the following classroom activities
    encourage the development of these qualities:

    a) The teacher 'presents' some vocabulary using pictures,
       mime, explanation or translation.
    b) The teacher asks the class to research a topic and (using a
       bilingual dictionary) to look up six words of key relevance
       to the topic that they know in their own language but
       whose meaning they are unable to express in English. In

Task

the next lesson he asks the students to pool the information that they acquire through this.

c) The teacher asks the class to 'prepare' a reading passage by looking up unfamiliar words at home before it is studied in class.

d) The teacher distributes a reading passage to the class. After a set period of time he asks individual students questions about the information contained in the text. He expands and corrects the answers elicited.

e) Students are appointed to find passages for the class to study. The teacher devises comprehension tasks. Working in groups, students choose tasks and collaborate in answering them.

f) Students visit the school library in class time and select books to read. Time for reading is provided in class and ultimately class time is also devoted to discussion of what the students have read.

g) Time in class is devoted to 'competition' activities in which students answer questions about grammar and vocabulary by locating and reading the relevant information in reference grammars or dictionaries.

h) Grammar exercises are set for homework and the teacher subsequently goes over these in class.

i) Students are asked to write a composition at home after the language and the topic have been prepared in class.

j) The teacher decides to abandon the course materials for a period of time. Instead the class is engaged in working on a project to produce a series of handouts presenting information about their town in English. He provides models for the class to read (from tourist brochures about British cities), and cassettes of expatriate native speakers discussing problems they may have (real or 'contrived') about finding things to do in their leisure time.

Example *Item (a):* Ostensibly this approach is likely to encourage dependence on the teacher rather than the development of autonomous learning (an autonomy-encouraging approach might involve the learners selecting vocabulary items they want to learn, researching vocabulary in dictionaries or working out the meaning of words from context and the grammatical characteristics of the words from analogy with other English words they know).

However, even within this teacher's approach there is a little room for encouraging autonomy. For example, giving students time to recall or guess words in response to a picture would be more helpful in this respect than simply 'telling' the students the word.

3 In what ways do you or might you develop learner autonomy in your own classes?

Notes

Discussion Task 2

Autonomy and learning

Timing   c. 45 minutes

Suggestions for procedure

Each of the three questions can be dealt with separately.
Participants can discuss the questions in small groups before
presenting their impressions or conclusions to the whole group.

Question 1
Plenary discussion may be kept short to avoid repetition of
points.

Question 2
One group can be selected to present its conclusions to the whole
group (using an OHP transparency if this is available), and any
additional comments or disagreements can be invited.

Question 3
This question may warrant the most extensive discussion. The
plenary discussion may begin with participants 'shouting out'
items that they have brainstormed.

General discussion and possible outcomes

This Task aims not to persuade participants of the value of
learner autonomy, but to raise the topic and explore ways in
which this may be encouraged if it is deemed appropriate.

The issues which the Task prompts may well give rise to the
discussion of autonomy and responsibility in teacher
development. This can be exploited to encourage participants to
discuss their attitudes towards the procedures adopted within the
seminar or programme of development they are attending, and
the rationale which underlies these.

The attributes of 'good' learners are discussed in Ellis (1985)
pp. 122–3.

Notes

Question 1

Responses to this question are likely to depend on the educational and intellectual traditions within which participants work. It should not simply be taken for granted that developing skills of autonomous learning necessarily facilitates learning, or that this is universally appropriate.

Question 2

(b), (f) and (g) appear to be most conducive to the development of autonomy, and (a) and (d) the least conducive. Depending on the circumstances which are cited, arguments both for and against (c), (e) and (h) may be cited.

Question 3

Responses will depend on both the experience and the reading of the participants. The list of activities provided in Question 2 may act as a stimulus to this brainstorming exercise.

Discussion Task 3

Motivation and learning

Aim   This Task aims firstly to raise the issue of what motivation is and to encourage evaluation of its importance in relation to other factors which affect learning. Secondly it looks at ways in which a teacher can affect motivation, and in this respect may be of particular relevance to teachers who feel that motivation is a problem within their classes.

TASK

Section A   *General issues*

Motivation is sometimes characterised as being *integrative* or *instrumental.* These terms apply principally to the context of a community which speaks a language which, in the wider context, is regarded as a minority language (for example, but not necessarily, an immigrant community). *Integrative* motivation refers to the wish to identify with the larger community, while *instrumental* motivation refers to the *need* to learn (for example, for educational or occupational purposes).

1   Do these terms/concepts have any relevance in the circumstances in which your students are learning?

2   Do you consider that the two types of motivation are compatible?

3   In what other ways might you characterise types of motivation?

4   In your experience of learning and teaching languages, how important do you consider motivation as a factor in overall success? (You might compare motivation with other factors such as intelligence, personality and contact with the foreign language outside the classroom.)

5   Motivation is normally seen as being an important component in successful learning. From your experience, to what extent is the converse also true – that success, itself, appears to engender motivation?

Section B   *Motivation and the classroom context*

1 Brainstorm ways in which the teacher can positively affect the motivation of her students. It may help you to think of these in terms of *short-term measures* (i.e. within individual lessons) and *long-term measures* (i.e. over a term, year or course).

2 Compare your list with the following and add points to your list as appropriate.

Reject any points in this list that you disagree with.

Short-term

a) Challenge students to think.

b) Ensure maximum student participation in lessons.

c) Set up a need to communicate.

d) Show interest in the students' opinions/experience and relate the content of lessons to this.

e) Make the learning experience 'enjoyable'.

f) Ensure that there is sufficient variety of activity, focus (of interaction) and pace.

g) Establish the aims of the lesson and the objectives within it.

Long-term

a) Make the aims and goals of the course clear well in advance and draw the attention of the students to the achievement of these.

b) Show interest in the students and encourage/be open to their interest in you.

c) Integrate the cultural dimension of the language (not necessarily in terms of English as a *national* language) – bring in and use materials such as maps, books and brochures and be prepared to provide background information to the materials and to explore the cultural implications of metaphor, etc.

d) Involve students in discussions about your approach and respond flexibly to their expectations.

e) Identify needs and take these into account.

f) Devote time and attention to group dynamics (e.g. choose activities not only for reasons of language learning but also because they may foster positive communal feeling).

g) Regularly demonstrate progress through repeating activities/exercises/tests or showing them what they did some time before.

h) Ensure that initial learning activities lead to 'success', i.e. by selecting tasks and activities which enable learners to achieve concrete goals.

3   Attempt to rank items in your list according to how important you think they are.

4   For each of these items think of concrete examples of how the precise objective might be realised.
Example *Short-term: Item (a):* If a student asks for the spelling of a word, instead of simply supplying the answer, the teacher might encourage the class to try to work this out from the pronunciation or through analogy with similar words whose spelling is known (techniques such as this need to be used judiciously in some circumstances, however, as a refusal to give a straight answer to a question could also be frustrating for some learners).

[This exercise is adapted from material in the Correspondence Course which forms part of the RSA DTEFLA Distance Training Programme operated by International House (Eleventh Edition 1991, Unit 6, p. 20).]

Notes

Discussion Task 3

Motivation and learning

Timing   Section A c. 20 minutes
Section B c. 20 minutes
Total   c. 40 minutes

Suggestions for procedure

Section A   *General issues*

These questions can be discussed in small groups before a
general plenary 'airing' of opinions and impressions.

Section B   *Motivation and the classroom context*

Question 1
A 5-minute limit can be put on this brainstorming exercise,
followed by a brief period of participants 'shouting out' their
solutions.

Questions 2 & 3
These questions can be discussed in small groups. It may be
unnecessary or even tedious to 'go over' these questions in a
plenary format.

Question 4
Groups can choose to select certain items from the list to
consider, or these can be divided between them by the trainer.
They can also be given the opportunity to ask each other for
assistance with regard to any items for which they may have
been unable to think of examples.

General discussion and possible outcomes

This Task aims to encourage participants to explore issues of
motivation, but of necessity, conclusions drawn are tentative.

c

Notes

Skehan (1989) devotes a chapter to motivation (Chapter 4), in which he reviews research into the sources of motivation and the influences on it. This is valuable additional reading. He concludes by suggesting directions in which further research should go, and leaves the overall feeling that much that is commonly taken for granted with regard to motivation is somewhat impressionistic.

Section A *General issues*

Answers to these questions will depend on the circumstances with which participants are familiar. However, it is likely that some of the following points may be made in the discussion:

Question 1
In many circumstances in which foreign languages are formally 'taught', integration into a host culture is not at issue.

Question 2
Although these two types of motivation are often considered to be qualitatively different, there is no reason to assume that they are incompatible.

Question 3
The terms 'extrinsic' and 'intrinsic' are also sometimes used to characterise types of motivation.

Question 4
This is often considered to be of paramount importance. However, while most successful learners would appear to be motivated, it appears not to be so clear that all motivated learners are successful.

Question 5
The causal relationship between motivation and success is something of a cliché. The converse is less commonly considered, but is not necessarily less applicable.

Section B *Motivation and the classroom context*

Answers to these questions will also depend on the experience and working circumstances of the participants.

Discussion Task 4

Learning strategies

Aim This Task encourages you to develop your awareness both of some of the processes involved in learning, and of ways in which teachers can influence the strategies their students employ.

TASK

A learning *strategy* is a measure that the learner actively (although not necessarily consciously) employs to facilitate or advance learning. Each of the following comments by learners describes a learning strategy.

a) When I read a text in which much of the language is unfamiliar, I 'guess' – I use my general knowledge of the world and knowledge about the particular topic to help me to understand.
b) When I come across a new word and I think I understand it and know how to pronounce it, I try to find opportunities to use it to see if I really can.
c) When I get 'stuck' reading something because the syntax or clause structure is so complicated, I try to translate that bit mentally to help me sort it out.
d) I use my bilingual dictionary a lot to try to find ways of expressing what I can already say in my own language.
e) When I'm reading I ignore unfamiliar words unless they crop up over and over again and I know I'm missing something important.
f) When I'm in the bus I look at my index cards. They have an English word on one side and an example sentence, the pronunciation and an explanation or word in my own language on the other.
g) I notice other students' mistakes – particularly if they're not speaking to me – and sometimes I realise I make that mistake myself. I try to remember the mistake and what the person should have said.
h) I like to repeat things over and over so that I can memorise them.

57

i) I go up to tourists and pretend I am lost so that I can get into conversation with them in English.
j) I rehearse to myself what I want to say before I have to say it.
k) When I don't understand I keep nodding and pretending to understand so that they carry on speaking and I get a 'second chance' to figure out what they want to say.
l) When I don't understand I ask them to say it again more slowly.

1 Which of these strategies do you use in learning languages?

2 Add any further comments which exemplify learning strategies to this list of learners' comments. Refer to your experience both of learning languages yourself, and of observing learners in your classes to help you think of further instances.

3 Learning strategies are sometimes divided into four categories:

– *Metacognitive* These relate to the planning and overall organisation of the language learning experience, and entail making choices from a repertoire of options including choices about which other strategies to use in a particular situation and for a particular purpose. For example, learners employ metacognitive strategies when they decide to use a dictionary to research the language needed to perform a particular task, or when they choose to focus on contextual clues to understand the meaning of unfamiliar language and to ignore unfamiliar language whose meaning is not derivable from context. These, in a sense, are the most sophisticated strategies in that they involve a knowledge of language learning behaviour, and of the options available to the learner.
– *Cognitive* These involve the direct experience of learning. For example, learners employ cognitive strategies when they consciously apply 'learned' rules in order to construct an utterance or when they focus on contextual clues to understand the meaning of unfamiliar language.
– *Social* These involve creating opportunities for using language.
– *Communicative* These involve achieving communication, often when there is a need to use or understand language which is unknown.

Task

Which of the items in your expanded list of examples of strategies belong to which of these four categories? (There are areas of overlap and in some cases it can be argued that an item belongs in more than one category.)

Example *Comment (a):* It describes both a cognitive strategy (the process) and a communicative strategy (the purpose).

4 Can you think of any strategies which your students employ which may actually *hinder* learning?

Example Looking up and trying to understand every word in a text which is lexically dense and abstruse probably amounts at best to inefficient use of time, and may in fact encourage the learner to depend too much on 'knowing' words in the process of deriving meaning from a text.

5 To what extent do you consider teachers of foreign languages should be responsible for developing the use of good learning strategies among the learners in a class?

6 In what ways can teachers develop these strategies?

Example *Comment (a):* The teacher can encourage the class actively to anticipate the content of a text on the basis of clues (such as where the text is from, the title, headings, diagrams), and can set a time limit on the reading, which obliges the students to activate extra-textual knowledge in order to derive aspects of its content.

7 It could be argued that communicative strategies have a short-term pay-off, but that over-reliance on them might lead to the learners lacking the motivation to learn the language itself. To what extent do you agree or disagree with this point of view?

Discussion Task 4

Learning strategies

Timing   c. 45 minutes

Classroom-based Task 2 involves practical research into issues dealt with in this task.

Suggestions for procedure

Question 1
Participants can share their experience in small groups.

Question 2
Participants may be asked to 'shout out' items from the lists the groups compose. If participants are having difficulty thinking of additions, the trainer may want to bring the brainstorming activity to an early conclusion and offer one or two further items himself. Five minutes is probably sufficient time to be devoted to this question.

Questions 3–7
These can be discussed in small groups. This may be followed by a brief plenary discussion in which participants compare their views. A representative from one group can be asked to summarise the conclusions of the group with respect to each question. Further comments can be invited question by question.

General discussion and possible outcomes

The system of categorising strategies employed in this Task is derived from Rubin (in Wenden & Rubin, 1987, pp. 22–7) and Uhl Chamot (ibid., p. 77). However, as this exercise reveals, the system is not watertight. There are three problems in particular:

1   The distinction between cognitive and metacognitive is unclear when one looks at specific instances of strategies – in the case of comment (j) for example, it might be considered

as metacognitive if it refers to preparing a lecture, but cognitive if it refers to split-second rehearsal of utterances.

2   The system is not a closed one. A strategy can be both cognitive and communicative, for example, the strategy exemplified by comment (a).

3   It could be argued that communicative strategies are not learning strategies at all since the goal is immediate comprehensibility with no necessary long-term pay-off (this might be true where *over*-reliance on these strategies removed the incentive to develop linguistic skills and other strategies).

Skehan (1989, p. 98) in his discussion of research into learning strategies acknowledges some of the problems inherent in any discussion of this nature:

> 'If, now, we review the whole of the learner-strategies research, we have to say that the area is at an embryonic stage. Conflicting results and methodologies proliferate. There are few hard findings.'

Discussion of strategies the learners may employ to facilitate communication naturally leads to a consideration of 'error'. Many of the specific strategies considered here in themselves give rise to error, which has significant implications for the way in which teachers will respond to this in class. This theme is developed in Discussion Task 6 and Classroom-based Task 3.

Question 1
Responses to this question will depend on the individual experience of participants.

Question 2
Unless there is obvious confusion about what constitutes a 'strategy', anything the groups propose should be acceptable. Wenden & Rubin (1987, p. 77) provides a useful checklist of strategies which may be of help to the trainer.

Question 3
The following is a probable system for categorising the comments (an asterisk indicates inclusion in more than one category):
Metacognitive: d, f, g*, h, j
Cognitive: a*, c, e, g*
Social: b, i
Communicative: a*, k, l

It could be argued that any of these strategies are also metacognitive in that the learner is consciously aware of their use and, by implication, their use may be the result of a deliberate choice. (g) is an interesting example in this respect as the 'noticing' and 'realising' may be unconscious (cognitive), but the 'trying to remember' suggests a conscious decision is involved.

Question 4

Questions such as this sometimes give rise to the danger of arousing dogmatic responses. According to individual styles of learning, certain strategies may or may not be appropriate and productive to the particular learner. It is important that in citing any examples, participants are aware that this is not definitive but, rather, a matter of identifying what is most probable.

Question 5

Increasingly, teachers see this as being part of their responsibility. Their function is not necessarily to determine the strategies employed by learners, but rather to increase awareness of the range of strategies available to them and to give practice in these so that learners can choose from a wider repertoire. Ellis & Sinclair (1989) is an example of material designed specifically for this purpose.

Question 6

Participants may refer back to the list of comments as a stimulus to this brainstorming exercise.

Question 7

This question aims to encourage thinking about the issue, and it may be inappropriate for the trainer to advance a particular point of view.

Discussion Task 5

Learners' roles

Aim This Task presents a perspective on classroom learning which is often overlooked. It is intended that this should develop your awareness both of the range of options available to learners and of the ways in which these may determine the response of the teacher.

TASK

Some models of learning/teaching regard learners essentially as *sponges* who soak up knowledge offered to them by the teacher.

In fact, learners probably perform a variety of roles in the classroom, of which *sponge* may at different points in lessons be one.

1   Make a list of other roles the learner may perform.
    Example Experimenter

2   Compare the items on your list with those below and make any adjustments to your list accordingly if you want.

Sponge	Experimenter
Researcher	Struggler
Negotiator	Path-follower
Obeyer	Initiator
Explorer	

3   Look at the following descriptions of classroom activities. For each activity indicate the main role of the learners as well as any relevant subordinate roles.

   a) Students work in pairs. Student A has a picture of an empty room. Student B has a picture of the same room, but furnished. Without looking at each other's pictures Student A has to attempt to draw in the detail so that her picture resembles that of Student B. Student A therefore has to ask Student B about the picture.
   b) Students work individually. They complete an exercise in which the infinitive form of each verb is given in brackets and they have to choose and insert the appropriate tense

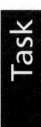

form. This is a diagnostic exercise, prior to studying these tense forms in class.

c) Students work individually. They complete an exercise in which the infinitive form of each verb is given in brackets and they have to choose and insert the appropriate tense form. This is a practice/testing exercise, subsequent to having studied these tense forms in class.

d) Students work in pairs or groups of three. They complete an exercise in which the infinitive form of each verb is given in brackets and they have to choose and insert the appropriate tense form. This is a practice/testing exercise, subsequent to having studied these tense forms in class.

e) Students listen to a recorded conversation in order to find the answers to specific questions. They subsequently discuss their answers to these questions in small groups and then listen again.

f) Students repeat a sentence in chorus after the teacher, trying to imitate the pronunciation.

g) Students read different texts on a common subject at home, and then pool their knowledge in class.

Example *Activity (a):* Negotiator (Struggler)

4   Individual learners may prefer certain roles to others. Think of learners that you know and attempt to identify which roles they prefer.

5   In what ways can the teacher accommodate individual preferences with regard to roles?

6   In what ways can the teacher encourage learners to experiment with unfamiliar roles?

Discussion Task 5

Learners' roles

Timing   c. 40 minutes

Suggestions for procedure

Participants can work on this Task in small groups. Time may be made available for a brief plenary comparison of responses to Question 4.

General discussion and possible outcomes

This topic can be followed up and extended by referring to Nunan (1989) pp. 79–84.

Questions 1, 2 & 4
Responses to these questions will reflect the experience of participants.

Question 3
The following is a possible system of attributing roles using the unadapted list of categories offered in the Task:

Sponge	Experimenter: b
Researcher: e, g	Struggler: a
Negotiator: a, d, e, g	Path-follower: c, d, f
Obeyer: f	Initiator
Explorer	

The examples offered here give little provision for the learner as *sponge*, *explorer* and, least of all, as *initiator*. This begs the question of activities and approaches which favour these roles. Learners act as *explorers* where they are encouraged to pursue individual interests (linguistic or personal) with little guidance, and to report back to the class subsequently. Almost by definition, teachers cannot encourage learners to initiate other than by establishing a relationship which makes it clear that they are pleased to respond to initiatives from the learners. Learners

Notes

appear to act as *sponges* when they listen to the teacher or another student explaining. However, in a sense, if learning is taking place it is probably necessary that the learners are not simply 'absorbing' but are actively relating the input to existing knowledge and classifying this.

Question 5

Individual learners may prefer roles which are more passive or more active, which involve working more individually or with other students in the class. Teachers can attempt to vary the tasks they set and the learning activities to allow for these preferences.

Question 6

Teachers can also introduce activities which specifically encourage students to reflect on the roles they perform in the class and on those that they prefer. For example, they might ask students to describe the way they see themselves as learners by choosing from a list of items such as those provided in Question 2 of this Task (with some monolingual groups this may involve use of the learners' first language).

The roles learners instinctively prefer may, in some cases, reflect what they are used to or what they understand is expected of them by the teacher.

Discussion Task 6

Learners' language

Aim   This Task provides a series of frameworks to facilitate analysing learners' language, and introduces you to some of the relevant terminology. It also aims both to raise awareness of the role of error in language learning and to help you develop a more principled basis for responding to errors and mistakes.

TASK

Section A   *Fluency and accuracy*

Accuracy describes the learner's use of grammar, vocabulary and phonology, and the extent to which this is free from mistakes. *Fluency*, on the other hand, describes the learner's ability to convey (or to understand) a message as it is intended. Accuracy is a component in this, but so too is the ability to organise ideas over a substantial stretch of language, to employ strategies to convey meaning when the learner does not know the required language items, and to 'keep the discourse moving' so that there are no long gaps while the learner thinks of what to say or write.

Look at the two accompanying samples of writing by foreign learners of English or listen to two extracts of different learners speaking.

1   Read through (listen to) both samples quickly. Are you able to say which learner communicates in English more effectively (fluency)? What factors in the use of language do you base this judgement on?

2   Attempt to count mistakes. To what extent does the frequency of mistakes mirror your subjective judgement as to which is the 'better' communicator?

Section B   *Categories of error*

1   As far as possible, try to classify the mistakes you have

identified in the previous section of the Task using the
following three categories:
– serious
– intermediate (i.e. intermediate between serious and trivial)
– trivial
Discuss the criteria you found yourself employing in
attempting to do this exercise. How easy or difficult did you
find the exercise?

2   As far as possible, try to classify the mistakes you have
    identified using the following categories:
    – discoursal
    – grammatical
    – lexical
    – stylistic
    – other
    How easy or difficult did you find the exercise? Does there
    appear to be any relation between your categorisation of
    items in this exercise and in response to the previous
    question?

Section C   *Errors and mistakes*

A distinction is often made between *errors* and *mistakes*.

Errors are considered to be evidence of the learners' developing
competence in the foreign language. For example, they may
indicate that learners are applying rules from their own first
languages to the use of English, or that they are applying rules
which they have internalised but which are in some way
intermediate between their own first languages and the language
they are learning.

   Despite an inevitable degree of variability in performance,
errors thus are generally systematic. Examples would be:

a) The systematic use of *did + infinitive* by a learner to indicate
    past time ('He did go home, and then he did turn on the TV
    and then he did fall asleep').

b) The systematic over-use of 'regular' past tense endings ('He
    goed home, and then he turned on the TV and then he falled
    asleep').

c) The systematic use of the present perfect to refer to single
    events in the past and the use of the simple past to refer to
    protracted and repeated events ('Before he has got married,

when he lived alone and he worked in the city, he went home every night, turned on the TV and fell asleep. Last night he has come round to dinner and he has fallen asleep again!').

Mistakes, on the other hand, are generally non-systematic and do not necessarily reflect the learner's underlying competence. Learners will normally be able to identify and 'correct' their mistakes if they are prompted to do so.

Refer to the accompanying examples of students' use of English. To what extent can you distinguish between *errors* and *mistakes*?

Section D   *Causes of errors and mistakes*

The following are sometimes cited as being among the 'causes' of errors and mistakes:
a) 'Interference' from the learner's first language
b) Over-generalisation of the rules of the target language
c) Responding to the demands of complex communication (simplification, omissions)
d) Carelessness

Using the accompanying samples of students' use of English as data to help you, try to answer the following questions:

1   How transparent are the causes of errors and mistakes?

2   In instances of opaqueness, would conversation with the learner help you to be clearer about the cause?

3   To what extent can the causes be considered as discrete?

4   In what ways and to what extent does an awareness of causes help the teacher to make decisions about how to respond to the errors and mistakes?

Section E   *Responding to learners' errors and mistakes*

The topic of responding to errors and mistakes in students' writing is dealt with in Discussion Task 23, Section F (*Correction of written work*, see page 225). To avoid duplication, the following refers only to learners' oral production in the classroom.

Task

1 Teachers can respond to learners' errors and mistakes in a number of ways. Look at the following list of responses and add any items you think are missing:

a) They can stop the student and either:
 – invite him to correct himself;
 – prompt him to correct himself by indicating the nature of the error or mistake or where it was in the sentence;
 – encourage other students to supply a 'correction';
 – supply a 'correction' himself.

b) They can make a note of the error or mistake and draw attention to it at a later stage individually or with the whole class.

c) They can choose not to respond.

2 The decision about how to respond is a complex one. Look at the following list of factors teachers need to take into account and add any items you think are missing:

a) The student's purpose in speaking (was he concentrating on accuracy or on fluency?).

b) The nature of the error or mistake (is this something the learner can correct himself?).

c) The personality of the student (is he confident?).

d) The ability of the student (is accuracy a priority for him?).

e) The ease with which the error or mistake can be corrected.

3 Look at the following examples and in each case say how you might respond. Make a note of any additional factors that your choice of response might depend on:

a) Students are working in pairs. The activity is designed to provide practice in a particular structure. Although they have already looked at the form and meaning of this, a student is still avoiding its use.

b) A student is telling a story to the whole class. He consistently (and inaccurately) uses the infinitive form of verbs, effectively speaking without tenses. The story was 'unplanned', and does not fulfil any objective pre-determined by the teacher.

c) Students are working in pairs, preparing a role play. It is clear that several students are confusing the pronouns 'he' and 'she'.

d) Students are discussing a topic which interests them in small groups. One student is struggling to express what he

Task

wants to say but cannot make himself clear and is becoming frustrated. You know what he wants to say.

e) Students are repeating a sentence from a tape in order to 'get their tongues round' difficult combinations of sounds. Several students seem to be unaware that what they are saying is very different from the taped model.

f) One student says something to the class and everyone appears to understand. However, you suspect that they have understood something different from what was intended and that the student who is speaking has not realised this.

Discussion Task 6

Learners' language

Timing   Section A c. 20 minutes
Section B c. 15 minutes
Section C c. 15 minutes
Section D c. 20 minutes
Section E c. 30 minutes
Total   c. 100 minutes

It is not necessary for all five sections of this Task to be used in the same session. Where time is limited, the sections of greatest relevance to participants' interests and teaching circumstances may be selected. Alternatively, different sections may be used simultaneously in a session.

The Task is intended to prepare participants to use Classroom-based Task 3.

Suggestions for procedure

Each section comprises material for discussion in small groups. During this discussion (particularly with regard to Sections B–D) the trainer may want to monitor carefully in order to clarify the concepts underlying the terms used. In these sections plenary feedback may be necessary only if general problems arise which need clearing up, or if participants are particularly interested in conclusions reached in other small groups. More substantial plenary feedback may be desirable for Question 3 of Section E. For each of the six examples given, a representative of a different small group may report back on the conclusions reached in their group, and comments can be invited from other participants.

Written compositions from Section 1 of the *Resources bank* may be used in this Task (see pages 290–4), but many trainers will prefer to obtain their own materials (for example, data from the participants' own learners) or ask the participants to provide them. Written materials are easier for the groups to examine, but where teachers are more concerned with teaching spoken English, use of taped extracts of learners speaking English may be more appropriate. The same materials may be used in each part of the Task, but participants may also prefer to look at a wider sample of materials, in which case 'new' materials may be introduced for use in Sections C and D of the Task.

General discussion and possible outcomes

This Task encourages the participants to analyse learners' language output by using conventional models of categorising non-standard language performance. One of the inevitable consequences of the Task is that participants will find the models clumsy to use. This is again (cf. Discussion Task 1) a reflection of the state of the art – the fact that these models are a tentative attempt to describe and explain processes which are not understood in their totality.

Participants who find that their raised awareness leads to unresolved questions can be encouraged to take advantage of the reading references provided in the Introduction to this chapter.

Section A   *Fluency and accuracy*

The outcome here depends on the characteristics of the learners whose language is investigated. In some cases, accurate use of language may betray a wish to 'play safe', and may belie a relatively limited communicative potential. In other words, there is no *necessary* correlation between fluency and accuracy.

Section B   *Categories of error*

Question 1
Participants are likely either to equate 'seriousness' with the extent to which errors impede effective communication or to equate this with particular types of error (for example, they may perceive grammatical errors to be more serious than errors of spelling, or spelling errors to be more serious than stylistic ones).

Teachers often have a tendency to regard grammatical errors as the most serious. However, it is interesting to explore why this may be so as these, often, are the ones which least interfere with effective communication.

Question 2
This question is intended to highlight for participants the criteria they instinctively employ in determining the seriousness of error

and to encourage them to question these. It may also draw attention to the extent to which these categories may overlap. For example, 'He said me he was ill' might be considered as either a grammatical or a lexical error, while the mis-use of cohesive devices such as 'furthermore' or 'as well as' might be considered either lexical or discoursal.

It is difficult to identify examples of 'communicative' error, but this is an obvious additional category. Learners (and indeed native speakers) may produce superficially accurate utterances without, however, managing to effect the purpose for which they are made.

Lexical and grammatical errors are often the most noticeable, but these are not necessarily the ones which interfere with communication.

Section C   *Errors and mistakes*

Responses to this question will depend on the examples of learners' output used and on how well participants know the learners who produced the material. However, participants are likely to conclude that it is often impossible to identify whether an instance of inaccurate usage represents an error or a mistake.

Errors will tend to be systematic and mistakes non-systematic. However, there is a danger of simplistically accepting the error/mistake model as being more adequate than it is with regard to explaining the processes of learning. The learner may be at an intermediate stage where he has access to the 'correct' rule but has not fully internalised it. Moreover, recent research suggests that the process of learning language is not a neat sequence of building up and internalising rules, but that a lot of language is learned initially in unanalysed 'chunks' (Pawley & Syder, 1983). This complicates any discussion of the distinction between errors and mistakes.

Section D   *Causes of errors and mistakes*

Question 1
Interference from the learner's first language may be transparent in some cases such as the use of 'false cognates' (words which look alike but which have different meanings or shades of meaning in the two languages). However, identifying causes of errors and mistakes often depends entirely on an intimate

knowledge of a learner's general learning experience and performance in using the language.

Question 2
Conversation with the learner may provide insight into the causes of errors and mistakes in some cases.

Question 3
The causes are rarely discrete. In any one instance, more than one factor may be responsible for the error or mistake, and it is often difficult to determine which factors are operating.

Question 4
Identifying the causes of errors and mistakes, although often difficult, can be very pertinent in terms of deciding how to respond. Only careless slips can be dealt with by on-the-spot correction. Errors of interference and over-generalisation provide a key to learners' current understanding of the language system and may provide the teacher with evidence on which to base decisions about what to teach explicitly. Mistakes which result from the effort to communicate may well disappear as the learner becomes more confident and experienced in trying to communicate.

Section E *Responding to learners' errors and mistakes*

Participants may like to follow up this section of the Task by reading the relevant sections in Gower & Walters (1983) pp. 146–51 or Harmer (1991) pp. 68–70, 237–9.

Questions 1 & 2
These questions are intended to prepare participants to approach Question 3. The trainer may want to evaluate and respond to additional items suggested according to the nature of these items.

Question 3
The following are possible responses (although participants may also advance sound reasons for preferring alternative options):
a) The teacher may interrupt the activity and remind the students of the aim of the exercise or he might make a note of what the student says and subsequently invite him to re-formulate it using the structure the activity was intended to practise.

Notes

b) The teacher might make a note of the student's errors and mistakes and subsequently ask questions to probe the extent to which the student was aware of these, and to try to ascertain the causes. He might leave the matter there, or might ask the student to re-tell part of the story using the correct tenses.

c) The teacher might respond as in (b) above, or he might gently interrupt to remind students to pay attention to the use of pronouns.

d) This kind of frustration can be very constructive and the teacher might simply give the student encouragement to persevere. Alternatively, if he felt that on this occasion the frustration might lead to the student's giving up and feeling discouraged, he might intervene and 'help' the student.

e) The teacher might stop the activity and ask students to listen more carefully, possibly indicating where in the sentence they are making mistakes. Alternatively, he might ask them to apply rules they have consciously learned to identify this source of error (for example, 'Think about which tenses we use to talk about the past. Now listen again . . . ').

f) The teacher might intervene and ask another member of the class to reflect back to the speaker what he thinks the speaker has said in order to alert the speaker and the other students to the 'hidden' breakdown in communication. Alternatively, he might make a note of this and refer back to it subsequently.

Among general points which might arise in the discussion are the following:

The value of correction altogether can be questioned. There is no general evidence to support the view that learners benefit from their mistakes being pointed out and corrected. However, individual learners may well feel that this is useful to them and, indeed, some learners may feel this is useful at some times and not at others.

Teachers clearly need to find out the attitudes of their learners to this question, and to monitor this constantly. They may also find it useful to explore the historical basis for correcting mistakes. Approaches to teaching which were strongly influenced by behaviourist theories of learning placed strong emphasis on correction as it was felt that uncorrected mistakes could lead to the development of 'bad habits', which would be difficult to eradicate. There is, in fact, very little evidence to support this view.

Notes

Any 'on-the-spot' correction is likely to take place in activities which are accuracy-focussed and teacher-centred. Correction would rarely be appropriate where the emphasis was on communication, as the correction would probably distract from the purpose of the activity.

Perhaps rather than thinking in terms of 'correction', teachers may prefer to think in terms of how best to help learners to develop their ability to communicate in the long-term. Only sometimes will this be best achieved by drawing their attention to mistakes, and this will probably be in cases where the teacher is aware that a learner is trying to formulate an accurate utterance, but is unsure about precisely what form this should take. Often this focus may not be so much on the mistake as on the rule or on the correct form, and may take place some time after the teacher has identified the problem.

Classroom-based Task 1

Task

Materials designed to develop learning skills

Aim   This Task aims to develop your awareness of materials and approaches which focus on the processes of learning. It also explores your own responses and the responses of your students to the use of these materials in class.

TASK

Refer to *Resources bank*, Section 3, Resource 10 (see pages 303–5). This extract is intended to help learners to develop their learning skills and comes from Ellis & Sinclair, *Learning to Learn English,* a book designed to help learners to develop effective and appropriate learning strategies.

Section A   *Analysis of the material*

1   What skills are targeted in this material?

2   How successful do you think this material is in achieving these objectives?

Section B   *Practical evaluation of the material*

Use this or similar material in class (you may need to prepare for this lesson/these lessons by teaching preliminary skills in previous lessons). Then devise a brief questionnaire to elicit from the students:

1   The extent to which they were aware of the objectives of the activity.
   Example
   Tick sentences in the following list which you think are true:
   In this lesson I learnt to organise my time better when I study at home.
   In this lesson I learnt to speak English better.

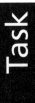

In this lesson I learnt to be more relaxed about making mistakes.
In this lesson I learnt some ways of remembering words I have studied.

2   The extent to which they valued the activity.

Example

Against each of the sentences you have ticked write a number 1–3:

1   This was very useful for me.
2   This was quite useful for me.
3   This was not useful for me.

Briefly give a reason for your choice in each case.

Notes

Classroom-based Task 1

Materials designed to develop learning skills

The Task can be used to extend and apply conclusions reached in the Discussion Tasks in this chapter. Discussion Tasks 2 and 5 are particularly relevant, and this Task can be prepared at the end of a session which uses one of these Discussion Tasks.

Suggestions for procedure

Section A   *Analysis of the material*

Questions 1 and 2 can be discussed by small groups of participants with or without plenary feedback on this. This may take place in the last 10–15 minutes of a session which has been based on one or more of the Discussion Tasks in this chapter.

Section B   *Practical evaluation of the material*

Time can also be made available for participants to prepare their 'experimental lessons' and the questionnaires together.

Two or three of the participants may be selected to carry out the research, and to prepare to report back on this to the whole group at some later stage after comparing and discussing the results between themselves.

General discussion and possible outcomes

Section A   *Analysis of the material*

Question 1
Skills targeted in this material include identifying personal learning styles and developing strategies which may not be a part of the learners' normal repertoire.

Notes

Question 2

Responses to this question will vary according to the beliefs and opinions of participants but they are likely to be positive.

Section B *Practical evaluation of the material*

The results of the experiment and questionnaire will depend on the materials chosen, the nature of the lessons and the characteristics of the learners.

Task

Classroom-based Task 2

Learning styles and strategies

Aim   This Task aims to encourage you to 'test out' assumptions and impressions about individual students' learning styles and strategies against the evidence you can obtain from your students.

TASK

Devise a questionnaire to distribute to students in one or more of your classes. It should contain 4–6 questions which focus on different aspects of learning styles and/or strategies. With monolingual classes of a low level the questionnaire may be written in the learners' first language.

Before collecting the questionnaires in, 'pre-select' three or four students whose results you want to analyse particularly carefully, and attempt to predict how they will respond to the questions. You may pre-select students each of whom appears to have a different 'level' of English, or you may choose those who appear to have particularly marked characteristics in their individual approaches to learning.

When students have completed the questionnaires but before you collect them in, hold a general discussion with the class on the topic covered by the questionnaire. Make general notes on the results of this.

Concentrate on the questionnaires submitted by your 'pre-selected' students. Compare the results of their questionnaires with your predictions. To what extent do these confirm or put into question your assumptions about the effectiveness of different styles and strategies?

The following items are intended to stimulate ideas for the possible content of a questionnaire:

Example *Styles*

1   Do you feel frustrated when you partially understand the meaning of a word or do you accept this and assume that with further study/exposure to the word its meaning will become clearer? Tick one of the following:
   a) frustrated   ....
   b) assume it will become clearer   ....

Task

2 Do you feel eager to use a new word you are unsure of in order to find out if the way you have used it is appropriate, or are you reluctant to use something until you are sure you can use it 'correctly'? Tick one of the following:

a) eager ....

b) reluctant ....

Example *Strategies*

1 Do you test your memory of the meanings of new words?

2 Do you sort out and make a neat copy of the rough notes you might make during an English lesson?

Notes

Classroom-based Task 2

Learning styles and strategies

The Task is particularly closely related to Discussion Tasks 1 and 4, and can be used to extend the issues discussed in these Tasks.

Suggestions for procedure

Participants can discuss this Task together in groups and collaborate on designing the materials. Two or three of them can be selected to carry out the research and to report back to the larger group subsequently, after comparing and discussing their conclusions together.

General discussion and possible outcomes

The term 'style' is used loosely in this Task. It is intended to encompass the range of personality types and learning characteristics dealt with in Discussion Task 1.

The precise outcome of the research will depend on the nature of the learners, and the particular assumptions participants choose to investigate.

Classroom-based Task 3

Task

Learners' awareness of errors and mistakes and attitudes towards these

Aim This Task provides a framework for you to investigate both the extent to which some of your students are aware of error, and also their attitudes towards error.

TASK

Select two learners who appear to be quite different in terms of their approaches to learning and check whether they are willing to take part in a small (and for them completely undemanding) research project. Choose one student who appears to favour fluent use of the language, and one who appears to put a high priority on accuracy.

At different times during their course of study, photocopy three or four examples of their written work (the freer the better) before you have corrected it. Near the beginning of the course also try to make a short recording of each of them chatting (two or three minutes each may be sufficient).

Towards the end of the course of study arrange a short 'tutorial' with each of them (15 or 20 minutes). Carefully plan the questions you will ask them and predict how well you think each of them will perform in the following exercise before the 'tutorial' takes place.

Ask each of them questions to elicit attitudes and awareness.

Example
How important do you think 'being correct' is?
How do you feel when attention is drawn to your mistakes?
Do you learn from this?
Do you like the teacher to correct mistakes or to give you the opportunity to do so?
How aware are you of mistakes you make?

Show them short extracts from their earlier written work and play them a short clip of themselves speaking. Ask them to identify and correct any mistakes. Indicate some mistakes that they have not identified. Can they recognise these?

85

Task

Use this data to help you draw up a short profile of each student under the headings *Attitude to mistakes/errors* and *Awareness of mistakes/errors.*

1   Does there appear to be any correlation between the information under the two headings?

2   Does the information you obtain confirm your subjective impression that one student was more accuracy-orientated and the other more fluency-orientated?

Notes

Classroom-based Task 3

Learners' awareness of errors and mistakes and attitudes towards these

The Task involves applying and researching issues considered in Discussion Task 6.

Suggestions for procedure

Since the recommended sample is so small (two learners), it may be useful for as many participants as possible to be engaged in this project. As, necessarily, it takes place over some time, it may be useful for the trainer or a member of the group to take on the responsibility for coordinating the activity and for keeping in touch with the participants carrying out the research.

General discussion and possible outcomes

It is likely that accuracy-orientated learners are more aware of their mistakes than fluency-orientated learners. However, this is not always the case, and participants who find this to be true may like to speculate about the reasons for this with reference to the individual students who took part in the project.

D

5   The teacher

Introduction to the chapter

1   Contents

2   General discussion of issues

The Tasks in this chapter focus on teaching styles, teachers' roles and teachers' use of language. In each case the aim of the Discussion Tasks is to help participants to become more aware of themselves as teachers, and more aware of their preferences, predispositions and general classroom practice. The material describes a range of possibilities in these respects, and participants can be encouraged to experiment with alternatives to their 'normal' behaviour in the classroom.

Classroom-based Task 4 aims to extend the participants' thinking about the use of the learners' first language in the classroom by encouraging them to explore the learners' reactions to its use (and/or non-use). Classroom-based Task 5 aims to help participants to become more aware of their own use of language in giving instructions as a basis, possibly, for making conscious modifications to the way they normally do this.

Discussion Task 10 and Classroom-based Task 5 are particularly relevant to teachers working in environments where the learners all share a common first language (or lingua franca). The other Tasks are intended to be of relevance and interest to all teachers.

3   Reading

Byrne, D. (1987). *Techniques for Classroom Interaction.* Longman.
Harmer, J. (1991). *The Practice of English Language Teaching.* Longman (Chapter 1).

Malamah-Thomas, A. (1987). *Classroom Interaction*. Oxford University Press.

Underwood, M. (1987). *Effective Class Management*. Longman.

The Tasks in this chapter involve the participants in introspecting and comparing experience. Reading is not essential, and these references are provided for trainers who, in preparing to use the Tasks, would like to remind themselves of some of the general issues raised in them, and for participants who would like to pursue particular interests which have arisen in their discussion.

The clearest and most straightforward introduction to this topic is the chapter in Harmer. Byrne and Underwood write at greater length, but are clear and to the point. Both of them cover issues of classroom management from a much broader perspective than that considered in these Tasks.

Malamah-Thomas provides a very different perspective. Her book, based around tasks itself, focusses on interaction from a more theoretical point of view and is of more tangential relevance to the Tasks in this chapter. Of particular value in the book is the range of instruments described for observing, recording and becoming more aware of the interactions which take place in classrooms.

Discussion Task 7

General teaching styles

Aim   This Task encourages you to reflect on your own
preferred styles of teaching, and to consider alternative
styles.

TASK

Section A   *General discussion*

1   Think of the activities you most enjoy and least enjoy in your
lessons. Are these activities in which you tend to play a
dominant role or a 'back seat' role? Do you see yourself in
the classroom more as a 'leader' or as a 'manager'?

2   To what extent do you feel that the tradition in which you
work allows you to teach in a style which feels comfortable
to you? (For example, some teachers may feel personally out
of sympathy with an approach which requires the teacher to
be very dominant.)

3   Has your teaching style changed during your career?

4   Do you envisage that it will change further?

5   Do you consciously experiment with adopting different
'styles'?

Section B   *Identifying personal styles and characteristics*

Look at the following list of adjectives which could be used to
characterise teaching styles and to describe teachers' qualities:

relaxed	patient	dynamic
resourceful	attentive	creative
innovative	caring	intuitive
hard-working	well-prepared	enthusiastic
authoritative	flexible	accurate
space-giving	clear	systematic
well-informed		

Task

1   In groups, ensure that you agree about the meaning of each term, and the distinctions between them.
    Example An *innovative* teacher is one who favours approaches which are original in themselves whereas a *creative* teacher may produce original materials but within a traditional approach.

2   Add any adjectives to the list which describe further qualities you feel are missing.

3   These adjectives are intended to describe positive qualities. Do you feel that any of them could have a negative side as well? In what way?
    Example A dynamic teacher may not provide the learners with sufficient 'space' to set their own pace and to initiate topics of personal interest.

4   Working individually, choose the four items from this list which you feel most accurately describe your own teaching style or characteristics. Put them into an order according to how characteristic of yourself you think they are.
    Explain to the other people in your group the reasons for the choices you have made.

Discussion Task 7

General teaching styles

Timing   Section A c. 20 minutes
Section B c. 20 minutes
Total   c. 40 minutes

Suggestions for procedure

In this Task it is important that participants work in groups where they feel comfortable. This is particularly important with regard to the final activity. The ideal group size for this Task is three.

Section A   *General discussion*

This part of the Task can be discussed in small groups.

Section B   *Identifying personal styles and characteristics*

It may be necessary for the trainer to clarify some of the terms. Unless the group is very large, this can probably be done in response to individual questions while the small groups are discussing the points.

The rest of the Task can be discussed in small groups. Plenary feedback may be desirable only if participants feel it would be useful and interesting.

General discussion and possible outcomes

This Task differs from most of the Tasks in this book in that it quite deliberately looks at the classroom from the point of view of the teacher rather than the learner. It also invites teachers to think of themselves in such a way that discussion should be closer to a model of sharing than of arguing or investigating.

Notes

This Task may give rise to questions about the difference between teaching *style/characteristics* and *role*. The role of the teacher depends on the aims and nature of a particular classroom activity, whereas the style embraces the more general predispositions of the teacher. Thus, a teacher can act as a *manager* (role) in giving instructions, and do this in a way which is caring/uncaring, patient/irritated, attentive/distracted, enthusiastic/bored, etc.

This Task focusses on the personal responses of individuals, which makes it difficult to anticipate any particular outcome.

In response to Question 3 in Section B of the Task, an argument could probably be advanced in the case of each of the adjectives, although some of the accompanying circumstances would have to be far-fetched.

Discussion Task 8

Teachers' roles

Aim   This Task aims to help you to develop your awareness
of the different roles teachers perform, and to consider
the appropriateness of different roles. It is intended to
help you to develop a more principled basis on which to
make decisions about the planning and teaching of
lessons, particularly with regard to the range of roles
available to you.

TASK

Section A   *Roles and functions*

Look at the following 'role definitions' and the list of some of a
teacher's functions.

For each of these functions, decide which role is most
appropriate (in some cases more than one 'role' may be
involved):

Roles

a) DIAGNOSTICIAN
b) PLANNER
c) MANAGER
d) PROVIDER

Functions

i)   To find out (as far and as consistently as possible) the needs,
interests, language difficulties and preferred learning styles
of the students.
ii)   To cater for these (as far as group exigencies allow).
iii)   To foster a group feeling (cooperation, liking, common
aims, mutual confidence, etc.).
iv)   To ensure that learners have clear short and long-term
learning objectives.
v)   To assess the progress of individuals and of the class as a
whole.
vi)   To ensure that learners are aware of this progress.
vii)   To encourage students to take responsibility for their
learning.

viii) To vary patterns of interaction within the lesson according to the precise aims and the nature/feeling of the group.

ix) To ensure that the students find their involvement sufficiently challenging.

x) To analyse and present realistic 'chunks' of the target language for students to process.

xi) To select and introduce activities and materials for language work.

xii) To help students develop positive, individual strategies for learning.

Example *Function (i) – Role (a):* The teacher is clearly acting as a diagnostician in performing this function, although the results of this diagnosis will subsequently form the basis for the teacher to act as a planner (b).

Section B   *Alternative ways of classifying roles*

For some purposes you might want a model which offers a greater number of categories than the one above. Make a list of further categories you might use to classify the roles a teacher performs.

Example Entertainer

Section C   *Roles and lesson activities*

Either:

Look at Lesson Plan B (*Resources bank*, Section 2, Resource 9, page 302). Using your preferred system for classifying a teacher's roles, specify the role the teacher is likely to adopt at each of the points marked 'R'. Compare your answers with those of other members of the group. How do you account for any differences?

1	7	12
2	8	13
3	9	14
4	10	15
5	11	16
6		

Example *1 Manager:* The teacher is involved here in the physical management of the classroom, organising the location and grouping of students in the room.

Task

Or:

Watch a 10-minute section of a videoed lesson. As you watch it a second time, record the changes which take place in the teacher's roles. Compare your list of changes with those of other members of the group. How do you account for any differences between the lists?

Discussion Task 8

Teachers' roles

Timing   Section A c. 15 minutes
             Section B c. 10 minutes
             Section C c. 35 minutes
             Total   c. 60 minutes

Suggestions for procedure

Section A   *Roles and functions*

Participants may want 5 minutes or so just to mull over the
categories, and in particular to reflect on the twelve functions
listed here. Some participants, at this stage, may want to modify
the categories provided in the Task. This is quite acceptable.

In small groups of three or four, participants match the roles
to the functions by putting one or more letters to a number (see
Example) and record this on an OHP transparency or large sheet
of paper to show to the whole group subsequently. They also
justify each choice they make.

Section B   *Alternative ways of classifying roles*

Participants can work on this in small groups (the trainer may
want to give a time limit of 5 minutes).

The trainer can elicit the additional 'roles' brainstormed by the
groups, write them on the board and provide a few minutes for
any participants to comment on suggestions made by other
groups.

It is possible that some groups may prefer to work with the
four-fold list of roles given here. This is acceptable.

Section C   *Roles and lesson activities*

First alternative (lesson plan):
Participants can work on this in the same small groups. The
trainer may want to give participants half a minute or so to read
the instructions and then ask if they need further clarification.

He may want to point out that in some cases the teacher is playing a dual or multiple role.

OHP transparencies, posters or re-constitution of groups can be used for participants to learn what conclusions were reached in other small groups and to comment on this.

Second alternative (video):
(Where video facilities are available and part of a lesson can be recorded, this option is to be preferred.)

1   Participants can individually record the changes of role which occur in the section of the lesson they watch.
2   In small groups they can then compare their conclusions with those of other participants.
3   In a plenary group, an appointed member of each small group can be invited simply to describe and account for any particular differences which arose during the small-group discussion.

General discussion and possible outcomes

Some of the realisations that participants may arrive at through this Task are:
-   The extent to which a teacher is involved in roles other than that of 'provider'.
-   The extent to which a teacher 'provides' more than just examples of new language.
-   The amount of time spent by teachers in lessons on 'management'.
-   The virtue of staying with a small number of categories to analyse a topic (groups who produce a long list of categories to describe roles may find that this is unwieldy in practice).

Section A   *Roles and functions*

The precise results of the matching exercise will inevitably vary from group to group, reflecting not only differences in teaching circumstances, but also reflecting differing assumptions about what is appropriate in any situation and differing interpretations of some of the terms.

The following combinations or 'matchings' are merely one person's individual response. This is not intended as an 'answer sheet':

i)	a	vii)	c
ii)	b (c, d)	viii)	c
iii)	c	ix)	c (b, d)
iv)	b (d)	x)	d
v)	a	xi)	b (d)
vi)	d	xii)	b, c (a, d)

Section B   *Alternative ways of classifying roles*

Although it is impossible to anticipate the full variety of categories the groups may produce, some of the following are likely to be included:
friend, judge, disciplinarian, police officer, facilitator, listener, counsellor, helper, monitor, leader, etc.

Section C   *Roles and lesson activities*

First alternative (lesson plan):
The roles performed at the different stages of the lesson by the teacher who wrote Lesson Plan B are debatable, and this debate is to be encouraged. In particular, participants can be encouraged not only to justify their choices but also to refer explicitly to how they themselves would approach a particular activity in the plan, and to compare this with each other.

As participants will be using their own taxonomies, it is not possible to predict the precise outcome. The following is one possible example of how the exercise might be completed using an unmodified taxonomy – (a) diagnostician; (b) planner; (c) manager; (d) provider:

1 c	7 d, a	12 a, b, c, d
2 c	8 c, a, d	13 a, b, c, d
3 c	9 c	14 c
4 c	10 a	15 a, c, d
5 a, c	11 c	16 c
6 d		

Second alternative (video):
The outcome of this will obviously depend on choices made with regard to the video extract.

Discussion Task 9

Teachers' language: Instructions

Aim   This Task looks at different ways in which teachers may give instructions and encourages you to consider alternatives to your normal approaches. It also explores some of the problems which may arise in giving instructions.

TASK

Section A   *A question of approach*

1   Consider the following:
   a) How carefully do you prepare the way you will give instructions in a particular lesson?
   b) In what ways do you give instructions?
      Example (With monolingual classes) The teacher may explain the procedure in English and ask a student to translate this into the learners' first language.
   c) What (if any) problems arise with regard to students understanding your instructions?

2   Comment on the following two points of view. Does either of them seem to be more acceptable than the other? (If you feel that this depends on particular circumstances, qualify your answer with specific reference to these circumstances.)

   a) **Teachers should aim to demonstrate to students as simply and as clearly as possible what they have to do. Non-verbal instructions are often more effective than verbal.**
   b) **The giving of instructions in the classroom is one of the few genuinely communicative acts which takes place. The teacher should thus exploit this opportunity by making her instructions as natural as possible. If they are complicated and difficult for the students to understand, learners and the teacher are consequently obliged to 'negotiate meaning' to achieve an authentic communicative purpose.**

Task

3   Evaluate the following instructions, keeping in mind any conclusions you may have reached in discussing the previous question:

a) Teacher: 'A. Now, I'd like you to get into pairs, A and B. A, I want you to ask questions to find out what is in B's picture. B, be careful not to let A see your picture. OK, here are the pictures. That's right, Maria, turn away from Aziza so she can't see it. Everyone, look at Maria and Aziza and see how they're sitting. That's right. Good.'

b) The teacher gets the attention of the whole class. Then she gives a picture to Maria and gestures to her not to reveal it to others. The teacher asks Maria three or four questions to find out what is in the picture. She then gestures to Wang (who is on the opposite side of the room) to continue the questions. She then uses gesture to divide the students into pairs and gives one student in each pair a picture. She says, 'OK? Now you.'

Section B   *Some common problems*

Look at the following situations and identify what might have gone wrong. What else could the teacher have done?

a) (Class of any level) The teacher hands out a passage for the students to read. She then tells them to read it very quickly in order to extract the gist. The students begin to read painstakingly.

b) i) (Lower-intermediate class) The teacher wants to teach the question *How long + present perfect continuous*. She wants the students to repeat 'How long have you been studying English?' but, instead, the students answer her 'Six months'.

   ii) (Lower-intermediate class) The teacher has drilled the question 'How long have you been studying English?', and now wants the students to ask each other across the class and to elicit the appropriate answers. However, the students simply keep repeating the question.

   iii)(Elementary class) The class is learning and practising the simple present. The teacher has drilled the question 'What time do you get up?' and now wants the students to ask other questions beginning 'What time do you . . . ?' However, the students keep asking 'What time do you get up?'

Task

c) (Elementary class) The teacher wants the students to do an exercise from their workbooks for homework. She explains that she wants the students to write the answers on a piece of paper to hand in. In the next lesson she discovers that most of the students have written their answers in the workbook. She cannot collect these in because they will need them for their next homework.

d) (Advanced class) The teacher has asked each student to prepare a short presentation on a topic of their own interest to give to the rest of the class. She discovers that many of the students have written down the text of the presentation and feel unprepared to give it without reading out what they have written.

Discussion Task 9

Teachers' language: Instructions

Timing   Section A c. 20 minutes
Section B c. 25 minutes
Total   c. 45 minutes

Suggestions for procedure

Section A   *A question of approach*

Participants can consider these questions in small groups.

In a plenary session, the 'secretaries' from three or four of the groups can tell the other participants the key points they have noted down, and time can be provided for any further related comments to be made or questions to be asked.

Section B   *Some common problems*

This section of the Task can be organised in a way similar to the above. However, in this case the 'secretaries' may want to summarise the discussion rather than pick out key points.

General discussion and possible outcomes

Section A   *A question of approach*

Question 1
The trainer may subsequently want to refer participants back to points made in response to this question to encourage them to evaluate their 'normal practice' in the light of issues raised in later parts of the Task.

Question 2
In responding to this question it is important that participants consider the advantages and disadvantages of both approaches, and circumstances in which each may be appropriate.

In the last few years the second point of view has come to supplant the first to some extent. Arguments for both points of

103

Notes

view can be advanced and factors which might be considered in this discussion might include reference to:
- the level of the class;
- the confidence and disposition of the learners;
- the complexity of the task;
- the time available.

Many teachers will probably adopt both approaches, even within one lesson, and will also mix the two approaches in different proportions.

Question 3

The first example of instructions illustrates (b) in Question 2, and the second example illustrates (a).

The first example (a) might be criticised for being prolix, abstract and difficult to follow. On the other hand, it is very 'human', and a teacher who is carefully monitoring the students' reactions may be able to pick up any problems they have in following the instructions.

The second example (b) might be criticised for being slick and clinical. It appears, however, to be very effective. Perhaps in the repertoire of a warm, humane teacher who communicates naturally with her students this approach is very valid. However, there might be a danger of its over-use by a teacher who was very preoccupied by the techniques of the classroom at the expense of the 'human' side.

Section B   *Some common problems*

Some of the following might be included among the points made:
a) The students were looking at the passage instead of paying attention to the teacher. Solution: give instructions before materials.
b) In (i) the students are confusing an activity with a precise linguistic aim with one whose aim is more concerned with communication. In (ii) and (iii), the students are confusing different linguistic aims. Solution: the teacher needs to signal the aim and focus of the activities more clearly. Perhaps she needs to teach and use clear and simple classroom instructions such as: 'repeat', 'answer', 'question'.

This kind of confusion often arises when the teacher is using communicatively plausible sentences (with first and second person pronouns) as examples of structures. An example is *How long have you been studying English?* To avoid this kind of problem, some teachers choose to teach new language through 'depersonalised' situations, using third person pronouns (the biography of a real or imagined person might be used in this case). This may be less plausible, but is also less prone to ambiguity and confusion.

c) The teacher could perhaps have shown them an example of what she wanted or, with a monolingual group, explained in their own language. The problem is probably one of the students' inability to understand these complicated instructions.

   With students at a slightly higher level, it is often helpful to ask a student to repeat the teacher's instructions back to the rest of the class in her own words to check that everyone has understood.

d) In cases such as this it is often difficult to know whether the problem originates from the lack of clarity of the instructions or from the unwillingness of the students to carry out the task. Where the task may be perceived by the students as 'difficult', 'threatening' or 'unpopular', after giving the instructions (and, perhaps, checking them by asking a student to repeat them back) it may be useful for the teacher to focus specifically on the students' attitudes towards carrying out the task. For example, the students can be asked in groups to discuss and report back on their feelings towards the task, or time can be made for them to make a brief individual written response. In the long run, time devoted at this stage to acknowledging sources of potential resistance to the task will be well spent. Reassurance can be provided for anxieties. If necessary the task itself can be adapted.

Task

Discussion Task 10

Teachers' use of the learners' first language

Aim   This Task encourages you to explore and consider reasons for and against the use of the learners' first language. It also asks you to devise guidelines for yourselves with regard to its use.

TASK

Section A   *Approaches and opinions*

To what extent do you agree or disagree with the various points of view expressed here?

a) The giving of instructions provides one of the few opportunities for genuine communication in the classroom. Use of the students' own language thus deprives them of a crucial opportunity for learning.

b) The use of translation to provide the meaning of new vocabulary encourages students to develop the mistaken assumption that there is a one-to-one correspondence between words in English and in their own language.

c) Using the students' first language for comprehension tasks enables students at a low level both to focus on more 'difficult' texts, and to focus on texts in a more structured and productive way.

d) If the teacher is worried about the class understanding his instructions or explanation, he can ask a student to translate what he has said to the others.

e) Instructions should be given in both languages – English first.

f) Students should be given the opportunity to discuss what they are learning in their own language – for example, having learnt how a particular idea is expressed in English, they may be asked to comment on the difference between this and their own language.

g) Students should be allowed to ask the teacher (in English) if they may say something or ask something in their own language. All other use of their language is prohibited.

Task

h) The learners' first language should be used in the classroom only very judiciously, and inexperienced teachers should work hard to develop alternative ways of making themselves clear, and only then contemplate using the students' language.

Section B   *General guidelines*

Use your responses to these comments as a basis for devising a set of guidelines on the use of the learners' first language in the classroom. Write this on an OHP transparency or on a large sheet of paper so that other members of the group can look at it and comment on it.

Discussion Task 10

Notes

Teachers' use of the learners' first language

Timing   Section A c. 20 minutes
Section B c. 20 minutes
Total   c. 40 minutes

Classroom-based Task 5 provides a framework for participants to explore their students' reactions to issues considered in this Task.

Suggestions for procedure

Section A *Approaches and opinions*

Participants can consider these points of view in small groups, choosing to discuss only those which particularly interest them. Plenary feedback may consist of 'secretaries' reporting back on points of particular contention or interest which arose in the discussion.

Section B *General guidelines*

The procedure for this is straightforward. This stage may, however, be omitted if the appropriate technology and resources are unavailable or, simply, if the participants feel they have exhausted the topic.

General discussion and possible outcomes

This Task aims to question both the unthinking over-use of the learners' first language and the dogmatic avoidance of its use. The discussion will probably need to make reference to specific groups of learners, specific teachers and specific activities and objectives in lessons. There are no 'right' or 'wrong' points of

Notes

view – what is important is that participants argue their opinions convincingly with reference to specific learning/teaching circumstances.

Section A   *Approaches and opinions*

These are some of the kinds of points which might be made:

a) This may depend on the level, age and tolerance of the learners. However, it is generally true, and even when learners fail to understand the instructions initially, as long as the teacher is sensitive to this and is prepared to modify his language and 'negotiate the meaning' with the learners, this may provide a rich source of language development for them.

b) This is a frequently-voiced opinion. However, there is little evidence to suggest that this is true. In the initial stages of learning, it is inevitable that learners will exaggerate equivalences between the foreign language and their own language. But this may be a useful, temporary learning strategy.

c) Participants are likely to agree with this.

d) Participants are likely to agree with this.

e) This may help learners get used to instructions in English and can provide a useful temporary 'crutch'. However, knowing that the instructions will be repeated in their own language may also encourage the students to 'switch off'.

f) Participants are likely to agree with this.

g) A lot of teachers employ this principle and are pleased with the results.

h) This is generally true. There is a danger that the teacher, himself, may become over-reliant on the use of the students' first language and lose or fail to acquire the skills of making himself comprehensible to his students in the foreign language.

Section B   *General guidelines*

The guidelines will vary from group to group but the kinds of points which might be made are:

– Use the students' first language when there is an obvious breakdown in communication.

– Prepare instructions very carefully at the lesson-planning stage in order to ensure that they are clear in the target language.

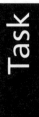
Task

Classroom-based Task 4

Analysis of teachers' language of instructions

Aim   This Task provides you with a framework in which to analyse and become more aware of the ways in which you give instructions. This may form the basis for making changes in your practice.

TASK

Record and then transcribe a section (or sections) of a lesson (or lessons) in which you give instructions to students. The transcript will probably need to be of about 200 words. (If you do not have access to recording facilities, you might like to invite a colleague to observe a lesson and ask him to transcribe as much of your instructions as possible.)

The following questions are intended as *examples* of some of the questions you might like to address in analysing the transcript(s):

1   To what extent do you explain, as opposed to demonstrate, what you want students to do?

2   To what extent (if at all) do you use the learners' first language?

3   How simple/complicated is your use of the target language in relation to the students' linguistic ability? You may like to consider factors such as *sentence length*, *use of idiom and vocabulary*, and *speed of speech*.

4   Do you repeat or modify instructions?

5   Do you use any means to check that students have understood the instructions?

Classroom-based Task 4

Analysis of teachers' language of instructions

The Task may be used to extend and apply issues considered in Discussion Task 9.

Suggestions for procedure

Participants may like to prepare the questions to ask themselves together.

As this Task looks at individual characteristics of the participants, a formal 'feedback' session may be inappropriate. However, participants who carry out the Task may appreciate a time being arranged (perhaps at the beginning of a session which will focus primarily on another topic) at which they can comment on their findings if they should want to do so.

General discussion and possible outcomes

The conclusions participants reach will be individual and personal. The trainer may wish neither to 'force' participants to carry out the Task, nor to share their findings with others.

Classroom-based Task 5

Teachers' use of the learners' first language

Aim   This Task provides a framework within which you can test out your assumptions about your learners' attitudes and responses to the teacher's use of their first language.

TASK

Identify your 'normal' use of the learners' first language in class, and plan a lesson in which you will consciously depart from this 'normal' practice. For example, if you tend to avoid the learners' first language, in this lesson carefully prepare ways of using it in giving complicated instructions and/or in teaching the meaning of 'difficult' language. If you normally make extensive use of the first language, on the other hand, consciously avoid its use by carefully preparing alternative means of giving instructions and/or teaching the meaning of language items.

Devise a brief questionnaire to use after this lesson. This should aim to elicit the learners' awareness of the difference and their attitudes towards this.

Example

1   Did you notice that there was anything unusual about this lesson? What?

2   In this lesson did you understand instructions:
   a) More clearly than usual?
   b) As clearly as usual?
   c) Less clearly than usual?

3   In this lesson did you understand the meaning of the language you studied:
   a) More clearly than usual?
   b) As clearly as usual?
   c) Less clearly than usual?

4   Write one or two short paragraphs to answer the following questions:
   – Do you like the teacher to use your first language in the classroom or do you prefer the language you are learning to be used exclusively? Why?

Notes

Classroom-based Task 5

Teachers' use of the learners' first language

The Task develops issues considered in Discussion Task 10.

Suggestions for procedure

Participants may like to plan the lessons and prepare the questionnaires together.

Participants who carry out the research may like to compare their findings and plan how they will present these to the group at the session which has been arranged for this purpose.

General discussion and possible outcomes

It is very difficult to anticipate the outcome of a project such as this as the results will depend on the particular groups of learners involved, and possibly also on the predispositions of the teachers and on their inherent or acquired strengths with regard to use (or non-use) of the learners' language in the classroom. It is important also to bear in mind that the effect of experimenting in itself may affect the perceptions of the learners positively or negatively.

Depending on the findings, the quality of the research and the attitudes of the participants, the trainer may find herself persuading participants to consider more seriously the results of the research on the one hand, or even persuading participants to approach the findings with a greater degree of scepticism on the other.

6   Planning

Introduction to the chapter

1   Contents

2   General background for the trainer or 'session leader'

The Tasks in this chapter focus on two broad aspects of planning.
Discussion Tasks 11–13 and Classroom-based Tasks 6 and 7 are
primarily concerned with the *content* of lessons (choice of materials and
activities and the rationale for these choices), while Discussion Task 14
and Classroom-based Task 8 are more concerned with the *process*
(interaction between the learners and the rationale for different
configurations).

The aim of these Tasks is to raise the awareness of participants with
regard to:

– Their own approaches to planning their teaching and the assumptions
  underlying these approaches.
– The range of approaches to planning available to them.

There is no sense in which the specimen lesson plans and schemes of
work which accompany these Tasks are intended as models. It is
assumed that the nature of any kind of plan will depend on a range of
variables including, of course, the personal preferences of individual
teachers themselves.

These Tasks tend to assume that teachers plan the content of their
lessons in detail. It is sometimes argued, however, on both pragmatic
grounds and on grounds of principle, that the precise content of lessons
should not be determined in advance.

On pragmatic grounds it is rarely feasible for a full-time teacher to devote the amount of time which is described here to preparing every lesson. Indeed, it can also be argued that over-careful planning can inhibit a teacher from responding flexibly to the needs which arise spontaneously during lessons, and can inhibit the learners themselves from initiating and determining the content of the lessons as they develop.

These and other objections to the careful planning of lessons may be advanced by participants. In this event, the trainer may wish to focus discussion on the circumstances in which careful planning may or may not be advisable, taking into account variables such as:
- The teacher (degree of confidence, experience, etc.).
- The learners (expectations from a 'lesson', goals of study, etc.).

However, underlying this material is the assumption that even if thorough and detailed planning of lessons is sometimes unrealistic or counter-productive, the *exercise* of planning carefully and exploring approaches and options in planning is valuable. There is a sense in which the 'unplanned lesson' does not exist – teachers cannot but carry with them into the classroom assumptions about what is and is not feasible and appropriate. By focussing very specifically on conscious planning, they may modify these assumptions and so affect the content and organisation of so-called 'unplanned lessons'.

3 Reading

Harmer, J. (1991). *The Practice of English Language Teaching*. Longman (Chapter 12).
Gower, R. & Walters, S. (1983). *A Teaching Practice Handbook*. Heinemann (pp. 60–5).

While no reading is essential to the use of the Tasks in this chapter, both Harmer and Gower & Walters provide useful background for the trainer in preparing to use the Tasks, and for participants as a follow-up to the activities.

Both Harmer and Gower & Walters describe formulas for planning individual lessons. Inexperienced teachers may find these of particular help.

Discussion Task 11

Schemes of work

Aim   This Task encourages you to reflect on your own practice with regard to planning schemes of work. It also invites you to compare and evaluate two examples of schemes of work and to analyse a teacher's account of devising these.

You are encouraged to consider alternative approaches to your customary practice by relating insights gained from your discussion and analysis of the materials to your individual preferences and your specific teaching circumstances.

TASK

Section A   *Personal experience*

A 'scheme of work' is an outline of the lessons planned for a particular class over a period of time. The precise period of time will depend on the length of the individual lesson and on how often the class meets.

1   How far ahead do you usually plan?
2   In how much detail do you usually plan ahead? Does this vary from class to class? What factors affect the amount of detail you specify in your schemes of work?

3   How do you ensure that your classes get an appropriate balance of the following?
   – activities aimed at developing the different 'skills' (listening, reading, speaking, writing)
   – fluency-orientated activities aimed at communication
   – activities with a specific linguistic focus

4   Do you usually show your schemes of work to your students? Why (not)?

5   How might the following affect the organisation and content of a scheme of work?
   – the nature of the course (intensive or part-time)

- the age of the learners
- the level of the class

Section B   *Analysing and evaluating schemes of work*

Look at the two schemes of work in the *Resources bank* (Section 2, Resources 6 and 7, pages 295 and 296). They were prepared by different teachers for different classes.

Both classes are fourth year groups in Spanish secondary schools. The students have four one-hour lessons of English a week, and the coursebook for each class is *Headway Upper Intermediate.*[1]

Compare the two schemes of work and comment on:
- the balance of 'skills'
- the balance between focus on:
  - 'skills'
  - language work
  - fluency-orientated activities
- the overall integration of activities
- variety
- revision
- homework

Example Both schemes of work appear to give priority to *speaking* firstly, and then *listening* as the skills which deserve the most attention. Both teachers appear to pay only very secondary attention to *reading*, and only Lindsay (Scheme B) seems to pay any explicit attention to *writing*. It is interesting to note that Jack (Scheme A) classifies the giving of presentations as *speaking* whereas most members of the class are presumably *listening* to the presentations. It would be interesting to discover whether he deliberately exploits the involvement of the rest of the class in this.

Speculate about the answers to the following questions on the basis of these two schemes of work:

1   Which teacher seems to be guided more by the coursebook?

2   Which of the teachers appears to be more systematic in their planning?

[1] Soars, J. & Soars, L. *Headway Upper Intermediate* (*Student's Book*), Oxford University Press, 1987.

117

3   One of these teachers is relatively inexperienced. What features of the two schemes of work may enable you to identify whether this is Jack or Lindsay?

Comment on any features of either of these schemes of work which you find interesting. Which one do you prefer? Why?

Section C   *Devising schemes of work*

Read the following account of how one teacher devises and uses schemes of work.

'All my classes have four 60-minute lessons of English a week and I plan these in detail lesson by lesson. But I also draw up a plan month by month, or in three-week blocks – at least after the first month with the class I do. During the first month I tend to do this more week by week.

I begin by jotting down what I think the class needs – like for my examination classes that usually means lots of grammar and writing practice. But I had a non-examination class at the same level last year, and for them this meant lots of practice in listening and speaking, and lots of communicative tasks where I really dealt with language only as problems came up.

Sometimes I actually do express these needs in terms of rough percentages. So, for example, I might end up with 20% oral fluency, 20% listening, 30% project work, 10% vocabulary, 10% grammar, 5% pronunciation and 5% revision. The percentages relate to time devoted to these in class – I know that everything we do in class really belongs to more than one of these categories, but I still find this a handy way of starting off.

Of course, over the year these percentages may change a lot. For example, in the first term I may be doing lots of language-based work because that's what the students say they want. But then they may begin to get tired of this, and so I progressively increase the proportion of time devoted more explicitly to skills development.

If I am using a coursebook I then look at that and I decide roughly how much I will cover over the next month. Bearing in mind what I have decided the class needs, I decide what to leave out of the coursebook and I think about other materials I may want to use. Then I draw up a grid for the four weeks with a 'box' for each of the lessons and I start noting down very briefly what I intend to do when. I leave quite a lot of blank spaces,

Task

usually 30–45 minutes' worth in a week. This is for catching up if we get behind or for slotting in things that come up.

I find drawing up the scheme of work like this really helps me when it comes to planning individual lessons because then I don't feel I have to rack my brains about *what* I am going to do. I used to just work through the coursebook but I think, actually, that even the best coursebook needs to be adapted to any particular class, and so now I find myself using it more flexibly than I used to.'

Refer again to the two schemes of work used in Section B of this Task.

1 Who do you think is speaking here, Jack or Lindsay?

2 Make notes under the two headings given below and compare the points with your own beliefs and practice:
The teacher's assumptions   *What the teacher does*
and beliefs
Example
1 S/he believes coursebooks   1 S/he uses a system of
   need to be adapted.   percentages to characterise
                                     the classes' needs.

3 Which of this teacher's assumptions and beliefs do you share? If you agree with any of these assumptions and beliefs, explain why. How would your own description of how you devise schemes of work differ from this teacher's?

E

Discussion Task 11

Schemes of work

Timing Section A c. 20 minutes
Section B c. 20 minutes
Section C c. 20 minutes
Total c. 60 minutes

Classroom-based Task 6 involves participants in applying and practically evaluating some of the conclusions they may reach in using this Task.

Suggestions for procedure

Sections B and C of this Task may be used simultaneously by different groups of participants. In this event the procedure will need to be adapted accordingly. In particular, an opportunity will have to be made for participants to exchange their conclusions at greater length. This may involve plenary discussion or may be achieved through re-constituting groups.

Section A *Personal experience*

Participants can discuss these questions in small groups. The trainer may like to canvass the groups after a while to find out whether or not participants would like to compare their experience in a plenary format. Unless there is a strong demand for plenary discussion, participants may simply move from this section of the Task to the next.

Section B *Analysing and evaluating schemes of work*

1 If possible, the trainer can make copies of *Headway Upper Intermediate* available in the session or can give them to participants to prepare in advance.
  In small groups participants can be asked to look at Units 4–5 of the book, and (bearing in mind a particular group of

students) roughly plan or discuss how they would plan a scheme of work based on this material. They may prefer to work individually for 5–10 minutes before comparing their conclusions in groups of three or four.

2 Participants may then work collaboratively on the Task itself. During this activity the trainer may invite one confident and perceptive participant to prepare to give a summary of her conclusions to the whole group.

3 This participant can report back her conclusions to the group.

4 An opportunity can be provided for anyone to comment briefly on this.

Section C   *Devising schemes of work*

As this section of the Task involves quite a lot of reading it can be prepared at home before the session. Alternatively, time (c. 10 minutes?) can be provided during the session for silent reading and reflection, followed by a further 10 minutes for making notes individually.

Participants can compare their notes and comment on their own beliefs and practice in pairs or threes. The trainer can monitor to ensure that appropriate points are made.

As this is a relatively 'closed' activity there may be little need for a plenary session to discuss Questions 1 and 2. Unless she has identified problems while monitoring, the trainer might simply ask whether there are any questions and deal with them herself.

Participants may, however, like to have some plenary feedback on other people's responses to Question 3.

General discussion and possible outcomes

Section A   *Personal experience*

It is assumed that this section of the Task will lead to participants questioning their own practice and considering alternative approaches to planning schemes of work.

There are no 'right' or 'wrong' answers to these questions, but the following are among the kinds of points which might be made in response to Question 5:

- more time might be set aside for revision in schemes of work for a part-time course
- young learners might need more variety of content – more frequent changes of activity to hold their concentration
- the higher the level of the class, the greater the range of activities one might expect to see in a scheme of work

Section B *Analysing and evaluating schemes of work*

These schemes of work are each for 12 hours of lessons. Some institutions may ask teachers to prepare schemes of work for periods of a term, or even a whole year. The problem of planning so far ahead is that, according to the responses of the learners, many teachers will want to cover material more quickly or slowly than they initially plan, or to make changes to the projected content of the course.

Although this section of the Task focusses very much on the materials provided, the trainer can usefully direct the attention of the participants to their own and each other's practice by exploiting opportunities to compare these schemes of work with their own.

The teacher who devised Scheme A appears to have a clear overview of what he wants to achieve over the three weeks, and he selects from the coursebook what is appropriate to his overall scheme. He appears to be clear about the focus of different activities (headings clearly given), and there is both considerable variety within the 12 hours and an awareness of how different components link together. It is interesting that he leaves gaps – time which he does not account for in advance.

Scheme B follows the coursebook more closely, and there is less variety in the scheme and less supplementing from resources external to the coursebook. This teacher might well be less experienced than her colleague – or possibly she had less time to spend on the exercise.

See the example answer given in the Task itself for the kinds of specific points which may be made in the small-group discussion.

Section C *Devising schemes of work*

It is possible that participants will react against the very schematic way in which Jack works, or describes his work.

Notes

They may have alternative suggestions for ensuring that the content of learning is balanced and appropriate over a period of time (e.g. retrospective checks). Trainers may want to encourage constructive, personal disagreement of this kind.

Question 1
The teacher is Jack. There are concrete indications of this (leaving blank spaces), but also the care and thought which has been applied to the use and organisation of course materials and other activities in the scheme of work is reflected in this description.

Question 2
Among the points made might be the following:

The teacher's assumptions and beliefs
Familiarity with a class makes it easier to plan ahead.
Learners have identifiable needs.
These needs should inform the content of their classes.
Learners' perceptions of their own needs constantly change.
The teacher deviates in practice from what is planned.
Planning schemes of work facilitates lesson planning.

What the teacher does
Draws up schemes of work about one month in advance.
Also plans lesson by lesson.
Supplements what is in the coursebook.
Omits some of the material in the coursebook.
Leaves blank spaces in the scheme.

Question 3
Responses to this question will depend on the experience and opinions of the participants.

Discussion Task 12

Task

Planning individual lessons

Aim   This Task encourages you to consider procedures which may help you to develop your skills with regard to planning individual lessons.

TASK

Section A   *Personal experience*

1 How much time do you usually spend planning lessons?

2 What does this depend on?
You may find it helpful to think about:
- the content of the lesson
- the kind of material you are using
- the nature of the students in the class
- your familiarity/relationship with the class

3 How do you record your lesson plans? (e.g. A notebook for each class? Loose sheets of paper? Annotations in the coursebook?)

4 In how much detail do you usually plan lessons?

5 What do you write in a lesson plan? (e.g. Aims? Anticipated problems? Questions you will ask students? The answers to questions?)

6 How closely do you tend to follow your plans in practice? What reasons might there be for departing from a plan or even abandoning it?

7 Do you keep old lesson plans? Why (not)?

8 If you keep them, when and how often do you refer back to them?

9 Has your approach to planning lessons changed during your career as a teacher? How? Do you envisage further changes?

10 What do you see as being the objectives of planning lessons? (You may like to imagine that you want to persuade a colleague who never plans lessons at all.)

Task

Section B *Evaluating lesson plans*

Lesson plans are usually written for the teacher himself and may be very brief. However, when teachers are 'formally' observed as part of an institutional scheme of teacher development and/or assessment, it may be useful for the teacher to make some of his assumptions explicit for the observer.

Compare the two lesson plans in the *Resources bank* (Section 2, Resources 8 and 9, pages 297–301 and 302). Both of them have been devised for the benefit of an 'observer'.

1   The plan for Lesson A contains a certain amount of detail which may be considered 'background' to the lesson itself. How useful/necessary do you think it is to consider these issues systematically in planning lessons?
Would you normally make this explicit for yourself?
How useful is it to do so?

2   The plan for Lesson B divides the 'content' part of the lesson into Teacher Activity and Student Activity.
In planning a lesson which was not to be observed, how much attention would you pay (explicitly or implicitly) to each of these factors?

3   In either lesson plan is there information which you feel is superfluous?

4   In either lesson plan is there information which you feel is lacking?

Discussion Task 12

Notes

Planning individual lessons

Timing   Section A c. 20 minutes
               Section B c. 25 minutes
               Total   c. 45 minutes

This Task can be used in conjunction with Discussion Task 13 and Classroom-based Task 7.

Suggestions for procedure

Section A *Personal experience*

In small groups participants can firstly choose two or three questions that they feel it would be interesting to discuss. There is no need for a 'secretary'.

After 10–15 minutes the trainer can check whether the groups would like more time for their discussion or whether they feel they have exhausted the issues.

The group can re-convene as a circle (two concentric circles if the group is very large or the room very small) and the trainer can invite participants to reflect on and 'voice' points that have occurred to them during the discussion in small groups.

The trainer can then invite anyone to speak. His role then will be to ensure that everyone listens, and that this becomes a sharing of experiences and thoughts rather than a session in which ideas are challenged or reacted to.

Section B *Evaluating lesson plans*

Participants can discuss the questions in small groups. The trainer can monitor the groups and note any points that he feels could usefully be brought to everyone's attention.

When the participants feel they have exhausted the activity, the work in small groups can come to an end. The trainer can then clear up any general points and check whether there are any questions from participants in the groups.

General discussion and possible outcome

Section A *Personal experience*

As the aim of this section of the Task is a general sensitisation to the issues through an exchange of experience, ideas and practice, it is important that anyone who finds themselves in a very small minority (e.g. the one person who never plans at all!) does not become a scapegoat for the group. Every point of view should be valued and listened to, and in this respect it may be important that the trainer sets an example of attentiveness and tolerance.

Among the kinds of points made might be the following:
- More time may be devoted to planning:
  - when the teacher feels unsure of himself (e.g. by less experienced teachers)
  - when using unfamiliar materials
  - with very demanding classes
- For some teachers there is a kind of evolutionary cycle whereby they plan in very great detail to begin with, but then plan less and less until something 'happens' (for example, a criticism might be made that the teacher is lazy, students might begin to be dissatisfied or the teacher might simply enjoy the teaching less), at which point they go back to planning in great detail. And so the cycle continues.
- Planning ensures that there is some system and balance in the students' learning.
- Planning ensures that the teacher can answer questions accurately, and can provide explanations when required.
- The knowledge that they are well-prepared gives many teachers confidence.
- Although a teacher may have planned a lesson in great detail, he also needs to be sensitive to demands which arise in the lesson. The lesson plan may thus be a springboard rather than a 'script', and there will be many occasions when the teacher and the class depart from what was intended.
- There are cases when teachers may go into a lesson and 'see what turns up', or take the initiative from the students. The ability to do this probably depends on the confidence and experience of the teachers, and on their having a good relationship with the class.

Notes

Section B   *Evaluating lesson plans*

Although it is intended that participants evaluate how the lessons are planned rather than the content of the lessons themselves, to some extent it is inevitable that discussion touches on the latter. The trainer may want to anticipate that this happens and to decide in advance on the extent to which he wants to pursue this.

These lesson plans are not 'model' plans. However, participants may find it useful to consider these categories and formats in planning their own lessons.

Question 1

It is important to consider these issues in planning any lesson. However, it would be in very rare circumstances (normally when being 'officially observed' or assessed) that a teacher made so much explicit on paper in this way on a regular basis.

Nonetheless, teachers involved in programmes of professional development and training may find it useful to make these aspects of planning explicit in order to provide themselves with a framework in which to think through and test out the rationale and assumptions underlying what they intend to organise in the classroom.

Question 2

This division might be particularly useful for a teacher who tended to see his lessons too much from the point of view of the teacher (rather than the students). However, more detail of the students' participation than provided here might then have to be recorded.

Question 3

There appears to be little that is superfluous in either plan, although participants may argue that some of the detail does not need to be written out.

Question 4

Participants should be prepared to argue and justify any points they make in response to this question.

Discussion Task 13

Task

Lesson aims

Aim   This Task encourages you to explore the thinking which underlies and precedes the detailed planning of lessons. It looks at different ways of defining aims, and questions the extent to which it is feasible to specify in advance what learning will take place in a lesson.

TASK

Section A   *General sensitisation*

1   To what extent is it possible or desirable to anticipate or specify the outcome of a lesson in terms of what students will learn?
     In what kinds of lesson is it more or less difficult to specify this outcome?

2   Do you normally define the aims of the lessons you teach in terms of the activity the learners are engaged in, in terms of your assumptions about what the learners will learn in the lesson or in some other way?
     In how much detail do you specify aims?

Section B   *Evaluating lesson aims*

Look at the examples of aims as expressed by six teachers on lesson plans and answer the following questions:

a)   To practise reading.
b)   To present and practise the present continuous for future arrangements.
c)   To enable students to make excuses.
d)   To help students to refuse invitations appropriately and confidently by referring to their arrangements using the present continuous, e.g. *I'm sorry, I'm seeing the doctor then.*
e)   To help students to become more confident about their listening skills by demonstrating to them that they can infer and pick out key information from a text, much of which they cannot understand.

Task

f) *Main aim:*
To enable students to describe their daily routines using some of the commonest verbs in the simple present (first person).
Subsidiary aims:
To develop a better class atmosphere by encouraging students' interest in each other's lives.
To develop students' listening skills (listening to the teacher talking naturally while using pictures to convey meaning).
To sensitise students to rhythm and weakening of syllable values, and to encourage them to attend to this in oral production.

1   Which of these aims do you consider to be most appropriately expressed?

2   Which teachers do you think define aims in an appropriate amount of detail?

3   Which teachers seem to think of the lesson from the students' point of view?

4   Which teachers are most likely to have modified the aims of their lessons in the process of planning?

Section C   *Application*

Write out in full the aims of a lesson that you have recently taught and exchange this with another member of the group.

Comment on how these aims are expressed, and what this reveals about the teacher's approach.

Discussion Task 13

Notes

Lesson aims

Timing   Section A c. 15 minutes
Section B c. 15 minutes
Section C c. 15 minutes
Total   c. 45 minutes

This Task can be used in conjunction with Discussion Task 12 and Classroom-based Task 7.

Suggestions for procedure

Section A   *General sensitisation*

These questions can be discussed in small groups.

A 'secretary' from one or more of the small groups can report back on any points of particular interest which arose in the discussion. Other participants can be invited to comment on these.

Section B   *Evaluating lesson aims*

Participants can discuss this section of the Task in small groups.

Using a prepared OHP transparency or simply using the board, one of the groups can present its findings to the whole group. Other participants can ask for clarification or justification, or can disagree.

Section C   *Application*

This is a personal activity which requires no general discussion. Participants can exchange what they have written and a few minutes can be given for them to clarify with each other any points arising.

Notes

General discussion and possible outcomes

Section A *General sensitisation*

Question 1

Some participants may argue that it is important to anticipate what students will learn in a given lesson, and to base the substance of the lesson on this. Aims may thus be specified in behavioural terms (what students will be able to 'do' as a result of the lesson), in linguistic terms or in terms of the skills and sub-skills they may develop in and as a result of the lesson.

Other participants may argue that, whatever the intentions of the teacher, what the students will learn in a lesson will be individual to them, and will often be difficult to specify or define.

In a lesson which focusses very specifically on the meaning and use of aspects of grammar or vocabulary, it is easier to anticipate the outcome for the students than, for example, one which is based on communicative tasks. It is important, nonetheless, to bear in mind the danger of assuming that what the teacher teaches is exactly what is learnt by the students.

Question 2

Responses to this question will depend on the experience and opinions of the participants.

Section B *Evaluating lesson aims*

Despite the danger (cited above) of assuming too close a correspondence between teaching and learning, it is sometimes useful to think of the aims of a lesson in terms of what the learners may have achieved/learned/developed by the end of the lesson or, ultimately, as a result of the lesson.

While it is not necessarily the case that the teachers of (a) and (b) have not thought through their lessons from the point of view of the learners, the way they have expressed their aims gives no indication of an awareness of *learning* objectives and of the role of the learners. These statements are more like summaries of the content of the lessons than statements of aims.

(c), (d) and (e) look at what the students are going to achieve through the lesson, but (c) provides no information about how the content of the lesson is going to facilitate this.

One of the arguments in favour of specifying aims very clearly is that this ensures the usefulness of the lesson, and allows the teacher to check that the precise content of the lesson is congruent with these aims. In determining the content of the lesson and then checking this against full and detailed projected aims, teachers often find that there is a lack of congruence. They can then choose either to modify the aims or the content. This may well have happened in the case of (f) – subsidiary aims often develop through the process of planning the content to achieve a broad, main aim.

Precise answers to the questions are very much a matter of opinion. The following, however are possible answers to Questions 2–4:

Question 2
(d) and (e). (The degree of detail given by (f) suggests a 'public lesson plan' – a plan given to an examiner or superior attending a formally observed lesson.)

Question 3
(c), (d), (e) and (f).

Question 4
(f).

Section C   *Application*

The outcome of this section of the Task depends on the experience of the participants.

Discussion Task 14

Planning patterns of interaction in lessons

Aim This Task helps you to become more aware of the rationale underlying the range of choices available to you with regard to grouping students for different activities.

TASK

Section A   *Rationale*

1   Make a list of arguments that a teacher might advance against the use of pairwork and groupwork in the classroom.

2   Make a list of arguments that students might advance against the use of pairwork and groupwork in the classroom.

3   Make a list of arguments you might use in order to persuade teachers and students who were resistant to the idea of working in pairs and groups and who advanced the points you have listed in answering Questions 1 and 2.
   Example An argument which might be advanced **against** the use of pairwork and groupwork is that this may encourage students to speak in their own language.

Section B   *Patterns of interaction and activities*

Look at the following list of some of the activities students might engage in in the classroom. Indicate by placing a tick in the appropriate column whether you think the most appropriate 'grouping' for the activity would be pairs (P), groups of three to five (G) or individual work (I). Discuss the reasons for your decisions.

Task

	P	G	I
Doing coursebook grammar exercises			
Doing coursebook vocabulary exercises			
Reading comprehension passages			
Answering comprehension questions			
Preparing arguments for a discussion or written composition			
Writing dialogues			
Brainstorming a lexical field			
Doing a revision test			
Talking about topics of personal interest			
Using a dictionary to research vocabulary relating to a specific topic			
Repeating words and phrases to improve pronunciation			
Role-playing a situation to practise exponents of a particular function (e.g. 'inviting')			

Discussion Task 14

Notes

Planning patterns of interaction in lessons

Timing Section A c. 20 minutes
Section B c. 20 minutes
Total c. 40 minutes

Classroom-based Task 8 extends and applies issues considered in this Task.

Suggestions for procedure

Section A *Rationale*

Participants can consider these questions in small groups. In each group a 'secretary' can make brief notes. These notes should not summarise the discussion but, rather, should record any points of disagreement or special interest.

In a plenary session, secretaries from three or four of the groups can tell the other participants the key points they have noted down, and time can be provided for any further related comments to be made or questions asked.

Section B *Patterns of interaction and activities*

Participants can work on this activity initially in small groups.

Members of different groups can compare and discuss their conclusions through the use of OHP transparencies, posters or by re-constituting groups so that individual participants can see the conclusions arrived at in other groups. Alternatively, the trainer might draw a chart on the board and collect answers from all the groups onto it (possibly using a different colour for each group).

If the participants do this section of the Task very quickly and seem not to be exploring the various alternatives and their rationales sufficiently, the trainer may wish to 'probe' with specific questions ('What reasons might there be for getting students to do X together?'), and may ultimately have to play 'devil's advocate', arguing an extreme case in order to provoke a reaction.

General discussion and possible outcomes

Section A   *Rationale*

For the sake of convenience, pairwork and groupwork are considered together in this exercise. In carrying out the activities, however, participants may find that they want to distinguish between them.

Different groups of participants may have very different attitudes towards pairwork and groupwork. The organisation of this part of the Task (concentrating on arguments which might be advanced against pairwork and groupwork before looking at the counter-arguments to this) may be particularly appropriate where there is some opposition to the idea of pairwork and groupwork among the participants. It is also appropriate where there is a variety of attitudes within the group or where attitudes within the group are largely neutral.

In cases where, however, participants may tend towards the indiscriminate over-use of pairwork and groupwork, the organisation of the activity might need to be adapted. For example, the following question might be included:

'In what circumstances would it be an advantage for learners to work: (a) individually, (b) as a whole class?'

(Answers to this question might refer to the expectations and preferences of the learners, the need for variety, aspects of classroom control and the need to identify individual features of the students' output.)

Among the arguments that a teacher might advance against pairwork and groupwork are the following:
- Students make too much noise.
- The seating in the classroom is inappropriate.
- Students will use their own language.
- This kind of interaction is contrary to:
  - Students' assumptions about education.
  - Students' assumptions about learning.
  - Normal educational practice in the students' culture.

Notes

Students might object that:
- They want to listen to the teacher.
- They do not want to listen to other students.
- They do not want to help other students.

Certainly, any teacher needs to be sensitive to cultural and institutional constraints and assumptions, and in some circumstances may wish to introduce pairwork and groupwork gradually and to a limited extent. However, it can also be argued that:
- Students learn from each other through collaborating on any task, through exchanging ideas and helping and correcting each other.
- All students in a class can take part in any practice activity.
- Students may become less dependent on the teacher.
- Some shy students may be prepared only to speak in pairs or small groups.

Section B   *Patterns of interaction and activities*

The activities indicated in this section of the Task are chosen because, although in many cases students may work on them individually, most of them can profitably be done as collaborative exercises.

The following shows one possible way of completing the exercise (equally sound alternatives may be argued by participants):

Notes

	P	G	I
Doing coursebook grammar exercises	✓		
Doing coursebook vocabulary exercises	✓		
Reading comprehension passages			✓
Answering comprehension questions	✓?	✓?	
Preparing arguments for a discussion or written composition		✓	
Writing dialogues	✓		
Brainstorming a lexical field		✓	
Doing a revision test	✓		
Talking about topics of personal interest		✓?	✓?
Using a dictionary to research vocabulary relating to a specific topic	✓?	✓?	
Repeating words and phrases to improve pronunciation			✓
Role-playing a situation to practise exponents of a particular function (e.g. 'inviting')	✓		

The rationale underlying this example answer is that classroom activities which focus on ideas benefit from the wider exchange possible in groups, whereas activities which focus very specifically on materials may be easier to carry out with pairs. Variety in itself, however, is a valid reason for determining the groupings and almost any answer would be acceptable as long as the participants were able to argue its case with reference to specific learning/teaching circumstances.

Classroom-based Task 6

Evaluating schemes of work

Aim   This Task provides you with the opportunity to put into practice and test out your long-term planning skills, and to learn from other teachers by collaborating with them.

TASK

Section A   *Preparation*

Choose a class that you are currently teaching and devise a scheme of work for a convenient 'block' of time such as a month or half a term. (This will depend on the number of hours per week allocated for a class.) If possible, collaborate on this with another teacher (or other teachers) with similar classes.

If you are currently teaching and have already prepared schemes of work for your classes, you may prefer to use one of these.

Section B   *Evaluation*

At the end of the chosen 'block' evaluate the scheme that you produced. The following headings may help to guide you in evaluating the scheme of work, but you may wish to add to this list or devise one of your own:
- Interest for the students
- Variety of activity for the students
- Balance (for example, of activities with a specific linguistic focus, of fluency-orientated communicative activities, and of activities designed to develop particular skills)
- Appropriateness to the class
- Integration of revision work
- Feasibility in use
- Deviation from the scheme in practice

Although there are obvious advantages to approaching this systematically (see below), even an impressionistic and subjective judgement can be useful if it is supported by reasons (for example, a hunch like 'I felt the whole month was a bit dull' can

Task

be a good starting point for investigating possible reasons for this and alternative courses of action).

Depending on the age and interest of your students you may like to engage their help in the evaluation of your scheme of work (however, they need to have quite a sophisticated understanding of classrooms and formal learning to take part in this). A way of doing this which provides interesting data is to ask the class to write individual paragraphs about their lessons over a given period. They can be 'prompted' with headings such as those listed above, and where feasible, learners with a low level of English may be asked to do this in their own language. To make the data more manageable, the conclusions of only certain 'pre-selected' students may be considered.

Features of the scheme of work can also be 'rated' by the students:

Example
3 = Good; 2 = OK; 1 = poor
Put a number 1–3 against each of the following to express your opinion of your English classes this month:

> There was variety in the lessons. ....
> There was variety from one lesson to another. ....
> We revised things we had learnt in earlier lessons. ....
> Etc.

Notes

Classroom-based Task 6

Evaluating schemes of work

This Task extends and involves the practical application of issues considered in Discussion Task 11.

Suggestions for procedure

Participants may wish to refer to the *Resources bank* (Section 2, Resources 6 and 7, pages 295 and 296) for examples of schemes of work. They may also wish to refer to the teacher's account of devising a scheme of work in Discussion Task 11, Section C (on page 118).

Section A   *Preparation*

In some groups several participants may work in specific circumstances which none of the other participants share. In such cases it is nonetheless often worthwhile to encourage participants to work together on devising a scheme of work as the discussion and negotiation which takes place in this process is valuable in itself. This may involve one or more of the participants in imagining the class and the circumstances.

Participants can devise schemes of work in pairs.

They can then move around and look at each other's work and ask questions as appropriate.

Section B   *Evaluation*

Time can be made available to participants to collaborate on devising a format for evaluating their scheme of work. If the participants plan to engage the help of their students in this, time can also be provided for designing the questions to ask them.

If there is to be feedback to the whole group on the evaluation of the schemes of work, the time for this needs to be allocated well in advance.

In case problems crop up to interfere with teachers implementing their schemes of work, the trainer may want to agree with specific individual participants to report back on their schemes of work and then to keep in regular contact with them to monitor their progress.

In the feedback session, participants can be given a free rein to report back on their work. If the technology is available, they can be supplied in advance with OHP transparencies or poster paper so that they can easily show their schemes of work to other participants. The trainer may have to be very flexible about the timing of this session.

Alternatively, the 'presenters' can be given a fixed period of time in which to report their findings, and this can be rigidly enforced.

General discussion and possible outcomes

Evaluating schemes of work is difficult, and even quite general comments ('I felt I could have placed more emphasis on vocabulary'; 'I need to spend more time seeing through what I'm doing and have fewer changes of activity') are valid and worthwhile. This is particularly the case if they are supported by observations made by the students themselves.

This Task will probably lead not only to accounts of the evaluation of the schemes of work in practice, but also to discussion of some of the problems inherent both in planning (for example, that circumstances may change after a scheme or plan has been made) and in evaluation (for example, that when people comment on something in the past their judgement may be affected by issues of the current moment).

Classroom-based Task 7

Evaluating lesson plans

Aim   This Task encourages you to test out assumptions and insights with regard to planning lessons.

TASK

Choose from the following according to the circumstances you work in and the resources available to you.

1   Write a detailed lesson plan and include in it the overall aims of the lesson as well as the aims of each stage. Make a copy of this, but doctor the copy so that the sections dealing with the aims of each stage are blank.

    Ask a colleague to attend your lesson and give them the copy of your lesson plan with 'missing aims'. Ask them to fill in the aims as they perceive them. After the lesson compare these with your own.

2   Write a detailed lesson plan and include in it the overall aims of the lesson as well as the aims of each stage. Make a copy of this, but doctor the copy so that the sections dealing with the aims of each stage are blank.

    Teach the lesson and then give the lesson plan with 'missing aims' to your students. Explain how the plan relates to the content of the lesson and then elicit what they think were the overall aims and those of each stage. In eliciting these observations, the following questions may be useful:
- What do you think you learnt?
- Why do you think I did this?

3   By arrangement, observe a lesson given by a colleague and retrospectively write the plan that you imagine this teacher was working from. Compare this 'retrospective plan' with the actual plan the teacher was working from. Explain in advance what you are planning to do.

4   Write a detailed lesson plan and teach the lesson. During the lesson write down the actual time on each occasion that you change an activity or begin a new stage of the plan (if a colleague is observing, they can do this for you).
    After the lesson:

Task

- Compare the actual timing of the lesson with your own prior estimation. Account for the discrepancies.
- As far as possible, evaluate the extent to which the aims you specified in the plan were achieved.
- Consider whether, in retrospect, any parts of the lesson were superfluous.
- Consider whether, in retrospect, there was anything 'missing' from the lesson. (For example, if the learners found a stage of the lesson unexpectedly difficult, this might suggest that a further stage of preparation for the activity could have been included – vocabulary might have been introduced – or, perhaps, instructions needed to be planned more carefully.)
- Consider any ways in which you departed from what you had planned and account for these.

Notes

Classroom-based Task 7

Evaluating lesson plans

This Task extends and involves the practical application of issues considered in Discussion Tasks 12 and 13.

Suggestions for procedure

The four activities in this Task are intended as alternatives. Participants can choose which is most suited to themselves and carry it out in their own time. If necessary, they can refer to the *Resources bank* (Section 2, Resources 8 and 9, on pages 297–301 and 302) for examples of lesson plans).

It is intended that carrying out the Task and reflecting on it is valid in itself, and it is not envisaged that formal feedback will take place.

However, if participants would like some sort of informal discussion of their findings, a session can be arranged for some weeks hence. In this case, it may be helpful to stress to participants that what they learned through carrying out the Task is more important than what they did and what happened.

General discussion and possible outcomes

Participants may feel that they want to choose an activity on the basis of the extent to which it is feasible to carry it out in their particular circumstances. Carrying out the second option, in particular, depends on having access to classes in which the students are particularly conscious of the way the classroom works from a teacher's point of view.

The following illustrates some of the kinds of points that might be made in an informal feedback session:

- 'I find that I tend to carry out activities because they are there in the coursebook, but that I don't think enough about whether they are really useful to the students.'
- 'I find it difficult to think through what the students need to do first in order to be able to carry out a particular task subsequently.'

Classroom-based Task 8

Students' attitudes to different patterns of interaction

Aim   This Task provides you with a framework within which to learn more about your students' attitudes to different patterns of interaction in the classroom.

TASK

Devise a very brief questionnaire (maximum 5 items) to help you discover the attitude of some of your students towards aspects of groupwork and pairwork.

Different members of your group may decide to explore different aspects of this question. For example, one teacher may compare the responses of different levels of students to one question only. Another may ask questions to see how the nature of the activity affects the students' preferences (see **Example** below), and yet another might explore how the students' preferences are affected by who they are paired with.

The following is an example of some of the kinds of items you might want to include in the questionnaire:

Example
Sometimes you work in class:
– On your own (e.g. silent reading)
– With the whole class (e.g. listening to the teacher)
– With one other student
– With other students in a small group

When you work on a grammar exercise from the coursebook, do you like:
– Working on your own
– Working with one other student
– Working with other students in a small group

Indicate your preferences by putting a number by each of the possibilities:
1   I don't like this.
2   I quite like this.
3   I like this a lot.

Classroom-based Task 8

Notes

Students' attitudes to different patterns of interaction

This Task extends issues considered in Discussion Task 14.

Suggestions for procedure

Participants may like to collaborate on devising a questionnaire. Time for this could be allocated at the end of a session in which Discussion Task 14 has been used.

Agreement needs to be reached with regard to:
- Which participants will carry out the investigation;
- The size and nature of their samples;
- The time and format of the session in which these participants will present their 'findings'.

General discussion and possible outcomes

Different learners and groups of learners may have very different attitudes. These attitudes may have been conditioned by their having had very little exposure or very little productive exposure to particular patterns of interaction (for example, some groups of learners may have had no experience of groupwork in the class).

The trainer, thus, may need to be particularly flexible in the feedback session. Depending on the findings, the quality of the research and the attitudes of the participants, he may need to contribute very little to the discussion. Conversely, he may also need to encourage participants to consider more seriously the results of the research on the one hand, or even to encourage them to approach the findings with a greater degree of scepticism on the other.

7   Teaching: Developing skills

Introduction to the chapter

1   Contents

2   General discussion of issues

OVERVIEW OF THE CHAPTER

The Tasks in this chapter concentrate on different aspects of reading, listening, speaking (oral fluency) and writing. The first Discussion Task looks at comprehension skills generally, and relates these to materials. The remaining eight Discussion Tasks deal with the four skills – for each skill there is a Task which focusses more on the processes involved, and one which focusses more on teaching methodology (these, however, are not completely discrete). Although any of the Tasks can be used independently, it is logical to use the 'process-orientated' Task before the 'methodology-orientated' Task (even numbers before odd numbers).

SUB-SKILLS AND HOLISM

These Tasks implicitly acknowledge that there are two quite different approaches to teaching these skills. The first is what might be termed the

149

'sub-skills' approach. In this approach classroom activities may not attempt to simulate authentic communication, but rather are designed to allow learners to practise particular components of the skills. For example, in a lesson focussing on reading, learners might use a text to practise a wide range of these sub-skills even though, in the 'real world', the text would not be read in some of the ways in which learners read it in the lesson.

In contrast, in a 'holistic' approach, discrete 'sub-skills' might never be practised in isolation. For example, exercises would be devised so that texts are always read in the way that they would be used in the 'real world'. It is assumed that if learners read a sufficiently wide range of texts, and in each case the exercise is designed to reflect how the text would be approached in the 'real world', they will develop the necessary skills.

In this material it is assumed that these two approaches are compatible and, indeed, complimentary. However, it is sometimes argued that the two approaches are not compatible. In particular some 'holists' argue that all skills-orientated classroom activities should attempt to simulate authentic use of these skills. Participants or trainers who feel strongly that only a 'holistic' approach is acceptable, nonetheless, should find that the Tasks enable them to argue their point of view. Ultimately, individuals who use the Tasks will form their own opinions about this.

INTEGRATION OF SKILLS

There are no Tasks focussing specifically on integrated skills. The division of skills into listening, reading, speaking (oral fluency) and writing is an expedient one, and is taken as the basis for organising this chapter. However, it is acknowledged that in practice these skills are not discrete, and the Tasks reflect this in that the activities discussed involve a combination of skills even though in each case one of the skills is given prominence.

LENGTH AND USE OF TASKS

The Discussion Tasks vary in length and many of them are significantly longer than Tasks in other chapters. Tasks 16–23 are each divided into between two and seven sections, and these sections can be used independently. Within a large, heterogeneous group of teachers, small groups may work simultaneously on different parts of a Task, although they can also be used in sequence.

APPLICATION

The issues raised in these Tasks should be of relevance to all teachers. Even very experienced teachers should be able to benefit from thinking about these issues and reconsidering their own 'normal practice'.

3   Reading

Pre-sessional reading for the participants is not essential for any of the Tasks in this chapter. However, the topic of 'Developing skills' is one which has an extensive literature of a very high quality. Participants may well want to explore the issues raised in these Tasks beyond the scope of the Tasks themselves, either before the sessions or to follow up the thinking and discussion which has taken place during them.

The following references will be of use to participants as well as to trainers who may want to read in order to prepare themselves for the use of the Tasks. A selection of the available sources has had to take place. There are many other excellent sources of useful, interesting and relevant background material, not least (and particularly in relation to the even-numbered Discussion Tasks) sections of modern 'skills books' and coursebooks for students which deal with these skills.

Brown, G. & Yule, G. (1983). *Teaching the Spoken Language.* Cambridge University Press.

Bygate, M. (1987). *Speaking.* Oxford University Press.

Byrne, D. (1988). *Teaching Writing Skills.* Longman.

Collie, J. & Slater, J. (1987). *Literature in the Language Classroom.* Cambridge University Press.

Grellet, F. (1981). *Developing Reading Skills.* Cambridge University Press.

Hedge, T. (1985). *Using Readers in Language Teaching.* Macmillan.

Hedge, T. (1988). *Writing.* Oxford University Press.

Nuttall, C. (1982). *Teaching Reading Skills in a Foreign Language.* Heinemann.

Pincas, A. (1982). *Teaching English Writing.* Macmillan.

Richards, J. C. (1990). *The Language Teaching Matrix.* Cambridge University Press.

Rixon, S. (1986). *Developing Listening Skills.* Macmillan.

Underwood, M. (1989). *Teaching Listening.* Longman.

Ur, P. (1981). *Discussions that Work.* Cambridge University Press.

Ur, P. (1984). *Teaching Listening Comprehension.* Cambridge University Press.

F

DISCUSSION TASK 15   MATERIALS DESIGNED TO DEVELOP
                       COMPREHENSION SKILLS

The main focus of this Task is on identifying some of the sub-skills of listening and/or reading which may be practised in particular materials. It may be used as an 'introduction' to Discussion Tasks 16–19, or as a means of consolidating and extending some of the issues dealt with in these Tasks. In either case, it may be more appropriate to link the background reading to Discussion Tasks 18–19 rather than to Discussion Task 15. However, the sources referred to in connection with Discussion Tasks 16 and 18 will also be relevant to this Task.

DISCUSSION TASK 16   FACTORS INVOLVED IN EFFECTIVE LISTENING

Richards, Chapter 3 (pp. 50–8 in particular) provides an excellent, condensed introduction to this topic. For a more extensive account and discussion of processes involved in listening, refer to Underwood, Chapters 1–4 (pp. 1–29) or Ur (1984), Chapters 1–2 (pp. 2–21). Brown & Yule, Chapter 3 (pp. 54–101) deal with the topic in yet greater depth.

DISCUSSION TASK 17   DEVELOPING LISTENING SKILLS

Richards (pp. 59–60) provides a short but very full taxonomy of types of task for developing listening skills. Rixon, Ur (1984) and Underwood provide a more extensive discussion and account of classroom approaches. Ur considers the processes underlying these approaches at greater length than Rixon, and deals very extensively with classroom activities (Chapters 4–5, pp. 35–166). Underwood, Chapters 5–7 (pp. 30–93) also provides a very comprehensive and systematic account of techniques and tasks which may be used, and in subsequent chapters explores the topic of selecting and exploiting materials with similar thoroughness.

DISCUSSION TASK 18   FACTORS INVOLVED IN EFFECTIVE READING

The introduction to Grellet (pp. 3–25) provides an admirably clear and concise account of a range of reading skills. Nuttall looks at these in greater detail and pays attention to a wider range of skills and sub-skills. The first eight chapters of Nuttall's book are full of insights and carefully detailed observations. Chapters 4–8 (pp. 31–124) are essential reading for anyone wanting to acquire an informed, in-depth understanding of the topic.

DISCUSSION TASK 19   DEVELOPING READING SKILLS

Richards (Chapter 5, pp. 87–99) provides a very brief but fascinating profile of 'an effective reading teacher', and Grellet (pp. 28–250) demonstrates a wealth of exercise types, each clearly related to specific sub-skills. Hedge (1985), Chapters 4–7 (pp. 62–119) and Collie & Slater, Chapters 3–6 (pp. 16–92) are of particular relevance to the issues raised by Question 5 in Section A of this Task.

DISCUSSION TASK 20   FACTORS INVOLVED IN ORAL FLUENCY

Richards (Chapter 4, pp. 67–76) provides his usual, impressively concise and clear general account of this topic. Bygate (pp. 3–50) deals with the topic at greater length. The first two chapters of Brown & Yule, however, still give what is probably the most detailed and comprehensive analysis of the topic (pp. 1–53).

DISCUSSION TASK 21   DEVELOPING ORAL FLUENCY

Ur (1981), although not a recent publication, still presents probably the best and most wide-ranging account of this topic.

DISCUSSION TASK 22   FACTORS INVOLVED IN EFFECTIVE WRITING

Richards (Chapter 6, pp. 100–17) looks briefly at aspects of writing skills (including coherence and cohesion), but is generally more concerned with approaches to teaching writing. Byrne is again more concerned with approaches to teaching writing, but comprehensively integrates into this discussion a concern for the processes and skills involved.

DISCUSSION TASK 23   DEVELOPING WRITING SKILLS

Richards (Chapter 6, pp. 100–17) gives a succinct account of aspects of this topic including a comparison of what he refers to as a 'product-focussed' approach and a 'process' approach.

Pincas and Byrne both write within the tradition of 'product-focussed' approaches. Pincas, though it is a short book, deals with a range of exercise types while Byrne is nothing if not comprehensive. Hedge writes firmly from the 'process' camp and argues her case eloquently, providing a wealth of practical examples.

Discussion Task 15

Task

Materials designed to develop comprehension skills

Aim   This Task introduces some of the processes involved in comprehension, and applies them in looking at published materials.

TASK

'Comprehension' involves extracting meaning from a text, from participating in a conversation or from listening to a person or people speaking. The kinds of meaning which are 'extracted', and the ways in which they are 'extracted' will depend on the purposes which underlie the reading, interacting or listening. Since these purposes vary considerably, 'comprehension', thus, can mean rather different things. For example, an academic might want to study one scientific paper or attend a lecture in order to learn everything which is specified and implied in it, whereas she might glance through another paper or attend another lecture only in order to reassure herself of the main points. In both these cases her objective is 'comprehension'.

Depending on the purposes for comprehending, a different range of 'sub-skills' may be involved. The following lists some of the sub-skills which may be involved in 'efficient comprehension'. The ability to:

a) Recognise the communicative function of a text (stretch of speech or writing) or part of a text. Examples of communicative functions are invitation, commiseration, persuasion, etc. (Note that a text or part of a text may express more than one function, and that the function(s) may be more easily identifiable in certain texts than in others.)

b) Obtain the gist (main ideas) from a text.

c) Identify specific details.

d) Distinguish main ideas from supporting details.

e) Recognise the speaker's (writer's) attitude towards the topic and towards the listener or reader.

f) Infer ideas and information not explicitly stated.

g) Anticipate or predict the 'content' of the text or the development of the discourse.

Task

h) Recognise familiar words.
i) Infer the context of the discourse.
j) Use the context to understand the meaning of unfamiliar words.

1   Add any further items to this list that you feel are appropriate.

2   Look at two examples of materials designed to develop aspects of comprehension skills. Either refer to examples of materials you use in your teaching or refer to the *Resources bank* (Section 3, Resources 11 and 12, on pages 306–9 and 310–11).
    Which of the above sub-skills are being developed or practised? How effectively?

3   Using the same materials, what additional comprehension tasks could you devise to develop some of the other sub-skills listed?

Discussion Task 15

Notes

Materials designed to develop comprehension skills

Timing   c. 45 minutes

This Task may be used either as an introduction to Discussion Tasks 16–19 or, if the issues dealt with in this Task are largely unfamiliar to participants, it may be used after these four Tasks as a means of consolidating, extending and applying their thinking and learning with regard to these issues.

Suggestions for procedure

The time required for the Task will depend on whether participants have prepared the Task at home before the session, and on whether all participants are working with the same materials or a variety of materials is used.

If a variety of materials is used, each small group can concentrate on particular materials. Then the groups can be re-constituted so that in each new group there is a representative to give feedback on the conclusions of the original group.

If trainers feel they want to have more 'control' over the analysis and discussion, each of the small groups can look at the same materials. The small-group discussion can then be followed by a brief plenary session in which a representative from one of the groups reports back on their conclusions. Questions and comments can then be invited from members of other groups.

Each of the three questions can be dealt with separately.

General discussion and possible outcomes

Question 1

Participants may be satisfied with the items on the list, or may wish to explore the skills in greater detail and add further items. These might involve more general aspects of comprehension such as 'mapping' new knowledge onto old to give meaning that is personal to the listener or reader, or may be specific to either listening or reading such as scanning a written text to locate specific information, or reading quickly to understand gist.

Question 2
This will clearly depend on the materials chosen. The following points relate to the materials in the *Resources bank*:
Resource 11   Identifying specific details (c).
Resource 12   Distinguishing main ideas from supporting details (d).
Inferring ideas and information not explicitly stated (f).
Identifying specific details (c).

Question 3
This will also depend on the materials chosen. The following points relate to the materials in the *Resources bank*, and serve as examples of the kinds of points participants might make:
Resource 11: Tasks could be devised both to develop *inferring the context of the discourse* (i) and for *anticipating the 'content'* (g). In the first place (i) a few seconds of a news item could be played, and students could be asked to predict what kind of text this is from the vocabulary and manner of speech (this might be organised as a multiple-choice exercise). In the second place (g) the students could be 'given' some of the words which occur in the items. They would then be asked to predict the content of the items. In both these cases students would listen to the tape before opening their books at the relevant page.
Resource 12: Comprehension tasks could be devised to develop the skill of *using the context to understand the meaning of unfamiliar words* (j). For example, students could be asked to find a word in the first paragraph which describes a kind of walk, and to specify whether or not this word suggests an element of difficulty (hike). An exercise which asked students to identify the names of all the living creatures in the text would combine practising this skill with that of *identifying specific details* (c).

Discussion Task 16

Task

Factors involved in effective listening

Aim   This Task encourages you to think about a range of personal factors involved in listening, and to consider ways in which these may facilitate or inhibit effective comprehension.

TASK

Section A   *Reflection on experience*

1   How would you rate your listening comprehension in relation to other abilities in the language?

2   Are there any circumstances in which it may seem better or worse?

3   Speculate about the reasons for your answers to Questions 1 and 2.

Section B   *Personal factors which may facilitate or inhibit effective listening comprehension*

Learners employ a variety of strategies in their attempt to understand the spoken language, and approach the task of listening with a variety of attitudes and expectations. Although some of these personal factors (strategies, attitudes and expectations) may facilitate understanding, others may be counter-productive.

In answering the following questions you may find it helpful to think of particular learners who appear to find listening comprehension either particularly difficult or particularly easy.

1   Make a list of personal factors which might inhibit effective listening comprehension and give reasons why this might be so.

2   Make a list of personal factors which might facilitate listening comprehension and give reasons why this might be so.

Task

3 Look at the following list of personal factors and indicate which you consider to be characteristic of effective and ineffective listening by writing either **E** (effective) or **I** (ineffective) against each item.
Example The learner is afraid of appearing silly by getting the answer wrong.   **I**

The learner:
a) Tries to understand everything.
b) Tries to listen word by word.
c) Tries to activate general knowledge of the topic to help him understand the discourse.
d) Guesses in order to help him understand when he misses information.
e) 'Thinks ahead' generally while listening (guesses how the discourse will develop/ what is going to be talked about).
f) Uses his knowledge of the language to narrow down the range of possibilities with regard to what the next key word or phrase may be.
g) Varies his attention during the listening process, concentrating on particular words which are stressed, and on stretches of speech which are pitched relatively high in the voice range.
h) 'Assumes success' (assumes that understanding is relatively easy and that there will be no serious breakdown in communication).

Notes

Discussion Task 16

Factors involved in effective listening

Timing   Section A c. 15 minutes
Section B c. 25 minutes
Total   c. 40 minutes

This Task serves as an introduction to Discussion Task 17.

Suggestions for procedure

Section A   *Reflection on experience*

Participants may like a few minutes to think about their individual responses to the questions before discussing them in small groups. Plenary feedback may not be necessary or appropriate.

Section B   *Personal factors which may facilitate or inhibit effective listening comprehension*

The organisation and distribution of time in this part of the Task will depend on how easy or difficult participants find answering Questions 1 and 2 in their small groups.

If they find answering the questions easy, these may be discussed briefly and participants can then be asked to 'shout out' any points they have made. Question 3 can probably then be dealt with quite quickly. The trainer can then provide his answers, or ask one of the groups to write up their answers on an OHP transparency or on the board, and can invite any comments or questions from other participants.

However, if the participants have difficulty in answering Questions 1 and 2, the trainer may decide to cut this activity short and refer participants to Question 3. There may then be some plenary extended discussion of the points made before participants are asked to go back to Questions 1 and 2 and to use their 'new' knowledge to help them to answer these questions.

If the trainer perceives that examples are needed to stimulate the brainstorming in Questions 1 and 2, these can be selected either from the list of possible outcomes (see below) or from Question 3 in this section of the Task itself.

General discussion and possible outcomes

Section A *Reflection on experience*

A very wide variety of points may be made. Among them one might expect to find some of the following:

- Comprehension improves when:
  - the listener is relaxed
  - the listener is physically alert
  - the content of the discourse is familiar
  - the speaker is familiar
  - the listener feels able to ask for clarification and knows how to do this
- Learners who are anxious about understanding spoken English seem to experience the greatest difficulty (this is obviously something of a 'vicious circle').
- Learners who try to understand every word may, in fact, understand less than those who tend, rather, to ignore what they do not understand.

Responses to these questions may also focus on aspects of their formal learning of the language. For example, participants may make reference to whether and how much the teacher spoke to them in the target language, and on the kinds of opportunities they had to listen to other speakers of the language.

Section B *Personal factors which may facilitate or inhibit effective listening comprehension*

Obviously, knowledge of vocabulary and grammar is a key component in understanding. However, for the purposes of this Task, attention is focussed on other factors relating more specifically to the processes of listening. Answers to the questions in this section of the Task are clearly only speculative.

Notes

Many of the points which might be made in response to Questions 1 and 2 are, in fact, expressed or implied in the exercise which constitutes Question 3. However, among some of the points made might be the following:

Question 1
Learners may be anxious and may lack confidence. They may be concerned not to appear 'silly' in front of their classmates by getting the answer to a question wrong. They may also lack exposure to/practice in listening to people speaking (or in listening to taped talks or conversations) in which non-standard accents are used, in which there is disruptive background noise, or in which the language is realistically representative of spoken English (for example, sentences may be ungrammatical and unfinished, speakers may hesitate and repeat themselves, more than one person may speak at the same time). Sound values of familiar words may differ from their expectations (particularly when certain syllables are weakened and run together).

Question 2
In responding to this question participants may in part indicate the opposite of the points made in response to Question 1.

Learners who appear to have a facility for understanding the spoken language may be more tolerant of not understanding everything than those who find this difficult. They may also anticipate what is going to be said, infer information, and listen selectively, using stressed syllables and stretches of speech in a 'high' intonation key to direct their attention.

Question 3
The following suggested responses to this question do not constitute 'correct' answers, but only probable answers. Participants may advance valid alternative responses, particularly if they link these to specific purposes for listening. For example, (a) is classified as *ineffective* because in most circumstances effective listening involves processing information, much of which may be 'given' or known to the listener already, and consequently attention needs to be selective. However, trying to understand everything would be an effective strategy if the task involved following instructions where every word conveyed essential information. Searching discussion of these issues is more important than agreeing on the answers.

Effective: c, d, e, f, g, h
Ineffective: a, b

Discussion Task 17

Task

Developing listening skills

Aim   This Task explores a range of techniques for developing listening skills, encourages you to evaluate their effectiveness in different circumstances and relates this to lesson planning.

TASK

Section A   *Reflection on experience*

1   Make a list of procedures you carry out in the classroom to help your students develop their listening skills. You may like to consider:
   - the kinds of materials you use
   - the kinds of listening tasks you set
   - the instructions you give
   - the activities the students are involved in

2   Think also of your experience as a learner of foreign languages. List any procedures you may have experienced which you felt were unhelpful or detrimental to developing your listening skills.

Section B   *Evaluating different approaches to developing listening skills*

1   Look at the following list of measures teachers might employ to develop listening skills. Indicate which measures you think are effective by writing **E** against them. Write **I** against any measures you think might be ineffective or counter-productive.

   Discuss the reasons for the decisions you make, and qualify them with reference to the needs and abilities of particular groups of learners and the aspects of listening skills you might wish to develop. In some cases a measure may be considered as either effective or ineffective depending on the circumstances (see the example overleaf).

Task

Example *The teacher instructs the class to listen carefully to every word.*   I
(Qualification: In most circumstances, effective listening involves paying attention *selectively*. However, listening carefully to every word *might* be effective – and indeed 'appropriate' – if, for example, the task involved dictation of an address.)

a) The teacher encourages the class to listen to herself or to other speakers of English.
b) The teacher arouses interest in the material before the class listens.
c) The teacher uses materials which incorporate features of natural spoken English (false starts, hesitation, repetition, changes in direction 'mid-stream', ungrammatical and unfinished sentences).
d) The teacher sets tasks which focus specifically on these features.
e) The teacher sets clear, realistic tasks which encourage the students to listen only for certain information.
f) The teacher makes it clear to students prior to listening that they will have the opportunity to discuss their answers in groups before speaking before the whole class.
g) The teacher encourages discussion of the processes of listening.
h) The teacher devises tasks which encourage the students to infer information which is only implied in the discourse.
i) The teacher encourages the students to guess how the discourse will develop.
j) The teacher encourages the students to use their knowledge of grammar and context to guess the next word.
k) When focussing on new language, the teacher gives realistic models, taking care to draw attention to the weakening and elision of syllables in a continuous stream of speech.
l) The teacher always takes care to speak slowly.
m) The teacher always takes care to use good quality tapes, and ensures that there is no distraction by the presence of background noise.
n) The teacher tries to use materials which provide good models of 'standard English'.

Task

o) The teacher always takes care to find out and record how many questions each student answered correctly.

p) The teacher teaches the students ways of interrupting a speaker to ask them to repeat, clarify or expand what they have said, or to speak more slowly.

2 Look again at the 'measures' which you decided were generally effective and classify them according to whether:

i) They encourage the development of confidence in listening and understanding.

ii) They are intended to aid the development of specific *strategies* to facilitate listening and understanding.

iii) They are intended to prepare the students to cope with some of the features of natural spoken English (as opposed to their experience of the written language).

3 In real life we listen for a purpose. Sometimes this is very general, for example for amusement or entertainment. However, this is often in order to derive specific information.

It is sometimes argued that materials and tasks which are used to develop listening skills in the classroom should simulate 'real, purposeful' listening.

Look at the following descriptions. Which of these do you think are examples of *purposeful* listening?

a) **Students listen to someone giving directions and trace the route on a map.**

b) **Students listen to a weather forecast and on the basis of this decide where they will spend the weekend if they want to have good weather.**

c) **Students look at photographs of the teacher's family and, while the teacher talks about the people, they have to identify them by name.**

d) **Before listening to a description of the town in which they are studying, students make a list of points they would expect to be made. As they listen to the description they tick the points which are, in fact, mentioned.**

e) **Students listen to a story and subsequently answer questions about the events.**

4 Look again at the five descriptions immediately above. In which of these would it be appropriate to use taped materials?

Task

5   Which of these five activities do you like best? Give reasons for your decisions.

Section C   *General considerations*

Consider the following questions. In your group see to what extent it is possible to reach a consensus.

1   How many times can a class be asked to listen to the same section of a tape?

2   Who should control the tape?

3   What are the learners *doing* during a lesson or part of a lesson devoted to listening skills?

4   How important is the use of video in the teaching of listening skills?

5   Is there any place for the use of dictation in teaching listening skills?

Section D   *Using taped materials – a possible procedure*

The following are some of the possible stages in a lesson in which the teacher's objective is to develop her students' listening skills. The order of these stages is jumbled.

1   Number them to reflect an order which you feel would be more satisfactory. Note that:
   – individual stages may appear more than once in the sequence
   – in any lesson some of these stages may be omitted and/or additional stages included

2   Explain your rationale.

   a) The teacher picks out ten seconds of tape and asks the students to identify the main stresses.
   b) Students listen to the tape and fill in a grid to record the main points.
   c) Students discuss this in pairs.
   d) Students speculate about the content of a tape on the basis of the title or a short excerpt.

Task

e) The teacher answers any questions about language on the tape.

f) The teacher teaches one or two key items of vocabulary.

g) Students listen to confirm their predictions.

h) The teacher plays the tape in sections while the students try to answer questions relating to detail.

i) Students read the tapescript.

j) Students discuss a topic related to the content of the tape.

Discussion Task 17

Developing listening skills

Timing   Section A   c. 15 minutes
Section B   c. 45 minutes
Section C   c. 15 minutes
Section D   c. 15 minutes
Total   c. 90 minutes

It is not necessary for all four sections of this Task to be used in one session. Where time is limited, sections which are of greatest relevance to participants' interests and teaching circumstances may be selected. Alternatively, different sections may be used simultaneously in a session.

This Task extends the issues considered in Discussion Task 16, approaching the topic from the point of view of teaching methodology. It can be used in conjunction with the previous Task.

Suggestions for procedure

Section A   *Reflection on experience*

Participants can discuss this section of the Task in small groups. If they find the brainstorming easy, the points may be discussed briefly and participants can then be asked to 'shout out' any points they have made.

However, if the participants have difficulty in the brainstorming exercise, the trainer may decide to cut this activity short and refer participants to Question 1 in Section B of the Task. There may then be some plenary extended discussion of the points made before participants are asked to come back to this part of the Task, and then use their 'new' knowledge to help them to do this brainstorming exercise.

Notes

Section B *Evaluating different approaches to developing listening skills*

Questions 1 & 2

These matching activities will probably be carried out quite quickly. The trainer can then provide her answers, or ask one of the groups to write up their answers on an OHP transparency or on the board, and can invite any comments or questions from other participants.

Questions 3 & 4

Participants can discuss these questions in small groups. A representative from one of the groups can report back to everyone on the decisions of the group if there is sufficient interest.

Question 5

Participants are likely to be curious to know what other groups decided in response to this question, and some time may be made available for a brief plenary discussion of this.

Section C *General considerations*

Participants can also discuss this section of the Task in small groups. In each group a 'secretary' can be appointed to summarise the discussion in note form. For each of the questions a secretary from one group can report back to everyone what the small group decided in order to open general discussion on that issue. At the end of this plenary discussion of the five questions, trainers may want to recap points made, clarify disagreement or make points of their own.

Section D *Using taped materials – a possible procedure*

This exercise can be done as a 'race'. Participants work in pairs, and the pairs compete with each other to finish first. The activity can be stopped when the first two or three pairs have finished, and pairs can be invited to compare their answers. The trainer can 'show' the group a possible answer to the exercise and invite comment or questions. It is important to make it clear that there is no single 'right' answer, and so argument about details of the sequence may not be productive.

General principles can be elicited from the whole group.

General discussion and possible outcomes

There is a danger in this Task that issues are over-simplified – the Task may appear to imply that there are 'right and wrong' listening tasks and activities or 'right and wrong' ways of organising a lesson. It is therefore important throughout the Task that participants both justify and qualify their answers to questions, making it clear which comments they make are generalisations, and specifying circumstances in which these generalisations are not applicable. These 'circumstances' will often relate to:
- the nature of particular learners
- the precise aim of the lesson with regard to different aspects of listening skills
- the purpose behind listening to different kinds of materials

Section A   *Reflection on experience*

Many of the points participants may brainstorm in this section of the Task recur in Section B. Additional points they may make include:

Question 1
Teachers may:
- provide the learners with practice in listening interactively to herself and to each other
- use tasks which focus clearly on practising and developing specific listening strategies
- arouse interest in the materials students listen to
- provide practice in listening for enjoyment (this involves both choice of the topic and, probably, choice of 'easy' material on occasions)
- also 'stretch' her students by providing more difficult materials and tasks
- use materials which contain 'natural' features of spoken English, background noise and the use of non-standard accents
- take care to present 'natural' models of language when focussing on grammar and vocabulary (i.e. with weak syllables weakened)
- provide clear instructions and realistic tasks

- allow students to discuss their answers to questions or tasks in small groups so that no one is 'put on the spot' to answer questions
- discuss listening processes and strategies with the class

Question 2
Participants may refer to:
- use of very difficult materials with insufficient preparation for the students
- use of only very simple materials or materials which provide unnatural models of language use
- unclear tasks
- 'putting students on the spot' to answer difficult questions

Section B *Evaluating different approaches to developing listening skills*

Although valid alternative points may be argued, the following are likely responses to the questions.

Question 1
Effective: a–k, p
Ineffective: l–o

Question 2
i) b, (e), f, (p)
ii) (b), d, e, g, h, i, j, p
iii) a, c, k

Question 3
The order is intended to reflect descending degrees of 'purposefulness' – (a) is perhaps the most purposeful and (e) the least.

Some participants may want to argue that 'purposefulness' is the most important criterion in evaluating a listening task. However, others may argue that other factors are more important. For example, the fourth description (d) is an example of an activity whose purpose is only pedagogic, and does not simulate 'real' listening. Nonetheless, the skills practised are real skills and students may be motivated by the task. In this case it may be as valuable as the more authentically 'purposeful' activities.

Question 4
Use of a tape would be particularly natural in the case of (b), and particularly unnatural in the case of (c).

Notes

Question 5
Responses to this question will depend on the individual preferences of participants.

Section C   *General considerations*

These questions are intended to encourage participants to think widely about a range of issues, and many individual, valid points may be made which it is difficult to predict. The following suggestions draw attention to some points which may be made:

Question 1
A tape may be listened to, in theory, an almost infinite number of times as long as each time they listen, the students are motivated to extract something 'new' from the experience. In practice, obviously, tolerance to this will depend on the group and on the nature of the material.

Question 2
This can be delegated to the students.

Question 3
A substantial amount of the time may be devoted to *thinking* and *speaking* about the tasks and about interpretations of what the students have heard.

Question 4
Where video is available this is very useful as, in normal conversation, we use visual clues to help us understand. The sound can be turned down on the television in order to focus the students' attention on these visual clues.

Question 5
Dictation can be adapted to form a very valuable source of listening practice. Students can dictate material (which they have, perhaps, written) to each other, or they can choose to write down sentences they particularly like from something they listen to. *Dictation* by Davis & Rinvolucri provides a wealth of examples of ways in which dictation can be used as a motivating and productive 'tool' for learning and teaching.

Section D *Using taped materials – a possible procedure*

The primary objective of this exercise is again not that participants 'get the correct answer', but rather that they think about and discuss the issues involved. There are many other, equally appropriate, possible answers, and in each case reference needs to be made to the objectives of the lesson and the kind of purpose for which people might listen to materials of the kind used.

The following two principles might be followed in instances where a teacher is concerned not so much with simulating real, purposeful listening, but rather is concerned to provide students with practice in a *range* of the sub-skills of listening. The basis for the order is thus essentially pedagogic:

– tasks focussing on meaning might precede tasks focussing on language
– tasks focussing on general understanding might precede tasks focussing on specific details

In this instance the following is one of many possible orders:

1 f   2 j   3 c   4 d   5 c   6 g   7 c   8 b   9 c
10 h   11 c   12 a   13 c   14 i   15 e   16 j

Participants who follow a strongly 'holistic' line with regard to skills development may argue that this section of the Task cannot be carried out without reference to specific materials and purposes for listening to them. (See *General discussion of issues*, page 149, in the Introduction to this chapter for an extended discussion of the 'holistic' position.) In this case, the exercise can be adapted so that participants order the stages in relation to a specified text and purpose for listening.

Task

Discussion Task 18

Factors involved in effective reading

Aim This Task provides you with a general introduction to various aspects of reading skills and strategies.

TASK

Section A   *General approaches to reading*

1 We read for a variety of purposes and, according to these purposes, in a variety of ways. Although reading always involves deriving meaning from a text, our purpose in reading determines the kind of meaning and the amount of meaning we look for.

The terms *skimming, scanning, receptive reading* and *intensive reading* are sometimes used to describe different kinds of 'reading skill'. Each of the following describes one of these kinds of reading skill. Write down the name of the reading skill by each of the four descriptions:

a) You read a poem by a poet you particularly like. You enjoy paying close attention to the poet's use of language.

b) You visit a library in the course of researching a particular topic. You quickly look through books and articles in order to ascertain whether they contain information on this topic and are therefore worth borrowing.

c) You are on holiday and sit down to read the latest thriller by your favourite writer. There is no pressure on you to finish it quickly.

d) While waiting for an appointment you pick up a magazine and discover it contains an article of great interest to you. You do not have time to read the article in detail but you want to extract as much information from it as you can in the few minutes you have.

2 Would you agree that language teaching sometimes favours *intensive reading* at the expense of developing ability in the other skills?

3 As stated and illustrated above, our purpose in reading a text normally determines the way in which we read it. Teachers

may want to simulate this in the classroom. However, a teacher may also want to use a text to practise *all* four of these skills (even though the task would then be 'inauthentic').

Do you consider that 'inauthentic' tasks of this nature are valid?

If you wanted to use a text to practise all four of these skills, in what order would you present tasks to practise each of them?

Section B *Effective and ineffective reading strategies*

1   The following strategies might be employed by readers in a foreign language. Mark each strategy according to whether you think it is generally effective (**E**) or ineffective (**I**). Qualify your decisions with reference to the circumstances in which these might be effective or ineffective, taking into account:
   – the needs, interests and abilities of the learners
   – the aims of the particular lesson
   – the purpose for reading a particular kind of text
   Example *Looking for unfamiliar words and underlining them.* I
   (Qualification: In many cases this would hinder efficient reading, in which attention needs to be paid to the information the reader *does* understand. However, after reading a text to derive the required information, underlining unfamiliar words and looking them up in a dictionary may be a useful way of extending vocabulary, which in the long term will help reading.)

   a) Mouthing the words.
   b Looking for a topic sentence in paragraphs.
   c) Trying to use the context to work out the meaning of unfamiliar words.
   d) Mentally translating everything.
   e) Mentally translating passages where complicated syntax or clause structure has led to confusion.
   f) Trying to identify implicit logical relationships between sentence and sentence, and paragraph and paragraph. (If these were *ex*plicitly indicated, words like 'however' or 'consequently' would be used.)

175

Task

g) Trying to distinguish between major and subordinate assertions.

h) Speculating about the content of the text on the basis of headings, pictures and the introductory sentences.

i) Choosing to use a combination of strategies (skimming, etc.) according to the nature of the text and the purpose for reading.

j) Using a dictionary to find the meanings of all new words.

2   True or false? *Faster reading aids comprehension.*

3   Which of the following diagrams most effectively describes the eye movements associated with efficient receptive reading?

a)

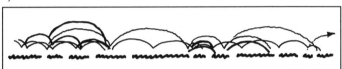

b)

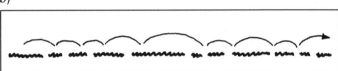

c)

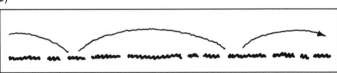

4   How can a teacher discourage learners from reading slowly and lingering over each word during the early stages of learning English?

Notes

Discussion Task 18

Factors involved in effective reading

Timing   Section A c. 30 minutes
                 Section B c. 30 minutes
                 Total   c. 60 minutes

This Task can be used in preparation for Discussion Task 19.

Suggestions for procedure

Section A   *General approaches to reading*

Question 1
The timing and organisation of this part of the Task will depend on the extent to which participants are familiar with these terms.

If the terms are familiar, the small groups can probably carry out the exercise in a matter of seconds and their answers can briefly be checked by the trainer. However, if the terms and concepts are unfamiliar to participants, the trainer may need to stop the small-group activity and 'teach' them, allowing time for questions and discussion.

Questions 2 & 3
These can be discussed by participants in small groups. There can then be a brief plenary discussion in which, if necessary, the trainer may clarify the issues these questions are intended to raise.

Section B   *Effective and ineffective reading strategies*

Question 1
Participants can work in small groups. A representative of one of the groups can be asked to record the group's answers on an OHP transparency or poster to show to the whole group. Other participants can then raise any further questions.

Notes

Questions 2 & 3
If the whole group is small (ten or fewer participants), individuals can advance answers to these questions to the whole group for plenary discussion. If the whole group is large, it may be more appropriate for participants to work on the questions initially in small groups.

Question 4
Participants can brainstorm their answers to this question in twos or threes before 'reporting back' to the whole group.

General discussion and possible outcomes

Section A   *General approaches to reading*

Question 1
There is a 'correct' answer to this question:
a) Intensive reading
b) Scanning
c) Receptive reading
d) Skimming

In their first language people may read poetry and legal contracts *intensively*, i.e. paying attention to the exact words which are used.

Novels and magazine or newspaper articles are normally read *receptively*, i.e. where the emphasis is on the informational content. This is sometimes referred to as 'extensive' reading, although the term 'extensive' can be misleading as it implies the use of long texts, complete texts or series of texts.

Scanning is a visual skill more than an interpretive one. 'Readers' look quickly through a text in order to find words ('shapes') which match a mental template of what they are seeking. The entertainments page of a newspaper would be scanned by a reader searching for the name of a particular film.

Skimming involves looking through a text quickly to derive the gist of something. It involves a degree of inference and interpretation. The review of a film might be 'skimmed' in order to ascertain how good the reviewer thought it was.

Question 2
In many parts of the world texts have traditionally been used in language teaching only as a vehicle for focussing on the language

Notes

contained therein. While this is a valid use of texts (the activity may contribute to improved language competence), in some cases it may be detrimental to the development of skills of reading such as extracting the maximum amount of information from a text in the minimum of time. A clear distinction may need to be drawn between the use of texts in the development of language competence on the one hand, and in the development of reading skills on the other.

Learners may need practice in choosing in what way to approach a particular text and in using the different skills of intensive reading, receptive reading, scanning and skimming judiciously in the process of 'reading' the text. The choice of these skills will depend on factors such as the nature of the text and the purpose in reading it, as well as on purely pedagogical factors (for example, which skills the teacher is concerned that the students should develop in a particular lesson).

The simple answer to this question, thus, may be 'yes', and many learners of foreign languages appear to be handicapped in their reading by their habit of reading slowly and over-attentively.

However, it is also true that during the 1970s and 1980s in many parts of the world there was a reaction against the exclusive practice of 'intensive reading' in the classroom. There was also a movement towards developing 'top-down' approaches to reading in which learners activate their knowledge of the topic and pay attention to the context to help them understand. As, in practice in the classroom, this often involves anticipating the context of texts, guessing, and increasing reading speed, many learners now have a lot of practice in skimming texts and relatively little practice in intensive reading. Consequently, it may now also be true that while some learners seem to practise only intensive reading skills, for others this aspect of their reading is seriously neglected. (Refer also to the discussion which relates to Question 3 of Section B below.)

Question 3
Some participants may feel that all reading tasks should simulate authentic, purposeful reading (see the extended discussion of this in *General discussion of issues*, page 149, in the Introduction to this chapter). However, there is also much empirical evidence to suggest that learners also develop their reading ability through activities which involve the use of skills which would not necessarily be appropriate to the reading of a particular text in the 'real world'.

Notes

Following the principle of starting from the general and working towards the particular, the following order is frequently followed by teachers who accept the latter position:

Skimming → Receptive reading → Intensive reading.

If practice is to be provided in *scanning*, it is logical that this should precede the other stages, although we may also scan a text we have already read in order to locate a particular part of it which we want to read again.

Section B *Effective and ineffective reading strategies*

Question 1

Although convincing arguments might be advanced for alternative answers in this exercise (circumstance-specific factors would need to be identified as in the example given), the following is a probable way of distinguishing the items.

Effective: b, c, e, f, g, h, i
Ineffective: a, d, j

Question 2

Some people are surprised to discover that research discloses that the answer to this question is generally TRUE. The purpose for reading a text nonetheless may still determine whether or not this is true in any specific instance. For example, in reading a densely worded, jargonistic legal contract prior to signing it, speed would probably not aid comprehension. In this case, appropriate 'comprehension' would involve deriving far more than the 'general idea' behind the words.

Question 3

Until recently it was widely believed that pattern (c) describes the eye movements of most people who appear to have good comprehension skills, and this belief was based in part on the observation that efficient readers are often also fast readers.

More recent research into eye movements, however, suggests that efficient readers not only read fast but also focus on a larger number of words in a text than less able readers. Their speed relies not only on their ability to activate their schematic knowledge to facilitate comprehension, but also on their ability to recognise words *automatically*. This research thus suggests that the correct answer to this question may be (b) rather than (c). (For a review of this research, see Grabe, 1991, pp. 385–6.)

Notes

Although no regressions (backward eye movements) are indicated in patterns (b) and (c), there will also be occasions on which efficient readers look back in a text. For example, a reader may do this to clear up ambiguity or suspected misunderstanding, or simply for pleasure or interest.

Question 4

Among the measures participants may suggest are the following:

- Providing a 'challenging' time limit for reading activities which makes it difficult for students to 'fix' on every word or small group of words.
- Making reading activities into a class 'race' for the same purpose.
- Momentarily 'flashing' sentences to the class which contain a simple instruction (for example, 'Get up and walk to the door'), or which require a shouted response of 'True' or 'False' (for example, 'There are five windows in this classroom'). This can be done using an OHP, showing prepared cards or by revealing prepared sentences on the board which have been 'hidden' under paper.
- Reading 'telegramese' to demonstrate that it is often not necessary to pay attention to every word in order to understand the sense of something.
- Discussion (and demonstration?) of the issue with students in their own language.

Discussion Task 19

Developing reading skills

Aim This Task invites you to explore and evaluate various practical techniques and procedures for developing reading skills, including aspects of task design and lesson planning.

TASK

Section A *General issues*

1 Comprehension and reading aloud
   Comment on the practice of reading aloud around the class as a way of developing reading comprehension skills.

2 Choice of reading material
   a) Make a list of criteria you might employ in selecting materials for developing and practising reading skills.
      Example The topic should be relevant to the interests and experience of the students.
   b) Who chooses the texts which are used for reading activities in the classroom?
   c) Comment on the suitability of the following text for developing reading comprehension skills:

Dear Carrie

I live in a small village, not far from Edinburgh. I came here only six months ago. The village has one street and only a few shops. It's very quiet. Three times a day there is a bus from the village to Edinburgh. It takes about 45 minutes. I like the village very much, but I haven't got any friends here. I am a single mother with two children, one boy and one girl. I'm 28 years old. The children are eight and six. I like sports and I like other people. I want to meet other people like me. Can you help?
Yours sincerely

Patty Dean

(from *Counterpoint Coursebook – Beginners* by Mark Ellis and Printha Ellis, published by Thomas Nelson and Sons Ltd)

Task

3 Presentation of texts
What are the advantages and disadvantages of the learners reading handwritten (as opposed to printed or typed) texts?

4 'Extensive' reading
How important is it that the students read outside the classroom and in their own time? How can they be encouraged to do this?

Section B   *Using a text – a possible procedure*

1 The following possible stages in a lesson to develop and practise reading skills are in a jumbled order. Number them according to what you would consider to be an appropriate order. (Note that in any lesson some of these stages may be omitted and/or additional stages included.)

a) **Students ask the teacher questions about unfamiliar vocabulary.**
b) **Students read very quickly in order to work out the answers to one or two general questions.**
c) **Students predict the content of the text from the title/picture/first line.**
d) **Students work out the meaning of selected words and expressions from the context.**
e) **The teacher teaches a few key words.**
f) **The teacher draws attention to some of the grammar in the text.**
g) **Students complete a detailed true/false exercise.**
h) **Students locate topic sentences in some of the paragraphs.**
i) **Students discuss topics related to the content of the text.**
j) **Students scan the text to pick out proper names.**

2 How many of these activities could be done by students working in groups or could be done individually and then discussed in small groups?

3 What would be the advantages of this?

4 What generalisations can you make about the principles underlying the order you adopted?

5 How many of these stages might it be realistic to plan in exploiting one text in one lesson?

G

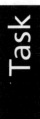

Section C   *Designing reading tasks*

1   Comment on the following sentence and the questions which follow it:

Splag grigged the flug spraggily in the scroog.
A Who grigged the flug?
B What did Splag do?
C Where did he grig the flug?
D How did he grig the flug?

2   Prepare a list of tasks which can be used to accompany texts in order to guide students in developing reading skills.
Example 1 'True/false statements'
(i.e. The text is accompanied by statements summarising information in the text. Some of these statements are accurate and some are not. Students evaluate each statement indicating whether it is 'true' or 'false'.)
Example 2 Putting jumbled pictures in order
(i.e. The text is accompanied by a series of pictures. Each picture represents the stage of a process or an event described in the accompanying text. Students put the pictures into an appropriate order or number them according to this order.)
Example 3 Personal response tasks
(An example of a personal response task would be an activity which involved students in reading a description of several hotels. Students would then describe and justify which one they would prefer to stay in, or they might select the hotels which would most suit the needs of certain people – either people that they know personally such as friends, colleagues or parents, or people whose profiles are presented in the task.)

Note that Examples 1 and 2 might be used to practise particular sub-skills of reading whereas Example 3 is more holistic in that learners use the text to achieve a particular communicative purpose, and different learners may employ different combinations of different skills in carrying out the task.

3   Final choice of tasks will often depend on:
– The nature of the text to be read
– The purposes for which it is to be read
– The precise skills or sub-skills the teacher aims to develop or practise

- The resources which are available to the teacher (e.g. books, photocopier, etc.)

Choose a text which you might use with one of your classes. Design tasks to accompany it and prepare to explain the rationale behind these tasks to other participants.

4 Prepare a brief list of guidelines you might draw up to give to teachers to help them in designing reading tasks.

Discussion Task 19

Developing reading skills

Timing   Section A c. 30 minutes
          Section B c. 20 minutes
          Section C c. 40 minutes
          Total   c. 90 minutes

It is not necessary for all three sections of this Task to be used in one session. Where time is limited, sections which are of greatest relevance to participants' interests and teaching circumstances may be selected. Alternatively, different sections may be used simultaneously in a session.

This Task is intended to be used after Discussion Task 18. Although prior use of Discussion Task 18 is not *absolutely* essential, it is important that participants have considered issues dealt with in this Task.

If trainers and/or participants are strongly committed to a holistic approach to teaching reading skills, they may want to omit Section B of the Task.

Suggestions for procedure

Section A   *General issues*

These questions can be discussed in small groups monitored by the trainer. Depending on the way in which the small groups answer the questions, the trainer can choose how long to devote to plenary feedback on these questions, and how much 'input' to give at this point herself.

Section B   *Using a text – a possible procedure*

Question 1
This can be organised as a 'race' for the participants working in pairs. The pairs who finish first can write up their chosen order for others to question or discuss. The trainer may also want to show the participants her own chosen order if this differs radically from that of the participants.

Notes

Notes

Questions 2–5
These can be discussed in small groups. Depending on the quality and number of points made, the trainer may subsequently want to clarify issues or add points in a plenary format.

Section C   *Designing reading tasks*

This section can also be discussed in small groups followed by a plenary discussion in which representatives of some of the small groups 'report back'.

Question 2
It may be useful for participants to have a written record of feedback on the brainstorming exercise. The trainer or an 'appointed' participant can list items on the board, or if photocopying facilities are available, a participant can act as 'secretary' and write down a list to be photocopied and distributed.

Question 3
The participants can be asked in advance to bring with them samples of texts they use with their classes. Alternatively, the trainer may provide the materials.

If different small groups work on different materials and all the groups present their work to the other participants, more time will need to be allocated for the plenary session.

OHP transparencies, posters or re-constituting groups can be used for this plenary feedback.

Question 4
Participants can prepare their lists in small groups. OHP transparencies, posters or re-constituting groups can be used to provide plenary feedback.

General discussion and possible outcomes

Section A   *General issues*

The following are some of the points that participants may make:

Notes

Question 1

Although this activity may have some use as a means of testing pronunciation (for example, if a natural dialogue is read), it probably does not help comprehension and, indeed, may have the opposite effect by encouraging students to read slowly, word by word. Moreover, it is important to bear in mind the fact that reading is normally a silent activity.

Question 2

a) Criteria mentioned by participants might include:
   - the difficulty of the language in relation to the abilities of the learners
   - naturalness of the language
   - length of the text
b) Conventionally, choice of texts is often determined by the course materials or they are chosen by the teacher. However, students can also be invited to choose materials for use in class. This is obviously easier to organise where the teacher has access to photocopying facilities and this involves no breach of copyright law.
c) The text is designed to provide a stimulus for writing and to revise specific language points. The authors make no claims that it is suitable for developing reading skills and, indeed, the unnatural, stilted nature of the language makes it unsuitable for this. Practice in reading sequences of short, simple sentences such as this provides little opportunity for learners to develop the skills they need to understand natural written English.

Question 3

In normal handwritten English many individual letters are often not clearly distinguished. For many learners (especially those whose first language uses a different script) this presents considerably more problems than reading printed text as they often need to guess a word from only those components which can be identified, and from the context of its use.

On the other hand, only by exposing them to the handwritten language can they develop the ability to read it. Moreover, they probably need to develop this ability, if only in order to read the teacher's writing.

It may be useful to provide them with 'authentic' exposure to handwritten English (through using letters, for example). It may also be useful to provide specific practice in this sub-skill, for example by providing a printed text and a parallel handwritten one in which a few changes have been made – the task for the learners is to identify the changes.

These points are particularly salient for learners whose first language is written in a script which is not Latin-based.

Question 4

Research suggests that the amount of time devoted to reading outside class has a very significant effect on the development of general language skills and reading skills in particular.

If the institution has library facilities, class time can initially be devoted to choosing books and developing the skills of predicting the content of a book from its cover, and from skimming through it. Class time can also subsequently be devoted to students 'reporting back' on the books they have read. (Depending on the class, this can be unstructured or structured in various ways and to varying degrees. For example, students can be asked to choose the character that they find most sympathetic in a novel and to describe him or her, justifying their choice.)

Some institutions also have 'class sets'. Students can be asked to read these at home and class time can be devoted to discussion of the content.

Hedge (1985), Chapters 4–7, pp. 62–119 and Collie & Slater (1987), Chapters 3–6, pp. 16–92 deal with these issues at considerable length.

Section B   *Using a text – a possible procedure*

This section of the Task pre-supposes a 'sub-skills' approach to developing reading skills as opposed to a 'holistic' one, in which the skills practised would be determined by the purpose for which a particular text would normally be read in the 'real world'. Any participants who take a strongly 'holistic' line may object to the assumptions implicit in this section of the Task (see page 149 of the section *General discussion of issues* in the Introduction to this chapter for a more extended discussion of this issue).

Question 1

There is no definitive answer to this question and the discussion and thinking which participants devote to this exercise may be more important than the order they finally choose.

The following is an example of an acceptable order (however, even radically different orders might be justified by reference to particular circumstances).

1 e   2 i   3 c   4 j   5 b   6 g   7 h   8 d   9 f   10 a

Question 2
The following stages could be organised as group activities or they could lead into group activities:
a, b, c, d, e, g, h, i, j

Question 3
Students would have the opportunity to discuss their opinions without fear of being 'publicly' wrong. Also, they are likely to refer back to the text to illustrate their arguments. There is thus a natural stimulus for reading more carefully.

Question 4
Although arguments might be advanced for not following these principles on particular occasions, the following generally apply.
– Begin with general comprehension and move towards a greater concern with details.
– Begin with a focus on meaning before paying attention to the language used in the text.

Question 5
This will depend on many factors such as the nature of the text, the time available and the level and motivation of the students.
   On average, many teachers might include perhaps four or five of these stages in one lesson.

Section C   *Designing reading tasks*

Question 1
This exercise is designed to illustrate the point that 'comprehension' questions need to be very carefully designed. A common weakness of 'comprehension' tasks is that the learners are able to provide 'correct' answers even if they have not understood the text.

Question 2
The following are among the kinds of tasks which might be mentioned.

Closed questions (e.g. Did he go to London?)
Open questions (e.g. Where did he go?)

Inferential questions (e.g. Do you think the person was really in love?)
Multiple-choice questions
True/false statements
Putting the jumbled paragraphs or sections of a text into the correct order
Filling in gaps in a text
Re-telling
Summarising
Drawing or completing pictures or diagrams
Putting pictures (or summarising words or statements) into the correct order
Giving (or choosing from several options) a title for a text
etc.

Teachers who pursue a 'holistic' approach to teaching reading skills may reject use of the tasks here which are contrived for the classroom, and may propose tasks which simulate 'real world' use of texts. For example, students might:
– read a catalogue in order to choose presents
– use an application form for filling in personal details
– read travel brochures in order to choose a holiday
    etc.

Question 3
The kinds of tasks participants devise will depend not only on the nature of the texts, but also on the points of view of the individuals with regard to the relative merits of 'holistic' and 'sub-skills' approaches.

Question 4
These guidelines may cover points from both 'sub-skills' and 'holistic' perspectives, or participants may choose to favour a particular point of view in devising the guidelines. (Holists may give priority to aspects of 'authenticity' while others may give priority to designing tasks which achieve specific aims in relation to defined sub-skills.)
   All participants will probably refer to and elaborate the need for clarity in task design, and the need for the tasks to *require* learners to process information which is both stated and implied in texts.

Discussion Task 20

Task

Factors involved in oral fluency

Aim This Task helps you to increase your awareness of a range of factors involved in oral fluency and to relate aspects of this to classroom practice.

TASK

Section A *Defining 'fluency'*

The term 'fluency' is sometimes used in different ways. Agree on what you understand by this term.

Section B *Reflection on experience*

Think of a foreign language you have learned, and preferably one that you speak quite well.

1 How would you assess your oral fluency in relation to other skills in the language?

2 Which aspects of your learning of the language most contributed to the development of your fluency?

3 What experience do you think would be most useful to you in order to enable you to develop your fluency yet further?

4 It is sometimes argued that fluency develops naturally in response to a *need* to communicate. To what extent is this point of view confirmed by your own experience of learning languages?

Section C *Problems with fluency for some learners*

The following are some of the problems of the 'silent learner' – the student who finds great difficulty in contributing to any kind of discussion in English, and who is reluctant to take advantage of opportunities to develop oral fluency:

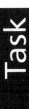

a) Inhibition/lack of confidence
b) Fear of making 'mistakes'
c) The feeling of having nothing to say on the subject
d) Lack of appropriate language
e) Lack of practice in conventions of conversational interaction

1 Brainstorm measures the teacher can take to help with each of these problems.

2 Look at the list of measures below. Add further items you have brainstormed to this list.

3 Write (a), (b), (c), (d) or (e) beside each of the measures in your revised list according to which of the above 'problems' it is intended to address.

i) Pre-teach key vocabulary.

ii) Thoroughly prepare for any discussion through brainstorming and exchange of ideas.

iii) Organise the class so that activities take place in small groups.

iv) Precede activities with extensive stages of preparation of some of the language the teacher has anticipated students may need to use during the activity.

v) Pursue and justify a policy of placing low priority on correctness and correction in certain activities.

vi) Teach exponents of *defining* (e.g. 'a thing which you do . . . with'; 'a thing for . . . ing') and of *eliciting* unknown words (e.g. 'What do you call a thing for . . . ing?').

vii) Provide 'stimulus' materials (e.g. texts on the topic to be discussed).

viii) Focus initially on information rather than opinion.

ix) Provide learners with specific training in communication strategies (e.g. circumlocution, hypothesising on the basis of features of the learners' first language or on the basis of the learners' existing knowledge of English itself).

x) Encourage and organise discussion of learning skills and objectives. Try to convince the learners of the value of trying to express themselves beyond their apparent linguistic limits, encouraging them to accept that 'mistakes are inevitable' in some activities in which the main focus is on oral communication.

xi) Analyse a (video) tape of native speakers involved in heated discussion, asking learners to pay attention to the speed and pitch of speech, body movements and gesture.

4   The items in the list of measures a teacher can take to help the 'silent learner' (i–xi) all aim to provide learners in some way with the confidence and skills to take advantage of opportunities to speak English.

It can also be argued, however, that in the development of oral fluency, specific measures such as these are less important than the fact of learners having a *need* to communicate and the motivation to do so.

In what ways can/do you create this need in your classes?

Section D   *Some features of conversational interaction*

A further aspect of normal interactive discourse is the negotiation of turns and topics, or in other words, who speaks when in a conversation and who says what.

1   Among a group of people involved in a conversation:
   a) How does someone indicate that they want to speak?
   b) How does someone interrupt?
   c) How does someone who is speaking avoid being interrupted?
   d) How does someone who has been speaking indicate that they have finished, or that they have reached a point at which they are willing for someone else to 'take over'?

2   A group of people are hotly debating a topic. One of the participants in the conversation wants to introduce a new 'angle' to the discussion. How might he successfully change the direction of the conversation?

3   Compare two linguistic/cultural communities with which you are familiar. What differences can you identify with regard to their respective conventions of participating in conversations?

Discussion Task 20

Notes

Factors involved in oral fluency

Timing	Section A	c. 10 minutes
	Section B	c. 20 minutes
	Section C	c. 40 minutes
	Section D	c. 20 minutes
	Total	c. 90 minutes

It is not necessary for all four sections of this Task to be used in one session. Where time is limited, sections which are of greatest relevance to participants' interests and teaching circumstances may be selected. Alternatively, different sections may be used simultaneously in a session.

This Task is intended to prepare participants to use Discussion Task 21. Section C of Task 20 in particular forms a 'bridge' between the two Tasks.

Suggestions for procedure

Section A   *Defining 'fluency'*

Participants can discuss this in small groups and write a summary definition. The trainer may need to ensure that participants are aware of the way in which the term is used in the context of this Task (see *General discussion and possible outcomes* below).

Section B   *Reflection on experience*

These questions can be discussed by participants in small groups. If participants are particularly curious about the conclusions reached in other small groups, or if the trainer has identified points of particular general interest in this discussion, a short plenary session may follow in which these points are 'aired' by participants.

Notes

Section C   *Problems with fluency for some learners*

Where the trainer anticipates that participants may be unfamiliar with conventions of conversational interaction, Section D of this Task (*Some features of conversational interaction*) can be used before this section.

Question 1

Participants can work in small groups.

The amount of time required for this brainstorming activity will vary. Where participants appear to be having some difficulty in coming up with ideas, the activity can be curtailed and the group moved on to address Question 3, which provides examples.

Where the activity is more productive, it can be curtailed when several of the small groups appear to have exhausted their ideas. Participants can then be asked to 'shout out' the ideas they have identified.

Questions 2 & 3

When some of the small groups have finished this activity the trainer can 'show' the participants her own answers using an OHP transparency or the board, and can invite questions or additions from the group.

Question 4

After ideas have been brainstormed in small groups, participants can be invited to 'shout out' items. The trainer or one of the participants can make a list of these on the board so that all participants have a complete record. Alternatively, where there is access to photocopying facilities, an appointed 'secretary' can make a list which will then be copied and distributed to everyone.

Section D   *Some features of conversational interaction*

Participants can discuss these questions in small groups before the discussion is 'opened up' to a verbal exchange of answers in a plenary mode.

Where there is access to the necessary technology and materials, it may be desirable to show the participants a few minutes of a video of people naturally discussing an issue (after participants have looked at the questions and before they have begun to answer them). In ideal circumstances there would be access both to a video of a discussion among native speakers of English, and to a discussion among speakers of some other language in that language. Scripted television programmes are probably not appropriate for these purposes as the conventions of conversational interaction will probably be artificial and different from those of normal interaction.

General discussion and possible outcomes

Section A   *Defining 'fluency'*

In these materials 'fluency' is used to describe the ability to communicate an intended message, or to affect the listener or interlocutor in the way that is intended by the speaker. The accurate use of language is a component in this ability, but over-attention to accuracy in the learning process may actually inhibit the development of fluency. Fluency involves the ability to adjust the message according to the responses of the listener or interlocutor, to construct coherent utterances and stretches of speech, to respond and to speak without undue hesitation. It also involves the ability to use strategies such as simplification, circumlocution and gesture to aid communication when the speaker may not have access to the vocabulary or grammar which would normally be appropriate.

Section B   *Reflection on experience*

The outcome of this part of the Task will depend on the experience and awareness of the participants.

It is likely, however, that high priority will be given to opportunities to use the language to communicate. In discussion of the 'need' to communicate participants may refer to the experience of being in a country where the language is widely spoken, but may also refer to classroom activities which simulate this need.

Notes

Section C *Problems with fluency for some learners*

There are no unarguably 'correct' answers to this exercise as any 'measure' is likely to facilitate different sub-skills of speaking to different extents. The following, however, represents one acceptable way of completing Question 3:

i) d	vii) c
ii) c	viii) c
iii) a	ix) d
iv) a	x) a
v) b	xi) e
vi) d	

In response to Question 4 participants are likely to refer to activities which involve an 'information gap' or 'opinion gap'. In these activities learners are obliged to share or exchange different information or opinions in order to complete a task. Discussion Task 21 looks at such activities more closely.

Section D *Some features of conversational interaction*

Some course materials teach specific exponents for use in negotiating
the turns and topics of conversation (for example, expressions such as 'If I could just come in here, . . . ' or 'Something I'd just like to bring up is . . . '). Although these expressions may be used in conversation, interaction is generally more complex than this.

Question 1
People indicate that they want to speak in a variety of ways. Eye movements and movements of the eyebrows are important, people tend to change their body position (frequently leaning forward although not necessarily so), and they tend to make 'affirmative noises' with increasing frequency and with mounting pitch and volume until they 'cut in' at a relatively high pitch and with a relatively rapid rate of speech. High pitch and speed are likely to be maintained by the person already speaking until it is clear that the right to speak has been conceded, and these features are also employed to 'fend off' interruption.

A speaker's eye movements are again important in signalling that he is willing for the conversation to be continued by someone else. The pitch often drops and the rate of speech slows down. Successful interruptions and 'take-overs' tend to occur at the end of clauses.

Question 2

Specific introductory expressions to indicate a change in topic ('Something I'd just like to bring up is . . . ') are unlikely to be used except, possibly, where conversation has come to a temporary pause or standstill. It is more likely that the new topic is introduced with no specific lexical marking, or even with an apparently misleading one ('And . . . ' or 'Yes, and . . . ' – expressions the speaker uses to 'pretend' to be continuing the same topic). The introduction of new topics, however, is frequently signalled in the intonation – the utterance begins on a very high intonational 'key'.

Question 3

The conventions of conversational interaction vary greatly between different speech communities. Even within Europe there are significant differences. For example, in some communities the person who wants to interrupt 'talks over' the person who is being interrupted, a strategy which is felt to be rude in most British English communities. In many non-European countries these conventions may be radically different. Age, social position and gender may all play a greater part in determining who speaks and who has the right to initiate topics, and people may expect to be named and explicitly invited to speak before they have a 'right' to participate in the conversation.

Discussion Task 21

Developing oral fluency

Aim This Task encourages you to explore and evaluate a range of techniques and activities for developing oral fluency.

TASK

Section A *Reflection on normal practice*

1 How much do your students speak in class?

2 How do you prepare speaking activities in class?

3 What materials do you use?

4 What particular problems do your students have?

5 In what ways do you encourage real communication to take place in your lessons?

Section B *Attitudes of some learners*

The following comments were made by students attending a 'conversation class'.

a) My teacher never corrects me so how can I learn?
b) I wanted a conversation class but all we do is play games.
c) Yesterday we talked about nuclear energy . . . but I didn't.
d) I know what to say but when it's my turn I can't.
e) I don't have enough words.

1 What do you think the underlying problems are?

2 What advice might you give to the teacher?

Section C *Activities – general*

Below is a list of various activity types designed to help learners to develop their oral fluency. Some of the types may overlap – for example, a jigsaw activity may involve an information gap (although the reverse is not necessarily true).

Task

a) Information-gap activities
b) Ranking activities
c) Jigsaw activities
d) Guessing activities
e) Problem-solving activities
f) Role play
g) Group discussion
h) Project-based activities
i) Prepared monologues

1 For each of these activity types (a–i) brainstorm an example activity.
Example *Activity A*: A 'spot the difference' exercise is an example of an information-gap activity. (Students work in pairs and each member of the pair has a slightly different picture. Without looking at each other's pictures they have to identify the differences between their two pictures.)

2 Match the items in the list of activity types (a–i) with the descriptions of (parts of) lessons (i–ix) below.

   i) Students work in small groups. Student A is given (or chooses) the name of a famous person. The other students have to discover the 'identity' of Student A by asking questions to which the answer is 'yes' or 'no'.
   ii) Students prepare a radio 'news' programme. They have access to newspapers and they appoint an 'editor', who is responsible for coordinating the preparation of 'stories' for broadcast. The programme is finally recorded onto tape.
   iii) Each student is asked to prepare to talk about a hobby or personal interest for two to three minutes. They must not read from a prepared text.
   iv) Students are given a possible list of adjectives describing personality. In groups they must agree on the three most important characteristics of a friend/a teacher/a spouse and put these in order.
   v) Students work in groups of four. Each student in the group has a different section of a text. Without showing the material to each other they have to decide on the order in which the sections occurred in the original, and pool their knowledge to answer general questions about the text.

201

Task

vi) The class reads a text about the dangers of smoking. They then divide into groups. Some groups ('doctors') prepare arguments to persuade someone to stop smoking. The other groups ('smokers') prepare their reasons for continuing to smoke. Finally the class is reorganised into pairs, each constituting a 'smoker' and a 'doctor'. The smoker has bronchitis and the 'doctor' tries to persuade her to stop smoking.

vii) The students work in groups. Student A is given a bizarre story and an explanation of the background. She tells the rest of the group the story. The other students ask questions to try to discover the background.

viii) Students work in groups with a series of statements on a topic they have read about. Together they have to try to reach a consensus on whether or not they agree with each of the statements.

ix) Students work in pairs. Student A has a very full diary and Student B has another. They have to find a time when it is convenient for them to meet.

Example *Activity (a) – Lesson (ix)*

3 Choose four of the activity types and brainstorm further kinds of material and activity which might be used.
Example The following are all examples of *information-gap activities*:
 – One student describes a picture to another student. The second student has to draw it.
 – One student arranges objects on the table and directs the second student to arrange similar objects in the same way. The students sit so that they cannot see each other's objects.
 – One student has a sequence of pictures which tell a story. The second student has the same pictures in a jumbled order. The first student describes the sequence to her partner. The partner has to arrange her pictures into the correct order.

Section D   *Activities – group discussion*

A teacher wants her students to develop the skills necessary for taking part in a group discussion. She also genuinely wants them to exchange their opinions about problems of *transport* in their home city.

1 What linguistic preparation might be appropriate?

2 In what ways might she organise this?

3 In what ways can she stimulate interest in the topic?

4 In what ways can she encourage shy members of the class to express their views?

5 What might she do about a very dominant student who is predisposed to monopolise any activity?

6 How might she choose to organise the classroom?

7 What might her own role in the activity be?

8 The following is an excerpt from a transcript of the teacher's lesson. What advice would you give to the teacher?

Teacher: Today we are going to talk about transport in our city. What do you think about this, Maria?
Student: Mmmm. I think is bad.
Teacher: Good. *It* is bad. What don't you like about it?
Student: The buses.
Teacher: Good. The buses. Do you think they are too slow or too expensive?
Student: Too slow.
Teacher: Good. Do you agree, Pilar?

Discussion Task 21

Developing oral fluency

Timing   Section A c. 15 minutes
Section B c. 15 minutes
Section C c. 45 minutes
Section D c. 15 minutes
Total   c. 90 minutes

It is not necessary for all four sections of this Task to be used in one session. Where time is limited, sections which are of greatest relevance to participants' interests and teaching circumstances may be selected. Alternatively, different sections may be used simultaneously in a session.

This Task follows up and extends many of the issues raised in Discussion Task 20, and can be used in conjunction with that Task.

Suggestions for procedure

Section A   *Reflection on normal practice*

These questions can be discussed by participants working in small groups. Unless the trainer identifies issues which she thinks it would be useful to raise with the whole group, or participants show a particular interest in the discussion of other small groups, plenary feedback may be unnecessary.

The discussion will be particularly productive if there is maximum diversity of experience within the groups.

If participants have already used Discussion Task 20, they may already have addressed the issues raised in Questions 4 and 5. In this case they may prefer not to discuss them again.

Section B   *Attitudes of some learners*

Again, plenary feedback may not be necessary. However, if the trainer feels that the small-group discussion is insufficiently searching, she may ask representatives from the different groups to report back on their discussion of one of the questions, and invite comments and questions from other participants. She may

Notes

also want to prompt the discussion by asking participants to elaborate on points they make. The way in which she does this will depend on the points made.

Section C   *Activities – general*

Question 1

If this brainstorming exercise appears to be fruitful in the small groups, the trainer can encourage them to 'move on' to Question 2 as they finish Question 1. However, if these terms are unfamiliar to them, or if the participants appear to be unfamiliar with a sufficient variety of activities, the brainstorming can be curtailed and the group directed to Question 2 as a means of providing input.

Question 2

The trainer can show the whole group the 'example' answer and invite comment and questions. Where members of the group are relatively unfamiliar with the topic, the trainer may find that she has to explain and demonstrate at this point, or ask participants who are more familiar with the topic to do so.

Question 3

Feedback on this activity may take some time, depending on the *diversity* of experience and knowledge within the group as well as the *amount* of experience and knowledge. The small-group activity can be curtailed when two or three of the groups have completed the task. In the plenary feedback, participants can, in a sense, 'teach' each other about any activities which are generally unfamiliar.

Section D   *Activities – group discussion*

Questions 1–7

It is intended that participants answer these questions in small groups. In monitoring this activity the trainer may decide how much time to devote to feedback, and whether this should be organised as a plenary session or by re-constituting groups. This decision may depend on how much participants have to say and how much diversity of opinion there is within the whole group.

If the small groups answer the questions in some detail, subsequent plenary discussion may be unnecessary even if the trainer feels that a few more points could have been made.

Notes

Question 8

After a brief discussion of this question in small groups (or with no discussion if participants seem relaxed and uninhibited in the plenary format), the trainer can invite participants to say what advice they would give the teacher.

General discussion and possible outcomes

This Task is primarily concerned with classroom technique. Discussion Task 20 considers the rationale which underlies this consideration of technique. Where participants have not used Discussion Task 20, the trainer may want to draw the attention of participants to this underlying rationale. In particular, participants may like to consider the argument that oral fluency develops largely in response to a real need to communicate (for example, in activities which are based on an information gap).

Section A *Reflection on normal practice*

The outcome of this discussion will depend on the kinds of experience the participants have.

Section B *Attitudes of some learners*

The following are among the points which are likely to be made in this discussion:

a) The student appears not to understand or value 'fluency', equating learning only with 'correctness' and probably seeing correctness as something which is achieved through 'being corrected'. She may also want the teacher to be present to monitor her performance whenever she speaks English.

   The teacher might be advised to discuss her own aims with the class and to engage their support for her policy. However, it is also possible that fluency is very low on the students' own agendas in learning English. In this case, the teacher might want to modify her approach.

b) It is possible that by 'games' the student means activities designed to encourage students to speak (such as information-gap, problem-solving or guessing activities). In this case, it would appear that it has not been made clear to the student (or that the student has not accepted) that these activities develop skills which are important in 'conversation'.

Again, the teacher might be advised to discuss her aims with the class.

c) It is possible that the student is shy, or that she had no knowledge or opinions about the issue.

The teacher might be advised to prepare the activity more thoroughly, with regard both to language and to ideas (see Section D of this Task). She might also make greater use of discussion in small groups, where shy learners may feel less inhibited.

The topic itself may have been inappropriate for this student.

d) Most language learners will probably recognise this phenomenon. The problem usually becomes easier with practice.

The teacher might be advised to discuss these problems directly with the class (in their first language where this is possible).

e) The problem here might be that the task is too difficult or that the teacher has prepared it insufficiently. However, it might also be the case that the learner has 'enough' words to express herself, but is reluctant to make mistakes.

Refer to (c) and (a) above.

Section C   *Activities – general*

It is not so much the aim of this section of the Task to introduce 'new' activities as to encourage participants to think about the range of activities they organise in their classes, and to think about types of activity that, perhaps, they have not yet used.

Questions 1 & 3
With most groups of participants the trainer will probably not need to add to the list of activities brainstormed, and may even need to limit them. However, the following book is particularly helpful if she wishes to remind herself of the possible range of activities, or wishes to suggest reading for the participants which may extend their knowledge of activities: Ur (1981) *Discussions that Work*.

Notes

Notes

Question 2
The following is the intended answer to this matching exercise:
a) ix   f) vi
b) iv   g) viii
c) v   h) ii
d) i   i) iii
e) vii

Section D   *Activities – group discussion*

Question 1
This will depend both on the level of the class and the extent to which the students are confident about trying to express themselves when they feel they lack some of the language which would be helpful to them in the activity. To some extent it will also depend on the kinds of transport used in the particular city or cities.

With a low-level class the teacher may want to ensure that the students know and can pronounce words such as *bus*, *underground* and *train*, prepositions such as *by* bus and *on* foot, expressions of quantity such as *a lot of*, *too much*, and terms such as *traffic jam*, *pollution* and *congestion/congested*. She may also want to ensure that they are confident in using some of the language of expressing opinions such as *I think* . . .

Question 2
Depending on how 'new' this language is to the class, it could be brainstormed in small groups, a gap-fill exercise might be used, or (with a monolingual class) a 'vocabulary' sheet might be given to students, giving the words with their first language equivalents, and notes about their usage and pronunciation.

Question 3
The teacher might ask students to think about their own journeys in the city and any problems they have, or ask them to compare travelling in the city with travelling in some other place. Students might read, listen to or watch a text or programme on this topic. They might look at pictures of problems, or, initially, brainstorm problems in pairs. The teacher might provide the class with statements describing transport in the city and ask students to decide which ones they agree or disagree with. She might ask students in groups to list specific arguments either in favour of or against a particular means of transport or a policy on transport.

Question 4

She might ask students to discuss this issue in small groups rather than as a whole class. She might also ask students to prepare what they want to say at home, and then ask a 'chairperson' in the group to pay particular attention to giving everyone in the group the opportunity to speak. It may sometimes help a shy student to give her the role of chairperson.

Question 5

She might speak to any such student individually before the activity and tactfully remind them of the need to give other students the chance to speak. Sometimes it may help to give such students this responsibility explicitly by appointing them as chairpeople.

Question 6

In any discussion where the main aim is fluency, dividing the class into small groups maximises the opportunity for students to speak and may reduce inhibition. With some classes the teacher may have difficulty in persuading students in small groups to keep to the task and to use the foreign language. However, it is worth persevering with this in most contexts.

In some classrooms the furniture militates against this organisation and school policy may also disfavour this kind of organisation. In these circumstances a degree of compromise may be necessary.

Question 7

In some circumstances the teacher may want to 'chair' the discussion herself, but this responsibility can often be delegated to students. The teacher can then monitor the discussion(s), noting points made which it may be useful to refer to later, noting language difficulties students appear to have and, perhaps, occasionally prompting them or (if the learners are children) disciplining them.

After an activity such as this some teachers feel that they are expected to provide feedback on mistakes they have heard. However, if the aim is essentially one of developing fluency it may be more appropriate to refer to the content of the discussion in any feedback rather than to the language used.

Question 8

This question is intended to consolidate points the participants may have made in response to the preceding seven questions. Points might be made about preparation, the organisation of groups, the role of the teacher and also about the nature of the

Notes

teacher's questions (which, on the whole, are formulated to elicit single words rather than discussion).

Discussion Task 22

Factors involved in effective writing

Aim Section A of this Task encourages you to reflect on your own experience of learning to write in a foreign language. Sections B and C aim to familiarise you with terms and concepts which are central to a consideration of effective writing. Sections D and E invite you to apply these terms and concepts in analysing writing tasks and samples of learners' written English.

TASK

Section A *Reflection on experience*

Think about your own experience of learning foreign languages.

1 What kinds of written tasks did you carry out?

2 What problems did you encounter in learning to write?

3 What helped you to overcome these problems?

4 Did you find that the act of writing itself contributed to your learning of the language? In what ways?

Section B *Some basic issues*

Effective writing involves conveying a message in such a way as to affect the audience as the writer intends.

Depending on the precise purpose in writing, this may, for example, involve seizing and maintaining the interest of the intended readers, conveying information clearly, delighting or amusing the readers or persuading them of a particular point of view. The writer needs to be able to imagine the readers and to assess their knowledge of the topic, their assumptions about the topic and their attitudes towards it and interest in it.

In achieving the purpose for writing, the writer makes choices about a number of factors. Look at the following list of some of these factors:

grammar   handwriting
vocabulary   paragraphing
cohesion   formulae
coherence   spelling
rhetorical organisation   capitalisation
layout   punctuation
underlining/italics

1   Add further factors to this list if you think there is anything missing. ('Style' is not included in this list as an independent item as this term normally refers to appropriate choices of *vocabulary* or *grammar*.)

2   Which of the terms in this list refer to:
   a) The organisation of functions within a text? (For example, a letter of initial complaint will conventionally begin with a description of the background, then state the problem, and will then indirectly request action.)
   b) The physical arrangement of information on the page? (For example, the fact that in a letter, the sender's address normally appears in the top right-hand corner.)
   c) The use of 'stock phrases'? (For example, 'Thank you for your letter of 16 July.')

Section C   *Cohesion and coherence*

Cohesion and coherence are central to all instances of language use, and indeed, to communication of any kind. However, it is in writing that learners of a foreign language often find that any problems they have in these areas become highlighted.

1   Look at the following extracts from compositions written by learners of English. Both students have problems with cohesion, which is why the texts seem odd even though mistakes of grammar and vocabulary have been corrected.

a)
> My landlady is an old woman. My landlady is very kind to me. She does not give me rice to eat. My landlady does not know I am used to eating a lot of rice. In my country people of my country need to eat a lot of rice.

Task

b)

> My landlady is called Mrs Jones. She
> lives on a ground floor of house. It is a
> very old house. Sometimes it rains.
> Water comes through a roof. My room
> is not at top of a house. My room
> is dry.

Rewrite these extracts so that they 'read' naturally.
   What problems does each student have with cohesion?
(Other mistakes have been corrected.)

2   Define 'cohesion' and make a list of words which commonly
    act as 'cohesive devices'.

3   Look at the following two sentences. Both are cohesive, but
    one has a problem of coherence. Which one?
    a) Yesterday I got up late and had a quick breakfast.
    b) Yesterday I got up late and bought a new car.

'Coherence' describes the logical relations between the ideas and
information embodied in discourse. In coherent text it is clear
how sentences relate to sentences, and paragraphs to paragraphs
(exemplifying a point made, countering a point made, extending
a point made, etc.). Coherence is helped by cohesion, but often a
writer assumes that the reader will use particular aspects of
general knowledge and knowledge of the specific conventions of
certain kinds of text to supply the necessary logical connections.
   In sentence (a) above, it is clear that the relationship between
'getting up late' and 'having a quick breakfast' is one of cause
and effect. In sentence (b), the two parts of the sentence appear
to be unrelated and it is difficult to infer any connection. In this
sentence there is a problem of coherence.
   The second of the sentences in (c) below is grammatically
similar to sentence (a) above. Again it is perfectly coherent.
However, in this case the relationship between the two parts of
the sentence is not one of *cause and effect* but of *equivalence* –
both parts of the sentence illustrate and expand the information
contained in the preceding sentence:
   c) I had a wonderful weekend. Yesterday I got up late and had a
      leisurely breakfast.

In both sentences (a) and (c) 'and' provides the cohesion.
However, the relationship it implies can be derived only through

the context and through knowledge (in these cases, of conventional human behaviour) which the reader brings to bear in the act of interpreting.

4 Look back at the preceding paragraphs in this Task. Define the relationship between the paragraphs beginning ' "Coherence" describes . . . ' and 'In sentence (a) above, . . . '.

5 In writing English, which appears to present more problems to your learners, cohesion or coherence?

6 Would this be equally true of the process of reading?

Section D *Writing tasks*

Look at the descriptions of writing tasks below. For each of them speculate about which of the factors listed in Section B of this Task might be particularly important in terms of the writer achieving his aims:

a) The task involves writing a note to someone who will be staying in your house while you are away. The note gives practical information about where things are and what the guest must remember to do or might want to do (for example, watering plants, locking windows before going out, using complicated kitchen equipment).

b) The task involves writing a formal commercial letter confirming an order which has been made by telephone.

c) The task involves writing an 'academic' essay discussing the advantages and disadvantages of a particular process or policy.

Section E *Writing by learners*

Analyse a sample or samples of writing by learners of English, paying particular attention to the factors listed in Section B of this Task.

What problems do they appear to have?

Which of these factors might the teacher focus on as a priority?

Choose samples from your own students' work or refer to Resource 5 (in Section 1 of the *Resources bank*, on page 294).

Discussion Task 22

Factors involved in effective writing

Timing   Section A c. 15 minutes
              Section B c. 15 minutes
              Section C c. 30 minutes
              Section D c. 15 minutes
              Section E c. 15 minutes
              Total   c. 90 minutes

It is not necessary for all five sections of this Task to be used in one session. Where time is limited, sections which are of greatest relevance to participants' interests and teaching circumstances may be selected. Alternatively, different sections may be used simultaneously in a session.

This Task is intended to serve as an introduction to Discussion Task 23, which concentrates more on ways of teaching writing skills in the classroom.

Suggestions for procedure

This Task introduces terms and concepts which participants may find difficult if the topic is new to them. The trainer may want to go through parts of the Task quite slowly if this is the case, ensuring that there is no confusion and, if necessary, providing his own examples to exemplify points made in the material. He may also suggest that some of the participants read around the topic before the session in which this Task is used. For a very short introduction to the topic, Richards (1990) is probably the best source. Pages 103–6 deal specifically with coherence and cohesion.

Section A   *Reflection on experience*

These questions can be discussed in small groups. Plenary feedback may be unnecessary unless there is a great disparity of experience and opinion among the participants.

H

Section B   *Some basic issues*

Questions 1 & 2

These can be discussed by participants in small groups and, if the discussion is productive, feedback on them can be brief. The trainer can record any additions suggested (Question 1) and show them his own answers to Question 2, and invite comment and questions.

However, if participants are less familiar with thinking about writing skills in these terms, he may want to introduce plenary discussion after Question 1 has been discussed in the small groups, and may have to take care to explain and describe some of the terms.

Section C   *Cohesion and coherence*

The trainer may want to introduce this part of the Task by inviting participants in pairs to attempt to write a definition of 'cohesion' and 'coherence'. If they find this difficult, the activity can be curtailed and the group can move on to working on Question 1.

To avoid lengthy and abstract explanation, after eliciting the definitions, the trainer may want to postpone further discussion of these until after the appropriate parts of the Task.

It is probably unnecessary to discuss the rewritten texts, but should the trainer want to do this, one of the small groups can write them on an OHP transparency to show the whole group if the equipment is available.

Question 1

Participants can work on the two brief texts in small groups. Plenary feedback on this discussion can be postponed until after discussion of Question 2, when participants may want to refer back to these texts to illustrate their definitions.

Question 2

At this point participants should be able to attempt a definition of 'cohesion', and provide examples. The definitions can be written on OHP transparencies or the board for discussion among the whole group. The trainer may also list the examples elicited on the board so that the whole group has a record of their collective brainstorming.

Questions 3 & 4

These can be discussed in small groups. The trainer may want to check the answer to Question 4 with the whole group if he has identified any problems.

Questions 5 & 6

The experience of individuals may be of interest to the whole group and, if the participants appear relaxed and uninhibited about speaking out, answers to these questions may simply be elicited after a few moments for individual reflection.

Alternatively, participants may prefer to discuss these questions in small groups.

Section D   *Writing tasks*

Participants can work on this section of the Task in small groups. A representative of one of these groups can present their conclusions as a stimulus for further discussion and comment in a brief plenary session.

Section E   *Writing by learners*

For this section of the Task all participants need to look at the same sample or samples of writing. Feedback may be organised through re-constituting small groups, or a representative from one of the groups may 'talk through' the conclusions his group reached. Other participants can then comment on these or add further points.

General discussion and possible outcomes

Section A   *Reflection on experience*

Participants' responses to these questions will depend on their individual experience of foreign language learning.

It is likely, however, that participants will refer to the value of positive encouragement from teachers and the usefulness of studying example texts and how they are written. They may also refer to the fact that the conscious processes of thinking about linguistic choices and the research that may take place in the act

Notes

of writing may have a positive effect on other aspects of language learning such as the development of linguistic knowledge.

Section B   *Some basic issues*

Question 1
Participants may want to be more explicit about the components of very general categories such as *grammar* (dividing it into syntax, clause structure, inflection, verb forms, etc.).

Question 2
This question is intended to ensure that the participants understand the terms. Trainers may wish to check whether there are other terms in the list which participants are unsure of. The following is the intended answer to the question:
a)   Rhetorical organisation
b)   Layout
c)   Formulae

Section C   *Cohesion and coherence*

Question 1
Participants should be able to identify the problems with cohesion as these are the features which make the language unnatural.

In Text (a) there is a lot of unnecessary repetition. The learner appears to have problems in judging how much information the reader needs in order to perceive the cohesive threads, and over-compensates by avoiding subordination and the use of pronouns. However, he also appears to have difficulty in using conjunctions and/or adverbs to mark some of the cohesive relationships ('My landlady is very kind to me. She does not give me rice to eat'). This relationship of 'concession' would normally be marked through use of 'although' or 'however'.

The writer of Text (b) has similar difficulties, but additionally has problems in operating the system of articles which would enable him to mark more explicitly information which is new, as opposed to that which refers back to something already stated in the text ('a roof' – *the* roof, i.e. of this house; 'at top of a house' – *the* house, i.e. my landlady's house, in which I live).

The texts might be rewritten as follows:

a)

> My landlady is an old woman, who is very kind to me. However, she does not know that people in my country need to eat a lot of rice, and so I am used to this. Consequently, she does not give me rice to eat.

b)

> My landlady, Mrs Jones, lives on the ground floor of a very old house. Although water comes through the roof when it rains, my room is dry because it is not at the top.

Question 2

'Cohesion' refers to the explicit linguistic signalling of relationships within a text. These relationships are commonly signalled by:

'Pro-forms'   (Not only pronouns but also 'pro-verbs' – I don't like cheese but my sister *does*; and 'pro-adverbs' – I haven't been to Japan but my sister went *there* last year.)

Conjunctions   although, as well as, so, because

Adverbs   however, nonetheless, furthermore, consequently

Substituted nouns   I like cats but my sister can't stand *the animals.*

Comparative forms   I have just seen a bad accident, but the one I saw last year was even *worse.*

Determiners   the, this, that, some of the

The example overleaf illustrates some aspects of cohesion in a text:

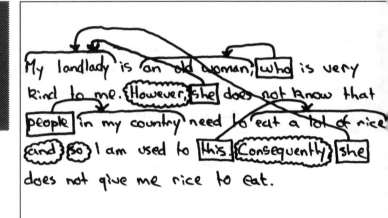

My landlady is an old woman, who is very kind to me. However, she does not know that people in my country need to eat a lot of rice and so I am used to this. Consequently she does not give me rice to eat.

Question 3
This is answered in the Task itself (sentence b).

Question 4
The function of the second paragraph is to *exemplify* the general point made in the first paragraph, providing examples of 'successful' and 'unsuccessful' coherence.

Question 5
Although conventions of organising parts of texts vary according to culture to some extent, people who can write coherently in their first language normally have the potential to transfer this ability to the foreign language. Coherence is more a question of logical thinking than of linguistic expression.

Problems of coherence frequently stem from an inadequate command of cohesive devices, however. As is implicit in the answer to Question 2 above, this 'command' involves more than just a knowledge of the words. It also involves a command of complex sentence construction and the multifarious ways of signalling definiteness in a text. Cohesion may present particular problems to speakers of non-European languages as the systems of cohesion in European languages are relatively similar.

Question 6
Some readers will use their knowledge of the topic and their general knowledge to perceive accurate logical connections even when they cannot identify the precise meaning or textual function of some of the cohesive devices. In reading, ignorance of cohesive devices is less likely to affect coherence. Nonetheless, knowledge of these greatly facilitates reading skills.

Section D   *Writing tasks*

The following is a likely answer to this question:
a) Primarily vocabulary but also grammar; paragraphing; underlining
b) Layout; formulae; grammar; vocabulary; rhetorical organisation
c) Coherence; rhetorical organisation

Section E   *Writing by learners*

Responses to this question will depend on the samples chosen. The following is a possible analysis of Resource 5 (Section 1 of the *Resources bank*):

The learner appears to have problems with all the factors listed in Section B of the Task except, perhaps, rhetorical organisation and coherence (underlining/italics is not a salient factor in this composition).

General features the teacher might choose to prioritise include: handwriting; punctuation; paragraphing; cohesion (note the repetition of 'present'); grammar (simple and complex sentence construction).

If the teacher is concerned with informal letters as a *text type*, he might also want to pay attention to layout and formulae.

Discussion Task 23

Task

Developing writing skills

Aim   This Task aims to extend your awareness of a range of factors involved in teaching writing skills, and explores factors relating to a variety of approaches.

TASK

Section A   *Reasons for writing*

The following are some of the reasons learners of English may be asked to write:

a) For *diagnostic* purposes.
b) To *develop linguistic competence* (for example, copying a model of new language or writing a short text to practise or test knowledge of language which has been taught).
c) To encourage the development of *fluency*.
d) To train/provide practice in aspects of writing skills per se, for example:
   i) Selecting characteristic features of particular text types according to the purpose in writing.
   ii) Including appropriate stages in the process of composition.
   iii) Assessing the knowledge, assumptions, attitudes and interest of the intended audience and addressing them accordingly.

1   How clear to your students do you make the purpose of any writing activity?

2   How might the purpose of a writing activity determine your approach to preparing the activity in class?

3   How might the purpose of a writing activity determine your approach to correction?

4   For which of these purposes might students be encouraged to write collaboratively?

Task

Section B *Preparation, motivation and communication*

1   Make a list of ways in which the teacher can motivate students to write by encouraging confidence and enthusiasm. **Example** She can get students to watch part of a selected TV documentary programme (in English or in their own language) as a stimulus for ideas to help them in writing.

2   How important do you consider it is that the writing task incorporates an element of real communication?

3   How might a task incorporate this element of real communication?

Section C *Teaching the features of particular text types*

Before asking the students to write an example of a particular text type you might want to go through some of the following stages. The order, here, is jumbled. Put them into an appropriate order and justify your decisions.

a)   Guided writing practice – the students write (parts of) a parallel text guided by prompts (e.g. pictures or sentences which summarise paragraphs).

b)   Exercises which practise particular features of the text type (e.g. ordering paragraphs in the text, combining sentences using a relative clause).

c)   Reading examples of the text type.

d)   Analysing texts to isolate characteristic features of that text type.

Section D *'Process' approaches to teaching writing skills*

In recent years attention has focussed on the *process* of writing, and the criticism has been made that teachers sometimes expect learners to produce written texts without allowing, encouraging or training them in the stages which are necessary for producing good texts.

1   The 'stages' of the writing process
    a) Complete the following chronological list of the stages

Task

writers might go through in writing something in which they are concerned with expressing themselves very exactly (for example, an essay or an important letter).

> 1 Mulling over and discussing ideas
> 2 Jotting down notes in no particular order
> 3
> 4
> etc.

Note that it would be inappropriate to go through all these stages in every instance of writing – the nature of the 'process' depends on the purpose for writing, the length of the text, the complexity of the ideas and the time available to the writer. Moreover, in practice these stages will rarely be discrete – there may be considerable overlap between them and there may be 'regressions' to earlier stages.

b) Think of different written assignments you might set your students. Specify one in which it would be appropriate to encourage them to work systematically through these stages, and one in which this would be inappropriate.

2   Choice of approach
To what extent is a process-based approach to teaching written skills compatible with a text-type based approach? (See Section C of this Task for an explanation of a text-type based approach.)

3   Technology
How might access to word processors affect the organisation of a lesson intended to develop process-writing skills?

4   Interaction
How might a lesson be organised so that students help each other in the processes of revision and re-drafting?

Section E *Designing writing tasks*

Agree on the characteristics and needs of a specific group of learners. Think of a particular kind of writing which they need to carry out and the difficulties that this might present them with.

Describe the lessons or parts of lessons in which you would help them with this aspect of the skill. Consider the kinds of preparation which would be of particular help to them, and the precise tasks you would set them.

Section F *Correction of written work*

1 In your own experience of learning foreign languages, what kinds of feedback did your teachers give you? How useful did you find this feedback?

2 Consider the following comments made by learners of English. In each case attempt to define in what ways the expectations and 'personal philosophies' of the teacher and the learner are similar or appear to differ.

Example *Comment (a)*: From her own experience as a learner or from her training as a teacher, the teacher may have internalised the view that red ink is perceived by learners to be intimidating or discouraging. She appears not to have questioned this, or at least she has not solicited the views of this learner's class. It may be the case that very few of her students share her reluctance to use red ink.

a) I wish the teacher would use red ink so that I could see things clearly.
b) I wish she would write in the corrections instead of using that code.
c) She corrects every mistake. It's really discouraging.
d) She seems to think that grammar and spelling are everything.
e) She writes really nice comments at the bottom.
f) She goes over our mistakes individually, one by one. It's such a waste of time.
g) She writes 'good' at the bottom, but I know it isn't.
h) I'd love to know what other students write.

Section G   *Grading compositions*

The following is a list of some of the factors which may be considered in grading a piece of written work. Add to the list if you wish:

length
correct grammar
originality of ideas
range of vocabulary used
range and complexity of structures used
appropriateness of style
spelling
handwriting
punctuation
organisation of ideas
relevance to the title

1   Put these factors into order of importance or group them according to how important you think they are. (If you find that this differs according to different groups of learners, you may wish to think of a specific learner or group of learners.)

2   In grading a composition, do you actually divide the marks available into categories (e.g. 5 for range of vocabulary, 5 for style, etc.), or do you give an impression mark?

3   Do you give two grades – one for content and one for language?

4   Do you prefer percentages, numbers out of ten, letters of the alphabet or another system of recording grades?

5   Refer to compositions written by some of your students or select examples from Section 1 of the *Resources bank* (on pages 290–4).
    Work out a scheme and grade the compositions. Compare and discuss the results of this.

Discussion Task 23

Developing writing skills

Timing   Section A c. 20 minutes
Section B c. 20 minutes
Section C c. 20 minutes
Section D c. 20 minutes
Section E c. 20 minutes
Section F c. 25 minutes
Section G c. 25 minutes
Total   c. 150 minutes

It is not necessary for all seven sections of this Task to be used in one session. Where time is limited, sections which are of greatest relevance to participants' interests and teaching circumstances may be selected. Alternatively, different sections may be used simultaneously in a session. This Task extends many of the issues dealt with in Discussion Task 22, and assumes familiarity with the terms introduced in that Task.

Section G of this Task may be of less relevance than the other sections to teachers who do not need to grade the work their students produce.

Suggestions for procedure

Section A   *Reasons for writing*

This exercise can be discussed in small groups. Representatives of the small groups can be asked to report back on their conclusions to the whole group.

Section B   *Preparation, motivation and communication*

This activity can be organised in a similar way to the above.

Question 1
The trainer may wish to make a list of the ideas suggested on the board so that participants have a record. Alternatively, where the group has access to a photocopier, a 'secretary' can be

appointed, who will write down the full list of ideas and photocopy it to circulate to all the participants.

Questions 2 & 3
A representative of one or two of the small groups can be asked to describe the group's conclusions, and further comments or questions can be invited.

Section C   *Teaching the features of particular text types*

Participants may carry out this activity very quickly, and the trainer may decide not to organise feedback with the whole group unless there is substantial disagreement within or between small groups.

Where small groups appear to be uncertain about an order, or where the trainer feels that the basis for their decisions about the order lacks principle, she can ask participants to argue their decisions in a whole-group format, insisting on the aspect of *justification*.

Section D   *'Process' approaches to teaching writing skills*

Question 1
One group can be asked to record their list on an OHP transparency, or to write it up on the board so that all participants can consider this and ask questions, add comments or disagree.

A representative from one of the groups may be asked to describe to the other participants the two assignments they have specified. There will probably be little need for extended discussion of this part of the question.

Questions 2–4
The amount that participants have to say in response to these questions may depend on their familiarity with process-based approaches, and also on their experience of using word processors and of organising collaborative writing activities with their learners.

Where these topics are generally familiar to the group and participants appear to have thought about them, participants may feel ready to discuss the questions in a plenary group. Where the topics are relatively unfamiliar, participants may be happier to discuss the questions in small groups initially. The trainer may also wish to 'prompt' discussion with some ideas of her own if she feels that this stimulus will be productive.

Section E   *Designing writing tasks*

Participants can work on this section of the Task in pairs or groups of three. As far as possible participants can work together with people who teach in similar circumstances to their own.

Descriptions of lessons and examples of tasks can be recorded on 'posters', so that participants can then circulate to look at the results of the work done by other pairs or small groups and ask for explanation or clarification.

Section F   *Correction of written work*

Participants can discuss this exercise in small groups. A 'secretary' can be appointed in each small group to report back to the whole group any points which are controversial or which are of potential interest to the others.

Section G   *Grading compositions*

The discussion of this part of the Task can be organised in a similar way to Section F above.

The materials used in Question 5 will depend upon access to photocopying facilities, the preferences and wishes of participants and whether they currently have classes who are writing compositions. Some participants may particularly want to use their own students' work, and to learn from the opinions of other participants about the quality of this work. Others may prefer to use materials which are provided by the trainer, or materials from the *Resources bank*.

General discussion and possible outcomes

Section A   *Reasons for writing*

This list of reasons for writing is a general one, and not all of them will apply in specific cases. In particular, some groups of learners will have no real, foreseeable reasons to write in English. In this case the 'per se' reasons (d) will not be relevant to their needs, and a teacher may decide not to provide training and practice in these skills. Other groups may have clearly identifiable and very specific reasons for wanting to write. In this case, the teacher may identify particular text types and audiences, and appropriate 'process stages', and provide training and practice only in those aspects of the skill which relate to the learners' identified needs.

Moreover, some participants may have reservations about the way in which 'reasons' are classified in this exercise. In particular they may question the value of 'fluency writing', in which the learners' concern with rapid and effective communication may be at the expense of accurate use of grammar and vocabulary. If these reservations are raised, the trainer may want to encourage participants to explore and list reasons 'for and against' including activities which concentrate on fluency in a programme of activities to develop writing skills.

Question 1
Responses to this question will depend on the experience and beliefs of the participants. It is possible with some groups, however, that this is something they have not thought about before. In this case, they may wish to consider the aims and the advantages and disadvantages of making the purposes of activities clear to students.

Question 2
Preparation with regard to *ideas* may be valuable in each of these cases. With regard to (b) and (d), linguistic preparation will also be important.

Question 3
In the case of (b) and (d), the main focus of correction will probably be on the language point and the characteristics of the particular text type and the way the audience is 'addressed' respectively. In the case of (a) and (c), 'correction' is possibly inappropriate. However, in the case of (c), some kind of personal response to the content of the writing will probably be appropriate.

A policy of 'not correcting' language mistakes in the case of (c) may have to be negotiated with the learners, and the teacher may feel that a degree of flexibility and compromise is necessary where the learners (and in the case of children, their parents) clearly expect correction of this kind.

Question 4
Collaborative writing is particularly appropriate in the case of
(b) and (d). In the case of (a) this may also be appropriate if the
teacher is concerned with obtaining a general view of strengths
and weaknesses rather than identifying individual characteristics.
In the case of (c) this will depend on whether the teacher feels
that learners are motivated to express themselves individually or
collaboratively.

Section B *Preparation, motivation and communication*

Byrne (1988), Pincas (1982) and Hedge (1988) all contain a
wealth of ideas on the topic of preparing writing tasks and
motivating learners.

Question 1
Encouraging students to help each other in preparing written
tasks often provides motivation and increases confidence.

Students can brainstorm ideas on a topic, organise points into
those in favour of a specified argument, those against and those
which are 'neutral'. Pictures (cartoons, magazine pictures, etc.)
can be used to stimulate ideas (for example, for stories), and
written tasks can also be based on other classroom activities such
as reading, listening, discussion or role play.

Writing for display on posters, or preparing newsletters or
class magazines may also provide motivation.

Question 2
Many learners are motivated by writing something which
obtains a 'real' response. Moreover, it can be argued that only by
writing something which requires a response and receiving it can
learners judge the effectiveness of their own communication
skills in writing. They are, in a sense, involved in 'negotiating
meaning' in much the same way as in oral interaction activities.

Question 3
Students can write letters to other students in the class, to
students in other classes, to pen-friends, to newspapers or
magazines or to information services (such as tourist boards in
English-speaking countries).

Some teachers ask their students to keep diaries in which they
will not only describe aspects of their lives outside the classroom
but may also directly address the teacher and ask for help or
advice.

Notes

Section C   *Teaching the features of particular text types*

It is now something of a cliché that *reading* is an important key to good writing. This exercise draws attention to the need to work systematically through a series of stages between the learners' first exposure to an example of a particular text type to the point at which they can competently write examples of the text type themselves.

The following is a probable order:
1 c   2 d   3 b   4 a

These stages may be covered only over several lessons.

Section D   *'Process' approaches to teaching writing skills*

Question 1
a) The following is a possible list of stages:
   1   Mulling over and discussing ideas
   2   Jotting down notes in no particular order
   3   Organising these notes and drawing up a rough plan
   4   Making a first draft
   5   Revising this draft and re-planning (possibly in response to suggestions from another person)
   6   Making a second draft
   7   Editing this draft
   8   Possibly writing a 'final' version

b) It is frequently argued that it is unrealistic or even potentially counter-productive to ask learners to compose a text without going through the stages which would be appropriate in the particular case.

   However, if the teacher wants to provide students with practice in writing texts which would normally be written quickly and with little thought (for example, certain kinds of messages or memos), working through these 'process stages' would be inappropriate.

   Examination essays also require the skill of preparing a 'final' draft very quickly, but it could be argued that this is an 'examination skill' rather than a natural 'writing skill', and that practice in this should be postponed until the learners are confident and competent in writing texts in the absence of this pressure.

Question 2

Although exponents of process approaches to teaching writing skills sometimes seem to imply that these approaches are incompatible with approaches based on analysis of examples of text types and their use as models, there is no reason why this should be the case. Encouragement to work through a series of stages systematically in preparing a text, and practice in this, can be integrated into the final stage of a text-type based approach to developing writing skills.

Question 3

Word processors facilitate the processes of editing and revision. Instead of preparing two or more drafts, all changes may be made to the original draft.

In countries where computer technology is readily available, the use of word processors is increasingly common, and their use in the classroom consequently prepares learners for the 'real world'.

Moreover, a learner's draft composition can be copied, creating a second document, and other learners can edit and change this copy. The original learner thus has easy access to suggestions which she may or may not incorporate into her original draft through moving text from the copied document to the original one.

Question 4

Learners can 'swap' their drafts for other students to amend. Either the original can be used or a copy can be made for other learners to work on. This is facilitated by the use of carbon paper, a photocopier or word processors, where the appropriate equipment is available.

Section E *Designing writing tasks*

Responses to this section of the Task will depend on the learners, their needs and the objectives of the lesson. However, participants can be expected to pay attention to ways of motivating the learners and preparing the tasks, to providing guided exposure to and practice in examples of the text type, consideration of the purpose and the audience, and provision for working through appropriate 'process stages'.

Section F   *Correction of written work*

Notes

Question 1

Responses to this question will depend on the experience and preferences of participants. However, it is intended to raise the issue of the extent to which learners are helped by attention being drawn to their weaknesses.

It is possible to argue that in some cases this may even be counter-productive. It may discourage some learners from writing altogether, and inhibit them from taking risks. It can be argued that the teacher should diagnose problems and provide remedial help and guidance, but actually correct very little on the page.

However, some learners clearly seem to like work to be corrected in detail, and they appear to learn from this.

Question 2

One general point which emerges from this exercise is that it may be desirable for teachers to discuss their approaches to correcting work with their students, and to vary their approaches according to the preferences of individuals.

a)   This is used as an example in the Task itself.

b)   The use of correction codes by the teacher is a widespread practice. Commonly, the teacher will use a symbol to indicate the line or the place in a line where a mistake occurs, and may additionally use symbols to indicate the nature of the mistakes (*'sp'* for spelling, *'wo'* for word order, *'t'* for tense, etc.).

The rationale for this practice is that it encourages students to think about their writing.

Some learners may prefer mistakes to be corrected in full and may argue that they still think about the underlying language rules and the reasons they made the mistakes. They may also complain that they are unable to correct some of the mistakes they made themselves – this is particularly true in the case of errors of vocabulary ('If I had known the word, I would have used it in the first place').

Teachers may find that it is useful to discuss their approach to correction with students and, perhaps, to vary their approach according to the wishes of individual learners. It is also interesting to note that use of a 'correction code' often gives teachers more rather than less work. Teachers who use a code may feel that it is necessary to collect work in a second time to look at how the learners have corrected their own mistakes.

c) The teacher may believe that mistakes can become 'entrenched' and that not correcting them is dangerous (there is little empirical or theoretical evidence for this still common assumption). She may also assume that learners expect every mistake to be corrected.

Other teachers may rigorously correct only mistakes of a certain kind, depending on the purpose for which the written task has been set. In either case it may be to the advantage of the learners for the teacher systematically to identify the attitudes and preferences of individual learners in her classes.

d) If the teacher has made it clear to the class that the purpose of a particular writing task is for learners to concentrate on grammar and spelling, to focus exclusively on these factors in correcting the work may be justified. However, if writing tasks are set for a variety of purposes, other factors may deserve more attention.

This learner appears to be frustrated by the teacher's unvarying approach. Another danger is that some learners may come to accept that spelling and grammar are 'everything', and neglect other factors (such as rhetorical organisation or style, etc.) in their writing.

e) Here, there would appear to be no conflict in the expectations of the learner and the teacher. Both of them attach importance to responding positively to work which has been submitted.

f) The teacher would appear to believe that this individual attention is necessary and welcomed by the learners. She might experiment with adopting alternative approaches. These might include encouraging students to correct each other's work, or might involve dealing with a number of mistakes with the whole class. In small groups, students might attempt to correct selected mistakes that the teacher has written on the board or on an OHP transparency. Alternatively, the teacher might write up a mixture of particularly 'good' sentences and sentences which contain mistakes – working in small groups the students would have to identify the 'good' ones and decide in what way they were 'good', and also identify and 'correct' mistakes.

g) This student is sceptical of the teacher's honesty even though the comment may, in fact, be sincere. Another student might welcome the comment and be motivated by it even if it were not strictly true.

   In the case of each student a teacher has to judge the extent to which they will be helped by some objective evaluation of the quality of their work against the extent to which they will respond positively to encouragement. It is possible that the teacher of this student simply tries to encourage the learners regardless of the quality of their work.

   Many teachers try to be sincere in their general, evaluative comments, but instead of referring to some norm based on the performance of a group of learners, evaluate each learner according to her own standards. Thus she might say that an objectively 'weak' piece of writing was good if it represented progress for that particular learner, while she might make a more negative judgement of a piece of work which was below par for a very able learner.

h) The teacher may feel that writing is a personal and individual activity, and that the work itself and her comments on it are 'private' to the person who has composed it. Some learners, however, may be willing for their work to be read by other students, or may be curious about other students' work. Depending on the preferences of the learners, the teacher may encourage students to read each other's work, and they may learn from looking at each other's mistakes and how they have been corrected. More importantly, perhaps, they may also learn from paying attention to the good qualities of each other's work.

   It would clearly be unacceptable to hold a student's work up to ridicule, but good work can be used as models for other students with many classes if this is handled sensitively.

Section G   *Grading compositions*

It is difficult to predict responses to this part of the Task as much of it concentrates on the particular experience and practice of the participants. Some of the alternatives presented may be unfamiliar to some participants, and it is intended that in this case this should encourage them to consider 'new' ways of approaching the correction of written work.

Notes

In response to Question 1 it is likely that some kind of distinction will be made about the relative importance of different factors. The following may be given particular importance:
range of vocabulary used
range and complexity of structures used
correct grammar
appropriateness of style
organisation of ideas

The scheme worked out by small groups in response to Question 5 will vary according not only to the priorities of the teachers and their learners, but also according to the conventions within which they work. For example, some teachers may be obliged to mark all work out of a total of 20, or to grade work with a letter A–E.

Some groups may want to devise a numerical scale, and then convert it into some other system of grading. For example, they might devise the following scheme:

	Possible totals
range of vocabulary used	15
range and complexity of structures used	15
correct grammar	15
appropriateness of style	15
organisation of ideas	15
overall 'impression'	25
	100

A = 80+   B = 60–79   C = 40–59   D = 20–39
E = 0–19

Classroom-based Task 9

Task

Students' awareness of comprehension sub-skills

Aim   Section A of this Task helps you to discover more about your students' perceptions of their own strengths and weaknesses with regard to reading or listening. Section B aims to help you to discover the extent to which your aims in dealing with specific comprehension sub-skills in a lesson are apparent to the learners and are perceived to be useful by the learners.

TASK

Section A   *Students' perceptions of their strengths and weaknesses*

1   *First lesson*
Devise a lesson which deals specifically with the skills of listening or reading. The students will read a passage about the skills or sub-skills of reading, or listen to a talk or discussion about the skills or sub-skills of listening (see Discussion Tasks 15–19 for ideas for preparing these materials, or select paragraphs from one of the books recommended in the notes accompanying these Tasks). One of the aims of the lesson will be that at the end of it the students will be able to specify several of the relevant sub-skills.

2   *First questionnaire*
Devise a questionnaire to elicit from the students individually how they perceive their difficulties in understanding either spoken or written English, using these sub-skills as a framework.
Example Instructions: Indicate how easy or difficult you find the following by writing a number (1–3) by each of the items:
      1 – Easy   2 – OK   3 – Difficult
Listening
a) Understanding several speakers speaking at once.
b) Understanding speakers with non-standard accents.
c) Understanding English spoken against background noise.

Task

d) Picking out detailed information from a 'talk' or discussion.

e) Understanding general information when you do not recognise many of the words.

etc.

3 *Interpretation and action*

Before looking at the results of the questionnaires, select two or three students who seem to find aspects of the skill particularly easy or difficult, and predict how they will respond in the questionnaire. Compare your prediction with the answers they give.

Try to identify the sub-skills which seem to cause the greatest difficulty to the whole class. This may help to guide you in preparing the second lesson.

Section B   *Students' perceptions of a lesson (optional)*

1 *Second lesson*

After a lapse of some lessons, plan a lesson which has clear and specific aims with regard to aspects of listening or reading skills (whether you use material from a coursebook, authentic material or design and prepare your own, you may need to devise the tasks to focus on 2–3 specific sub-skills). After the lesson, make a subjective evaluation of the extent to which you think you achieved your aims and try to predict how the students will answer the second questionnaire.

2 *Second questionnaire*

After the lesson, administer a questionnaire to discover:

1 The extent to which the students were aware of these aims.

2 What the students felt they learnt or developed through the lesson.

Example Instructions: Indicate whether you think you were able to develop or practise any of the following skills in this lesson by writing a number (1–3) by each of the items:

1 – Useful practice   2 – Practice (but not very useful)
3 – No practice

Listening

a) Understanding several speakers speaking at once.

b) Understanding speakers with non-standard accents.

c) Understanding English spoken against background noise.
d) Picking out detailed information from a 'talk' or discussion.
e) Understanding general information when you do not recognise many of the words.
   etc.

3 *Interpretation*
Compare the results of the questionnaire with your own subjective evaluation of the lesson.

Classroom-based Task 9

Notes

Students' awareness of comprehension sub-skills

This Task is intended to be used in conjunction with Discussion Tasks 15–19, and involves the practical application of ideas raised in these Tasks.

Suggestions for procedure

Part of a session can be devoted to the selection of participants to carry out this Task. Participants may also work together in groups to plan the two lessons and to prepare questionnaires to be used.

Times may be fixed for the participants who carry out the Task to meet in order to plan the presentation of their findings and conclusions, and for a 'final' session at which these will be presented to the whole group. The precise organisation of this final session will depend on how many people are involved, the time available and the findings of the participants.

Using both sections of the Task may make the exercise complicated. Section B is thus seen as an optional addition.

General discussion and possible outcomes

While it is not possible to predict the findings (as this obviously depends on the learners involved), it is quite common to discover that learners are unused to considering the nature of their difficulties and, initially, may assume that any problems in comprehension are primarily related to lack of vocabulary.

They may also be aware of the aims of a lesson in more 'global' terms than the teacher. Where this is the case, the question is raised as to whether comprehension skills are developed 'holistically' rather than (or as well as) in terms of the discrete sub-skills teachers may specify.

Notes

Where this is feasible, participants may like to use the second questionnaire over a series of lessons in order to discover whether learners become more conscious of the processes of comprehension and the discrete aims of lessons as attention is paid to these factors.

Classroom-based Task 10

Oral fluency

Aim Section A of this Task investigates the relationship between the amount that students talk and their competence with regard to oral fluency. Section B investigates the extent to which teachers concur in their estimation of ability with regard to oral fluency. Where there is disagreement between the teachers, this inevitably and usefully raises the question of what criteria are employed in estimating this.

TASK

Section A *Fluency and willingness to speak*

1 Set up an activity which involves students working in groups of four or five, and which obliges each student in the group to participate. Some kind of jigsaw activity might be appropriate.

2 Ensure that at least one group includes students with a range of abilities with regard to oral fluency.

3 Record this group carrying out the task.

4 Analyse the recording by timing how long each student speaks.

5 Ask a colleague who is unfamiliar with these students to listen to the tape. He should 'grade' the oral fluency of each student on a scale of 1–10.

6 (Optional) Ask another colleague who is unfamiliar with these students to listen to the tape. He should 'grade' the accuracy of each student on a scale of 1–10.

7 Use this data to explore the relationship between willingness to speak and fluency (and accuracy – optional stage 6 above).

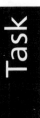

Section B   *Teachers' perceptions of students' fluency* (optional)

Carry out stages 1–3 above. Ask three or four colleagues to carry out stage 5, and ask each to write a short paragraph outlining the criteria they have employed. Compare the results. If possible, play the tape to the group of colleagues together so that once they have graded the students individually, they can discuss any reasons for disagreement.

Classroom-based Task 10

Oral fluency

This Task can be used in conjunction with Discussion Tasks 20 and 21, and involves the practical application of several of the issues raised in these Tasks.

Suggestions for procedure

Part of a session can be used to select participants to carry out this Task. These participants will need access to the appropriate technology (recording facilities) and to colleagues who are willing to help (other participants may also fulfil this role).

Times may be fixed for the participants who carry out the Task to meet in order to plan the presentation of their findings and conclusions, and for a 'final' session at which these will be presented to the whole group. The precise organisation of this final session will depend on how many people are involved, the time available and the findings of the participants.

Section B of the Task may make the exercise complicated and is, therefore, optional.

General discussion and possible outcomes

The outcome of this Task will depend on the learners involved, and also on the teachers who are asked to listen to the data.

It is, thus, not possible to predict the findings accurately. Nonetheless, it is likely that while some correlation will exist between perceived fluency and willingness to speak, there will also be individual variation in this respect. Teachers may be expected, broadly, to concur in their estimation of fluency, but again there is also likely to be some measure of individual variation. One teacher may attach greater or lesser importance to hesitation or speed of speech, for example, while another may be more concerned with how effectively learners manage to identify and 'repair' breakdowns in communication by finding other means to re-express a particular message.

Classroom-based Task 11

Writing skills

Aim This Task helps you to discover more about the effectiveness of a text-type based approach to teaching writing skills. Although this judgement will be subjective, it will also be more than merely impressionistic. The findings of this Task may encourage you to reflect on your assumptions about the relationship between teaching and learning.

TASK

1 Depending on the needs, interests and level of the class, select a text type which will be unfamiliar to most of the students (with an elementary class this might be a postcard, with an intermediate class it might be a memo or even some kind of narrative or description such as the opening of a novel, while with an advanced class it might be some form of more formal discursive composition).

2 Prepare the class to write an example of the text type by working on the content, but not on the form or language. For example, in the case of a postcard, students could brainstorm in small groups what information they would include in a card to an English friend who had recently moved away.

Ask students individually to write their example. Collect in the results and, without marking them, try to identify common areas of weakness. Do not return them to the students.

3 Devise activities firstly which encourage students to analyse examples of the text type, and subsequently to practise some of its characteristic features. This may take place over a series of lessons.

4 Ask students individually to write a further example of the same text type. (This stage will resemble stage 2 except that the form and language have now been prepared.)

5 Select four or five students of different abilities and compare the two versions of the composition. Count the number of improvements in the second version for each student.

6 Return the corrected versions of the second attempt to the students. Also return the uncorrected first version and ask the students to make any changes to it in the light of their subsequent learning.

7 Collect in these 'self-corrected' compositions and count the number of genuine improvements in the case of each of the 'selected' four or five students.

To what extent is it possible to generalise about the effectiveness of the lessons?

If there are aspects of the writing of particular students which reveal less improvement than you anticipated, is it possible to speculate about the reasons for this?

Classroom-based Task 11

Notes

Writing skills

This Task is intended to be used in conjunction with Discussion Tasks 22 and 23, and it involves the practical application and evaluation of approaches discussed in these Tasks.

Suggestions for procedure

Part of a session can be devoted to the selection of participants to carry out this Task.

Times may be fixed for the participants who carry out the Task to meet in order to plan the presentation of their findings and conclusions, and for a 'final' session at which these will be presented to the whole group. The precise organisation of this final session will depend on how many people are involved, the time available and the findings of the participants. However, as the data used in this Task is written by the students, where participants have access to photocopying facilities or to an OHP, some of the data itself can be made available to other participants in the 'feedback session', and their judgements and conclusions elicited.

General discussion and possible outcomes

While the precise outcomes will depend on the groups of learners involved, it is likely that there will be positive evidence of the effects of the teaching. It is also likely that there will be some individual variation in this respect, too. It may be interesting to see whether these students (who appear to have responded less to the teaching) are generally weaker than the others, or whether this approach to teaching writing skills perhaps favours learners with certain characteristic styles of learning more than others.

8 Teaching: Developing linguistic competence

Introduction to the chapter

1 Contents

Discussion Task 24   Contrasting approaches
Discussion Task 25   Task-based activities
Discussion Task 26   Example sentences
Discussion Task 27   Establishing the meaning of language items
Discussion Task 28   Introducing new language items and planning lessons

Classroom-based Task 12   Approaches to teaching grammar

2 General discussion of issues

A distinction is made in the organisation of this book between *developing skills* (Chapter 7) and *developing linguistic competence* (this chapter). A strict definition of *linguistic competence* might refer to the learners' knowledge of grammar and vocabulary and make no reference to their ability to use this knowledge in understanding and communicating in the foreign language. However, the term *linguistic competence* is used more pragmatically in this book, and the Tasks in this chapter include reference to the communicative use of grammar and vocabulary. There is thus a degree of overlap between the concerns of Chapters 7 and 8, and the distinction between them is to some extent an expedient one.

Some of the Tasks in Chapter 8 focus on particular approaches to teaching linguistic competence (Discussion Tasks 24 and 25, and Classroom-based Task 12), while others focus on aspects of teaching it which may be common in any approach (Discussion Tasks 26, 27 and 28).

The chapter does not directly address approaches which deny the value of explicit focus on language items (as in some 'purist' versions of communicative or task-based approaches), but reference is made to these indirectly in Tasks 24 and 25 and in the notes which accompany these Tasks.

The term 'language item' is used in this chapter to refer to words, expressions and grammatical exponents. Although, traditionally, a distinction is made between teaching vocabulary and teaching grammar, they are considered together here. This is not only because there are many features in common, but also, there may be as great a difference in approach between the teaching of any two items of vocabulary or any two items of grammar as between an instance of vocabulary and an instance of grammar.

Discussion Tasks 27 and 28 provide participants with the option of referring to Resource 14 in Section 3 of the *Resources bank*. This extract is chosen specifically because, although the book from which it is taken is not a recent publication, it has relatively universal familiarity, and the approach embodied in the material is still current. A more recent publication might be less widely known across the world.

3   Reading

No specific reading is required for this chapter, although reference is made in the Tasks or in the accompanying notes to the following:

Harmer, J. (1991). *The Practice of English Language Teaching.* Longman.
Leech, G. N. (1987). *Meaning and the English Verb.* London.
Nunan, D. (1989). *Designing Tasks for the Communicative Classroom.* Cambridge University Press.
Ur, P. (1981). *Discussions that Work.* Cambridge University Press.
Widdowson, H. G. (1990). *Aspects of Language Teaching.* Oxford University Press.
Wilkins, D. A. (1976). *Notional Syllabuses.* Oxford University Press.

Harmer is cited with regard to PPP models of presenting language (in which activities follow the sequence: Presentation, Practice, Production), and Nunan with regard to task-based approaches. Participants who are interested in following up the methodological issues dealt with in this chapter may find the appropriate sections in these two books of particular interest. Reference is also made to Widdowson in the notes which accompany Discussion Task 24. This is also in the context of task-based approaches.

Leech and Wilkins are cited in the notes which accompany Discussion Task 26 with regard to their use of the terms 'meaning' and 'function'.

Discussion Task 25 involves use of material from Ur (*Resources bank*, Section 3, Resource 13).

Discussion Task 24

Contrasting approaches

Aim   This Task helps you to increase your awareness and knowledge of approaches to developing learners' linguistic competence, and encourages you to consider the principles underlying different approaches. The Task also encourages you to experiment with alternative approaches.

TASK

The following two examples describe different ways in which the attention of learners may be focussed on new language, and they may be encouraged to use it.

   Read these and discuss the questions which follow.

Approach A

The following three stages are in chronological order:

a) The teacher draws attention to the meaning and form of one sentence, which provides a model of a particular structure. The students repeat the sentence while the teacher checks that they are saying it correctly. Using cues of some kind (pictures, word prompts, etc.), the teacher then elicits further examples of the structure from the students.

b) In pairs or groups:
    – the students do written exercises to practise the structure;
    – they engage in narratives or dialogues prompted by written or visual prompts which closely control the language they use, obliging them to use the structure.

c) The students engage in some written or spoken activity which is designed to create the opportunity to use the structure taught, but in which the primary focus is not on the structure itself. This might, for example, involve a role play or discussion, describing pictures or telling a story.

Approach B

The teacher sets up an activity whereby some students have access to information which has to be communicated to those who do not have this information. For example, Student A has a

Task

sequence of pictures which tell a story and Student B has the same pictures but in a jumbled order. Student B has to arrange his pictures in the correct order by listening to Student A and asking him appropriate questions.

At some point during or after the activity the teacher 'feeds' the students language (vocabulary and/or structures) which facilitates the task. If this language is 'fed' retrospectively, the task is repeated with parallel materials.

1 Do you teach in ways which resemble either of these examples? Do you or your students have any personal preferences with regard to approaches to focussing on new language?

2 What assumptions about the nature of language and the nature of language learning underlie each of these two examples?

3 To what extent are the approaches these instances exemplify compatible/incompatible?

4 How might the following factors influence the teacher's choice of approach as demonstrated in these two examples?
   a) The environment in which learning is taking place (in a country where English is/is not spoken).
   b) The objectives of the learners in learning English.
   c) The age of the learners.
   d) The experience and linguistic competence of the teacher.

5 Your aim in a particular lesson is that the learners (elementary) should develop the ability to talk about future arrangements using the present continuous (*We're flying to Bombay on Sunday*).

   What might be the content of a lesson using an approach which resembles *Approach A* and one which resembles *Approach B*? (Think about the materials, the activity of the teacher and the activity of the students.)

Discussion Task 24

Notes

Contrasting approaches

Timing   c. 45 minutes

This Task prepares participants to use Classroom-based Task 12, which provides the opportunity for them to investigate issues raised in this Task in the context of their own classes.

If participants are unfamiliar with task-based approaches to teaching language items, it may be useful for them to use Discussion Task 25 before they use this task.

Suggestions for procedure

Questions 1–4
These questions can be discussed in small groups, and a representative from some of the groups can then report back points of particular interest to the whole group for comment or further discussion.

Question 5
Some or all of the small groups can be asked to record an outline of the lessons they prepare on an OHP transparency or poster so that all the participants can see the results of the work of other small groups and make comments or ask questions.

Instead of all the small groups considering the application of the five questions to both approaches, some groups can concentrate on *Approach A* while others concentrate on *Approach B*.

General discussion and possible outcomes

Approach A is an instance of a 'Presentation, Practice and Production' (PPP) model of teaching new language, and the three stages described represent each of the 'Ps'.

Approach B is an instance of a task-based approach to teaching new language, which is one version of a communicative approach. Many different kinds of task might be used in this

Notes

approach, but all of them would involve learners sharing and exchanging information or opinions in order to achieve some kind of goal.

For a fuller discussion of a PPP model, see Harmer (1991, pp. 60–2). Harmer uses a more sophisticated paradigm, but one which is still essentially within the tradition of PPP. His 'general model for introducing new language' comprises the following stages: 1 Lead in; 2 Elicitation; 3 Explanation; 4 Accurate reproduction; 5 Immediate creativity. Stages 1–3 constitute Presentation, stage 4 constitutes Practice, and stage 5 constitutes Production.

For a fuller discussion of task-based approaches, see Nunan (1989, pp. 5–21).

Question 1

Responses to this question will inevitably depend on the experience, preferences and teaching circumstances of particular participants or groups of participants.

Question 2

In that PPP lessons pre-suppose the prior selection of a particular linguistic item (or items), they also pre-suppose a syllabus or programme of learning which specifies linguistic items and assumes that these are 'accrued' by learners.

A task-based approach may also be based on a similar syllabus or programme of learning.

However, it is also sometimes argued that such a programme may interfere with the learners' natural or conditioned predispositions to learn. It is argued that instead of an ordered programme of linguistic items, the sequence of tasks themselves may be used to facilitate learners learning items in their individual, predisposed orders (language items would not be specified, but linguistic competence would develop through the process of carrying out the tasks). Exponents of this 'strong' version of a communicative approach would argue that linguistic competence develops through learners 'exchanging meanings', being involved in interaction which has real communicative goals, in which language is used for a purpose. The term 'meaningful' language use is employed to describe this kind of interaction in which a task can only be completed through learners exchanging information and opinions – 'meanings'.

Prabhu (1987) is probably the most notable exponent of this point of view, and the principles Prabhu espouses are both described and evaluated succinctly by Widdowson (1990, pp. 143–6, 171–6).

Question 3

These two approaches belong to different traditions of learning and teaching and, in practice, they may not often co-occur. The more extreme exponents of a task-based approach might argue that they are incompatible. However, it can also be argued that there is no intrinsic incompatibility – tasks can be used to supplement a syllabus specified in terms of language items and, moreover, they can be chosen because they give rise to the use of certain language items, and used in order to provide opportunities for the practice of particular language items (in which case they would be subsumed into the 'Practice' stage of a PPP model).

Question 4

a) and b) Although answers to these questions will inevitably be to some extent only conjecture, participants may be able to support and justify their views with reference to their own experience as learners and teachers.

It could be argued that in an environment in which English is spoken, and in which many learners have developed a general ability to communicate but are hampered by inadequate understanding and command of grammatical systems, a PPP model would be appropriate. However, learners in such an environment who have not acquired this general ability to communicate, may have pressing and immediate needs to develop this ability above all. In this case a task-based approach may help them to achieve their immediate goals more efficiently.

Learners whose goal is not to communicate but to pass examinations whose focus is specifically grammatical may realise their objectives more efficiently through a PPP model.

c) Young learners who seem to depend less on their logical and analytical capabilities in the process of learning foreign languages may respond better to task-based approaches.

d) Teachers whose own command of the language they are teaching is poor, or those who feel that it is poor, may feel more comfortable using an approach which gives them maximum control over linguistic interaction in their lessons. They may prefer a PPP model, which allows them to anticipate the nature of the linguistic interaction and to prepare for this more carefully.

Question 5

It is important to note that many exponents of task-based approaches might quarrel with the use of tasks to fulfil a specific

Notes

linguistic objective as described here (see references to Prabhu above).

The Presentation and Practice stages of a PPP lesson might both, for example, involve the use of pages of a diary (5.00 Football practice; 8.00 Dinner/Mary, etc.). The Production stage might involve discussion and comparison of plans for the coming weekend or next holiday.

A task-based approach might, for example, also involve the use of diaries. Students could work in pairs and each of the members of a pair could have different diaries. The task would involve finding a time at which both of them were free to have a meeting.

Discussion Task 25

Task

Task-based activities

Aim This Task provides you with direct experience of features of task-based learning, and encourages you to reflect on this.

TASK

Your trainer will ask you to carry out a task as though you were students of the language. Do this and then answer the following questions:

1 This activity is based on an 'information gap'. In other words, the students have different information and have to collaborate on a task which involves them in exchanging this.
   What is the theoretical basis for preferring an activity like this to one in which the students have the same information and tell it to each other?

2 A teacher might set up this task with no input of new language at any stage (before, during or after the activity). What would be the aim of this part of the lesson?

3 What items of language might be taught prior to this lesson if the aim was that students have the opportunity to use particular words or structures?

4 Rather than teaching the language prior to setting up the task, the teacher might stop the activity at some point and teach the necessary language, or deal with this retrospectively. In what circumstances do you think it might be preferable to teach the language in the middle of the activity or retrospectively? If you adopted this approach, is there anything you would want to do subsequently?

5 How easy or difficult is it (or would it be) in your teaching circumstances to obtain materials of this type? How might the activity be organised other than by giving the students individual pictures?

6 What kinds of materials could be used for an activity like this at lower levels?

7   What instructions did the trainer give you in setting up this activity? Is there any way in which you would want to adapt them with your own classes?

8   Make a list of ways in which an information gap can be created and exploited in the classroom.
Example Students have pictures which are largely similar but which contain a few key differences. Their task is to identify the differences without looking at each other's pictures. (This is the activity used in this Task.)

Discussion Task 25

Task-based activities

Timing   c. 45 minutes

Participants who are unfamiliar with task-based approaches altogether may find it useful to carry out this Task before Discussion Task 24.

The material used in this Task is from Ur (1981) *Discussions that Work*, p. 55 (*Resources bank*, Section 3, Resource 13).

Suggestions for procedure

The activity can be set up by the trainer or by one of the participants who has been suitably 'primed'. Rather than explaining the procedure to one of the participants, she can:

1   Give one of the pictures to one of the participants, and keep the other picture herself.
2   Ask the participant two or three appropriate questions about her picture.
3   Divide the group into pairs and ask the members of each pair to number themselves 'A' and 'B'.
4   Explain that 'A' and 'B' must not look at each other's pictures.
5   Distribute one picture to all the 'A's , and the other to all the 'B's.
6   Tell them that the first pair to identify a certain number of differences should shout out 'finished'.
7   Tell them to carry on as in the demonstration (stages 1 and 2 above).
8   When two or three pairs have finished, ask them to tell the group the differences they have found and allow other pairs to add further differences to this list.

The participants can then discuss the questions relating to this activity in small groups. Representatives from some of the small groups can subsequently report back points of particular interest to the whole group. The trainer (or one of the participants) may want to compile a list of information-gap activities on the board in response to Question 8.

259

Notes

The amount of time allocated to answering these questions may depend on the prior familiarity of participants with activities such as this. Where they are largely unfamiliar with such activities, the group may prefer to focus on their experience of the activity and on Questions 1 and 5–8.

General discussion and possible outcomes

The following are some of the points that participants might make in response to the questions:

Question 1
A distinction can be made between an approach which is entirely based on activities like this and one in which activities like this are one of a range of kinds of activities, many of which have no information gap.

In the first of these cases, the theoretical basis is a view which pre-supposes that language is learnt through exchanging meanings in purposeful, goal-driven interaction rather than through the practising of pre-learnt forms.

In the second of these cases, the theoretical basis may be similar to the above except that the pre-supposition might be that language is learnt through exchanging meanings in purposeful, goal-driven interaction *as well as* through the practising of pre-learnt forms. On the other hand, other teachers may justify activities which embody a communicative purpose such as this in more modest terms. They might argue that their theoretical basis is the way that they create *motivation*, and provide learners with practice in dealing with the element of *unpredictability*, which is a feature of this kind of interaction.

Question 2
In addition to the points made in response to Question 1, the aim might be one of developing fluency rather than linguistic competence (see Discussion Tasks 20 and 21).

Question 3
The content of these pictures suggests that they are suitable for learners with a good vocabulary. They would probably thus also have a good command of the necessary grammar. The teacher might teach some of the vocabulary (skirting board, lead, kettle, dart board, peeling, etc.), and might also want to revise complex

Notes

prepositions ('in the top right-hand corner of', etc.), and possibly even the use of 'there is/are'.

Question 4

The activity might be essentially diagnostic, enabling learners to try out the linguistic resources they already have. The teacher would monitor students carrying out the task, and then might teach some of the language that they appeared to lack, before setting up a parallel task in which they were able to use it. Having faced the need for certain language in carrying out the task, the learners might also be more aware of the value of learning it and more motivated to learn it.

Question 5

The response to this question will depend on the circumstances in which participants work. However, it is worth bearing in mind that almost any line drawing can be adapted for use in this way by making a photocopy of it, and then altering details of this with white erasing fluid and a black pen. Pairs of pictures can also be produced on stencil machines where the teacher has some artistic ability or can solicit the help of someone else who has. As well as the teacher preparing these materials, pairs of learners can adapt line drawings which will then be used by other pairs to carry out a parallel 'spot the difference' activity.

Where there is no access to reprographic facilities, a large picture can sometimes be drawn in advance of the lesson on a board at either end of the room and then covered with newspaper. Students sit back to back so that each member of a pair faces the opposite direction, where they can see slightly different pictures once the newspaper is removed.

Question 6

Simple pictures might be chosen, and possibly ones with which learners are already familiar. Where an institution has access to a photocopier and this does not infringe copyright law, the procedure outlined in response to Question 5 above can be carried out with any pictures in the students' coursebook.

Question 7

Responses to this question will vary according to the circumstances in which participants work, and the way in which the demonstration activity was set up.

Notes

Question 8

The following may be among the activities suggested:

1   Student A is given or draws a picture or diagram. She then instructs Student B to draw what is on her own sheet of paper.

2   Student A arranges objects into a particular shape or builds some form of construction with them. Student B has the same objects and has to arrange them into the same shape or construction in response to instructions from Student A.

3   Students A and B each have different parts of a text or sequence of pictures. By asking each other questions and describing what they have, they have to decide on an appropriate order in which they might naturally occur.

Discussion Task 26

Example sentences

Aim   This Task helps you to develop your awareness of the rationale underlying a grammatical syllabus and the selection of grammatical items in materials for the language learner. It also aims to develop awareness of linguistic factors to take into consideration in teaching grammar.

TASK

Many language teaching 'methods' involve the use of sentences which provide examples of the characteristic use of a structure. These sentences may occur in texts which are specially written for the purpose of 'presenting' the structure, or in authentic texts. The teacher may explicitly direct the attention of the learners to the sentence or sentences, or may refer to them in response to learners' questions.

Alternatively, the sentence or sentences may be written up on the board, and the grammar explained. The teacher may also devise a 'situation' in which the sentence could be used and then introduce it orally or in a written form. (For example, he might teach 'menu', 'ashtray' and the names of certain dishes before using pictures and objects to 'create' a restaurant in the class, and to indicate that he is a customer. He would then present the following sentence as an example of requests before eliciting further examples from his students: *Could I have the menu, please?*)

Section A   *Selection and use of 'example sentences'*

The following sentences are all instances of 'example sentences'. Look at them and then answer the questions which follow.

a) It's going to rain.
b) Japan is much more expensive than Italy.
c) Mrs Brown drives more slowly than Mr Brown.
d) I've got three children.
e) He can't have lived there.
f) I hoped I'd get a pay rise after 6 months.

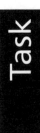

g) **Oil has been found in the Irish Sea.**
h) **I worked for the company for 5 years.**
i) **Whatever did you do that for?**
j) **It is important that she be admitted to hospital.**
k) **I'd rather you didn't tell anyone about this.**
l) **Thursday? No, I'm busy. I'm playing tennis with Jane.**

1   What language point is each sentence intended to 'present'?
    Example *Sentence (a): It's going to rain.* The use of 'to be
    going + infinitive' to express a prediction based on present
    evidence.

2   Put the sentences in order according to the sequence in which
    the language points might be taught. Then group the
    sentences according to the levels at which they might be
    taught (for example, Beginners, Elementary, etc.).
      Justify your decisions.

3   Choose two or three of these 'example sentences' and explore
    the factors you would need to bear in mind in using them in
    the classroom.
      The following checklist may help you in doing this (note
    that in the case of any particular sentence, only some of these
    factors may be relevant):
    a) **Form**
    b) **Meaning**
    c) **Function**
    d) **Appropriacy**
    e) **Pronunciation**
    f) **Spelling**
    g) **Collocation**
    h) **Possible confusion with similar or related forms**
    Example *(a): It's going to rain.*
    a) *Form* – present tense of 'to be' + going + infinitive
    b) *Meaning* – prediction based on present evidence
    c) *Function* – this would depend entirely on the context in
       which the utterance occurred. For example, it might be
       used as a form of advice or warning as in the following
       interchange:
       Speaker 1: I think I'll leave my umbrella here.
       Speaker 2: *It's going to rain.*
    d) *Appropriacy* – neutral (although in this instance the
       contraction suggests that this is a spoken utterance).
       Although the teacher may not want to draw the attention
       of the learners to this, he might also need to be aware that

in certain more formal registers such as news reports, this form is sometimes avoided for reasons of 'style'.

e) *Pronunciation* – the main stress in this utterance would normally not be on the auxiliary 'going to'. (In this utterance the main stress would normally be on the main verb. However, the context in which an utterance occurs might determine that in a longer utterance the main stress were on some other word such as an object or adverbial expression.)

   – in casual speech 'It's' might be weakened to /s/, and 'to' might be weakened to /t/ or /t'/

f) *Spelling* – no particular points to be made in this instance

g) *Collocation* – no particular points to be made in this instance

h) *Possible confusion with similar or related forms* – possible confusion with other ways of expressing future time

   – possible confusion with use of the same form to express premeditated intention (as in *'I'm going to see him on Tuesday'*)

Section B   *The use of 'example sentences' in course materials*

Look at two examples of materials which aim to develop linguistic competence in some way. The materials should be written by different authors, and should be as different as possible in approach, although it is desirable that they should focus on similar areas of language (one or two pages from two coursebooks would be appropriate for use in this part of the task).

1   Compare the way in which the authors use (or, possibly, do not use) 'example sentences'.

2   What assumptions are made by the respective authors with regard to the nature of language, the nature of learning, and the importance of focussing on discrete items of language as models of how these forms are used?

(If suitable materials are unavailable for this part of the Task, use Resource 14 from Section 3 of the *Resources bank*, on pages 314–17, and compare the authors' use of example sentences and the assumptions embodied in these materials with the use of example sentences and the assumptions embodied in materials you use or are familiar with.)

Discussion Task 26

Example sentences

Notes

Timing   Section A   c. 30 minutes
Section B   c. 30 minutes
Total   c. 60 minutes

Suggestions for procedure

Section A   *Selection and use of 'example sentences'*

Questions 1 & 2
Participants can discuss these questions in small groups. Some or all of the groups can record their conclusions on an OHP transparency or on large sheets of paper to use as posters. Participants can then look at the conclusions of other small groups and raise questions or make relevant comments.

Question 3
Plenary feedback on this question may be unnecessary. The trainer can monitor the work of the small groups and decide (in consultation with the participants themselves) whether feedback is desirable or useful.

Section B   *The use of 'example sentences' in course materials*

Participants can work on this section of the Task in small groups, and feedback may again be unnecessary unless participants express particular curiosity about the conclusions of other small groups.

If there is considerable heterogeneity within the larger group, the small groups may be formed according to similarity of teaching circumstances. As far as possible, each small group may like to work on materials they use with their own students.

General discussion and possible outcomes

Section A *Selection and use of 'example sentences'*

Question 1

Most of the answers to this question are fairly (but not always absolutely) definite. In each case, the participants should focus on the main point of the sentence, and take into account the relative complexity of language used. For example, in (i) it is unlikely that the linguistic 'point' is the use of the simple past tense, as this is unlikely to be introduced within a sentence with a complex question construction such as 'Whatever . . . for'.

a) (used in the example)
b) Intensification of comparative adjectives (much more)
c) Comparative adverbs
d) 'have got'
e) 'can't have', i.e. logical deduction about the past
f) 'would' used to express 'future in the past'
g) passive voice (present perfect)
h) The use of 'for' to express duration
i) 'Whatever' (used as an example to elicit the addition of 'ever' to other question words)
j) The use of the 'bare infinitive' after the subject in certain adjectival expressions
k) The use of the past tense to denote present or future time after certain forms (hypothetical meaning)
l) Use of the present continuous for future arrangements

Question 2

The precise order chosen and the way in which the items are classified will depend on the learners (including, possibly, characteristics of their first language) and the use of the names of 'levels' in any particular context.

The following is a possible order, but one which is no way definitive.

Beginners: 1 d   2 a
Elementary: 3 h   4 b   5 l
Intermediate: 6 c   7 g   8 f   9 e   10 i
Advanced: 11 k   12 j

In carrying out this activity, participants are likely to pay attention to the following factors:

Notes

1 The usefulness of the item in communication.
2 The simplicity of the item in structural terms.
3 The extent to which the item builds on and facilitates generalisations about the language.
4 Coverage, i.e. the extent to which the item can be used in place of other items which have not yet been learned.

Special needs of learners will also need to be considered. For example, learners who want only to be able to read technical texts in English may need to learn the use of the passive voice very early since meaning can easily be misunderstood if this is unknown. (k) and (l), however, might never be taught to these learners as their meaning is relatively transparent. These might be taught only to learners who place high priority on accurate production of English.

Question 3
Responses to this question will depend on the items selected. The trainer may perceive a need to clarify the following terms (with reference to forms not included in this list): *function, appropriacy, collocation,* and *possible confusion with similar or related forms.*

Function (c)
In this Task the term *function* is used to refer to communicative function, the effect an utterance has or is intended to have upon the interlocutor, audience or reader. The term *meaning* on the other hand, is used to refer to what Wilkins calls 'semantico-grammatical categories' or 'notions' (Wilkins, 1976, pp. 21–3). This is also how Leech uses the term *meaning* in *Meaning and the English Verb* (Leech, 1987). Language teachers sometimes refer to this grammatical meaning as 'concept'.

Whereas it is possible to define the different meanings that any one item of grammar has the potential to express with a large (but not absolute) degree of certainty, the function of any utterance is normally clear only from the context in which it is used. Factors such as intonation, nonetheless, help to clarify the function, and certain 'formulaic' expressions (for example, 'Please' or 'Why don't you . . . ?') are commonly (but not necessarily) used to express particular functions.

In the case of the sentence below, we are able only to guess at the function it is used to express without access to the wider context in which the utterance took place.

He *used to bring me flowers* every day.

Notes

It could be intended, for example, to invoke sympathy, to reproach or even to threaten. The 'meaning' of the structure in italics, however, could be stated as 'discontinued past habit' and is context-independent.

The following three dialogues illustrate how the function of an utterance may depend upon the context while the meaning of the grammar remains constant (in this case future possibility):

A Speaker 1:   I'm worried sick about John. He should have been here hours ago.

   Speaker 2:   *He may come tomorrow.* (Reassurance)

B Speaker 1:   Thank God Harry isn't here – he'd kill me.

   Speaker 2:   *He may come tomorrow.* (Warning)

C Speaker 1:   I'd better write to John and tell him.

   Speaker 2:   *He may come tomorrow.* (Advice, i.e. 'wait until after tomorrow')

Moreover, the function of any utterance or stretch or discourse may be open to interpretation, and two or more functions may be expressed simultaneously.

It is important, perhaps, also to note that the terms *meaning* and *function* are used differently by different writers. Bolitho & Tomlinson, for example, make no distinction between grammatical meaning and communicative function, referring to both as 'function' (Bolitho & Tomlinson, 1980, pp. 91–2).

Appropriacy (d)

Examples of this are the difference between '*Please be quiet*' and '*I don't want to be a nuisance, but I wonder if you could possibly make less noise?*', or between '*Can you please send me the stuff?*' and '*I should be grateful if you could despatch the goods.*'

Collocation (g)

In lexical terms this refers to the fact that we can say a 'strong wind' or 'high wind', but not a 'big wind'.

In terms of grammar it refers to factors such as that 'interested' needs to be followed by 'in', or 'object' (verb) by 'to'. It is also sometimes used to refer to the high frequency with which, for example, 'yet', 'already' and 'just' co-occur with use of the present perfect.

Possible confusion with similar or related forms (h)

An example of this would be 'he used to drive' when teaching 'he's used to driving'.

Section B   *The use of 'example sentences' in course materials*

Responses to this section of the Task will depend on the materials chosen.

Resource 14 is from *Building Strategies* (Abbs & Freebairn, 1984, pp. 84–7), and is typical both of many materials produced at that time and of many more contemporary materials. Instances of the target structures occur initially in a dialogue which has been constructed to make their meaning and use clear from the context in which they occur. Subsequently at the beginning of each of the two 'sets' included here example sentences are given, 'extracted' from the context of the original dialogue, and followed by exercises which ask the learners to use the structure with different vocabulary. In the case of Set 1, an element of role play is used to lend this activity a degree of contextualisation. In Set 2, the first practice activity involves making comparisons using the 'structure' which has been presented.

The assumptions which appear to underlie this material are that the learners' attention needs to be focussed on the grammatical form and meaning of discrete language items (and in the case of Set 1, on function), and that an element of oral practice of the language is important. An attempt is made to make this practice contextualised and 'natural', although the focus remains very much on the language items and there is no real information gap.

Discussion Task 27

Establishing the meaning of language items

Aim   This Task looks at two different approaches to teaching the meaning of language items, and provides an opportunity for you to consider the rationale for each, and reasons for using one approach or the other in specific circumstances.

TASK

Approaches to making the meaning of language clear can be divided into those which involve 'giving' and those which involve 'guiding'.

'Giving' describes the process whereby the meaning is 'transmitted' to the students in some way, and they are relatively passive recipients. 'Guiding' describes the process whereby students are involved in working out the meaning for themselves. In 'guiding' approaches, the learners may, for example, derive a rule from contextualised instances of the use of a particular language item.

Section A   *Giving or guiding?*

Look at the following examples of approaches to establishing the meaning of new language. Which ones are examples of 'giving' and which are examples of 'guiding'?

a) Teacher: 'If you want to invite someone to a party, you can say: "I'm having a party next week. Would you like to come?"'

b) The teacher gives a student feedback on an error: 'Good, Carlos, but it's not "I used my green shirt yesterday," it's "I wore my green shirt yesterday." Remember, we "wear" clothes.'

c) Teacher: 'Look at paragraph 3 and find a word which describes a negative personality characteristic.'

d) Teacher: 'Look at this dialogue on the board. The underlined verbs both refer to the future, but what's the difference in

Task

meaning? . . . No. Well, think about when they made the decision.'
The following is written on the board:

> A: Why *do you want* the corkscrew?
>
> B: *I'm going to open* that bottle of wine I bought yesterday.
>
> A: We *drank* it last night.
>
> B: Oh. Then *I'll open* a beer.

e) One student tells the others the meaning of a word.

Section B   *Opinions*

1   Consider the following opinions expressed by teachers and learners. To what extent do you agree with them?

a) 'Giving' approaches are boring.
b) 'Giving' approaches do not help the learners to remember the meaning of new language.
c) 'Giving' approaches are impossible with low level classes unless you explain in their own language. Otherwise, they just don't have the language to understand the explanation.
d) 'Guided' approaches work best when the meaning of something is complicated.
e) The danger in using 'guided' approaches is that the learners may actually work out the meaning inappropriately and thus understand something which is inaccurate.
f) 'Guided' approaches encourage learners to become more autonomous in their learning, and less dependent on the teacher.
g) 'Guided' approaches reflect more closely the natural mechanisms of language learning.

2   Choose either of these two approaches and list:
– the reasons for using it;
– any limitations or disadvantages in its use.

Section C *Application: Guiding students*

1 'Concept questions'

The teacher can use questions to check that students have understood the meaning of an item of language. It is often an advantage for these to be simple and direct. They can be formed by specifying the crucial, defining components of meaning in terms of statements, and then turning these statements into questions.

What questions might you use to 'check' the meaning of the following?

a) Selfish

b) She used to live in London. (used to + bare infinitive)

c) Shy

d) She wishes she were at home. (wish + simple past or 'subjunctive')

e) He's been painting the ceiling. (present perfect continuous)

f) He managed to open the window. (manage + infinitive)

g) He took it out on the cat. (phrasal verb: to take it out on X)

Example

a) Do selfish people enjoy giving things to other people?

b) Does she live in London now?

Did she live in London before?

Was this for a short time?

2 Devising tasks

Using a piece of material with which you are familiar, or using the dialogue from p. 84 of Resource 14 (in Section 3 of the *Resources bank*, on pages 314–17), isolate an item of language you might want to teach.

Write down exactly how you might 'guide' students to 'discover' the meaning of the item (the item might be a word or a structure, and you might 'guide' the learners by asking questions orally, or by giving them an accompanying written task).

Notes

Discussion Task 27

Establishing the meaning of language items

Timing Section A c. 15 minutes
Section B c. 15 minutes
Section C c. 30 minutes
Total   c. 60 minutes

Suggestions for procedure

Section A *Giving or guiding?*

Participants can carry out this section of the Task in pairs or small groups very quickly. The trainer may choose, simply, to tell them (or write up) the recommended answers to the exercise, and to invite comment or questions.

Section B *Opinions*

These points can be discussed in groups of three or four. If the discussion seems to be productive, feedback to the whole group may be unnecessary. However, where participants are curious about others' opinions, or where the trainer feels that participants would learn something important through this, representatives of some of the small groups can be asked to report back one or two points of particular interest from the discussion.

Section C *Application: Guiding students*

Some of the small groups may like to write down their response to this section of the Task on an OHP transparency, or on large sheets of paper so that it can be shown to the other participants for comments or questions.

General discussion and possible outcomes

The Task makes a distinction between two *approaches* to making the meaning of language clear. *Approaches* are not to be confused with *methods*. Although, historically, some methods have been dogmatic about whether learners should be 'given' the meaning of new language items or 'guided' to discover this themselves (*Audio-lingual teaching*, for example, clearly espoused a 'guided' approach), in this Task it is not assumed that any method should necessarily favour (or indeed proscribe) one approach or the other.

The distinction which is made here between 'giving' and 'guiding' is seen from the point of view of what the teacher does. From the learner's point of view the difference is less distinct as the individual process of successful learning may involve an element of working things out from examples and using these to derive a general rule even where the teacher has not consciously made provision for this. All learning may thus in a sense involve an 'inductive' component.

Moreover, learning the meaning of any item of language will often take place over a period of time. Through repeated contact with the item, encountering it in a variety of contexts and registering the response of other people to their own use of it, learners may gradually refine their understanding of it. Few items of language will be completely 'learnt' through classroom presentation – this, rather, is the beginning (or where learners have already encountered the item, a key intermediate stage) of the process of learning. It is sometimes argued that an approach to teaching which involves 'presentation' of language items per se may encourage learners erroneously to think that the item has been 'learned' while this learning is still only partial. This argument is used against 'giving' approaches in particular.

Section A *Giving or guiding?*

Giving: a, b, e
Guiding: c, d

Notes

Section B   *Opinions*

This exercise is intended to encourage participants to think about the issues, and to elicit their opinions. It is thus not possible to predict the precise points which will be made. It is likely, however, that participants will refer to some of the following:

Question 1

a) This view is sometimes advanced by both learners and teachers, and may be particularly true if the approach is used on an exclusive basis. However, it could also be argued that the over-use or inappropriate use of either approach could be boring. This will also depend on the preferences and predispositions of the learners, as well as on the nature of the language item in question. (The item may be relatively trivial and not merit the process of working out its meaning. Conversely, it may be difficult to devise means for this to be worked out.)

b) Many learners seem to find that their memory is aided by involvement in the process of working something out.

c) This may often be true. However (particularly in the case of certain kinds of vocabulary), there are various alternatives to verbal explanation such as the use of pictures and mime. It can also be argued that, with monolingual groups of learners, discriminating use of their first language by the teacher is efficient and desirable.

d) This is often true. Where the meaning is complicated it may be easier to illustrate this through guiding learners' attention to aspects of contextualised examples rather than explaining. An example of this is instances of language use which indirectly express the user/speaker's attitude, for example 'should have' (You should have told him).

e) Again, there may be some truth in this contention. However, the teacher can check the students' understanding of the item through the use of carefully phrased questions ('concept questions'). Moreover, it could be argued that real understanding of the meaning of many items is only achieved through continued exposure to it in the contexts in which it is used, and that the 'teaching' of the item is only the initial part of the learning process. In this case, it might be argued that there is no harm in partial or partially inaccurate understanding of an item.

f) This argument is based on the fact that learners are developing skills and approaches that they can apply without the help of the teacher, and is a key argument in the debate.

It might also be argued, however, that practice in the use of dictionaries and reference grammars (which 'give' the meaning of items) also contributes to the development of autonomy. It is thus important to distinguish 'giving' by the teacher, and 'giving' approaches in which the source of information is texts which are available to the learner outside the classroom.

g) This is true. It is often assumed that the processes of learning a second language should resemble those of learning the first language ('natural mechanisms'). This view is, however, unproven.

Question 2

The following are among the points which participants may be expected to make:

Giving

Reasons for using: speed; clarity

Limitations or disadvantages: may encourage dependence on the teacher

Guiding

Reasons for using: motivation; involvement of learners; may encourage autonomy

Limitations or disadvantages: may be unclear; may be time-consuming

Section C *Application: Guiding students*

Question 1

Asking students whether or not they understand an item of language does not necessarily test whether or not they do understand it. Concept questions are a more reliable way of testing this. They also serve to 'highlight' the key features of meaning.

It is often desirable to use the minimum number of questions which will fulfil this function, and to ensure that they solicit simple 'yes' or 'no' answers. Clearly, if they are asked in English, they need to be phrased in language which is familiar to the students.

The following are possible questions to use in the exercise:

a) (see **Example**)

b) (see **Example**)

c) Do shy people enjoy meeting strangers?
    Do shy people usually feel comfortable at parties?
d) Is she at home?
    Does she want to be at home?
    A little or a lot?
    (Does this refer to the present or the past?)
e) Is he painting the ceiling now?
    Did he finish doing this just now or a long time ago?
    Is 'painting the ceiling' a momentary activity?
f) Did he open the window?
    Was this easy?
g) Did he hurt the cat?
    Was he angry?
    Did the cat make him angry?

Question 2
Responses to this will depend on the materials chosen.
   In the case of p. 84 of Resource 14 (Abbs & Freebairn, 1984), if the teacher wanted to focus on the use of the comparative form of the adjectives she might ask the students to underline the sentence 'It's bigger than I expected. Noisier and dirtier too.'
   Students would then be asked to explore the context and use of their general knowledge to answer the following questions:
Is Milan big?
Is Milan noisy?
Is Milan dirty?

Did Barbara expect Milan to be big?
Did Barbara expect Milan to be noisy?
Did Barbara expect Milan to be dirty?

Was Barbara surprised? Why?
etc.

Learners might also be 'guided' to work out how the comparative forms are constructed by being asked to compare the simple adjectives with the (comparative) adjectival forms in the text.

Discussion Task 28

Task

Introducing new language items and planning lessons

Aim This Task relates discussion of aspects of developing linguistic competence to lesson planning. It focusses on some of the choices available to a teacher within a PPP approach, and on the rationale which might underlie these choices.

TASK

Think about an item of language that you have recently taught or will soon be teaching. In what ways might you make the form, the meaning and the function clear? What activities might you organise for students to practise using the language?

The following are some of the possible stages of a lesson or part of a lesson in which the teacher is concerned that the students should learn how to use this new item of language.

Look at this list and answer the questions which follow.

a) Students supply examples of the language relating to their own experience.
b) The teacher makes the function of the language item clear.
c) Students repeat the example or 'model' sentence exemplifying the language item.
d) The teacher makes the meaning of the new language clear.
e) The teacher uses visual or written prompts to elicit from the students 'substitutions' – further sentences using the same language.
f) Students do a written exercise focussing on the correct and appropriate use of the language item.
g) The teacher draws attention to the form.
h) The teacher asks questions to test the students' understanding of the meaning and/or function of the language item.
i) The teacher writes a model/example of the language on the board.

1 The order of these stages is jumbled. Number the stages according to the order in which they might occur in a lesson. You may want to make two separate lists, exemplifying two different approaches.

K

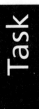

You may also omit or add stages if you wish. Before comparing these lists with those of other groups, decide what rationale underlies the sequence(s) you have chosen.

Example You might argue that (i) has to come first because a particular group of learners require the security of seeing and knowing what they are going to be learning.

2   Make a list of ways in which the teacher might accomplish stage (d).

Example (Vocabulary) Picture of the object.

(Vocabulary and grammar) Draw the attention of the students to the item used in a text and ask questions which direct students to work out its meaning from the immediate context in which it is used.

3   (Stage b) Some language items have an obvious and direct connection with a particular function (e.g. '*Why don't we . . . ?*' – suggestion), others have a more indirect relationship with a range of functions (e.g. Type 1 conditional – threat, warning, promise, bartering), others have no particular functional associations – the function would always depend on the context in which it is used (e.g. simple past).

Think of further examples of language items which fall into each of these three categories. How important is it to draw attention to function and/or meaning in each of these cases?

4   Which two completely different objectives might stage (f) be used to achieve (simultaneously or separately)?

5   Do you consider any of these stages to be either indispensable or quite unnecessary in focussing on new language in a lesson? Are there any other stages that you would consider to be indispensable?

Discussion Task 28

Introducing new language items and planning lessons

Timing   c. 45 minutes

Since this Task pre-supposes a model of teaching in which explicit attention is paid to discrete items of language, it might be inappropriate for use with any groups of participants who strongly objected to this approach.

Suggestions for procedure

Question 1
Some participants may be willing to perform this exercise 'in the abstract'. Others may wish to focus on teaching a particular item of language, in which case they may be given a few minutes individually to think about how they (would) approach teaching a particular item of language. They may then be asked in small groups to choose *one* of these items to concentrate on in answering the first question.

Participants may work on this exercise in small groups. Some of these groups may record the results of their discussion on an OHP transparency or on posters to show to the other participants, who may like to raise questions and comment on the order chosen.

Some groups of participants (particularly if they are relatively inexperienced as teachers) may prefer to make only one list.

Questions 2–5
A representative of each small group may record the main points of the discussion. One or two representatives may then report these points back to the whole group as a stimulus for general discussion.

General discussion and possible outcomes

Notes

Trainers and participants may like to refer to the notes which accompany Discussion Task 26 (*General discussion and possible outcomes*, Section A, on pages 267–9) in order to clarify the way in which the terms *meaning* and *function* are used in this Task.

Question 1

There is no right or wrong order. What is important is that participants have clear reasons for justifying the order they choose.

The following are examples of orders that might be chosen, and of the rationales which might be given for these:

Order 1: 1 d   2 b   3 h   4 g   5 c   6 e   7 a
          8 f   9 i

This order describes a conventional PPP lesson. The learners understand the meaning of the language they are learning before they are asked to produce it themselves. Their own use of the language is initially very highly controlled to avoid their making mistakes. This control gradually diminishes as the learners have more practice. The teacher writes a model of the language on the board only after the students have practised it orally. This order is very commonly used by teachers trained in the traditions of 'situational presentations', whose roots lie in audio-lingual teaching.

Order 2: 1 i   2 g   3 d   4 b   5 f   6 e   7 a

This order also ensures that the learners' use of language follows exemplification of the form and meaning of the item. However, their attention is initially drawn to the form rather than the meaning. As in the example given in the Task itself, this may be suitable for learners who require the security of seeing and knowing what they are going to be learning.

Question 2

Among the ways in which a teacher can make the meaning of language clear are:

Pictures (see **Example**)
Attention to textual context (see **Example**)
Translation
Explanation
Mime
A 'situation' (see Discussion Task 26, on page 263, for an example of a 'situation)

Question 3

Items which have an obvious and direct connection with a particular function are frequently formulaic expressions such as 'please', 'thank you', 'sorry', 'excuse me', or question forms (often employing modal verbs) which are ritually used in the context of some of the more obvious social functions (inviting, offering, suggesting, etc.). Nonetheless, the precise function is always only derivable through reference to the context of use. (Even formulaic expressions may be used to express context-dependent functions, for example, 'please' can mean 'I wish you wouldn't do that', and 'sorry' can mean 'I absolutely refuse to do that'.)

Language items which have an indirect connection with a range of functions include, for example, the present continuous used to make excuses or to justify refusing invitations ('I'm playing tennis then'), the second conditional in the first person to give advice ('I would buy the green one'), and the future continuous used to reassure someone that something is no trouble ('I'll be seeing him anyway'). There is nothing formulaic or fossilised about these uses, but these items are frequently used in this way because the meanings they express are appropriate to these functions.

Despite the inclusion of the present continuous and future continuous in the second category (above), most tenses can be used as examples of language items which it is difficult to associate with particular functions.

The meaning of any language item needs to be made clear in almost all cases, and where the item is associated with a particular function this is equally important. Indeed, it could be argued that some formulaic expressions have only functional (as opposed to denotative) meanings. (For example, 'sorry' used as an apology, to express indignation or to ask for repetition or clarification depending on the context and how it is said.)

Where an item has no direct functional associations, it can still be presented in a context where its functional use in that context can be made clear. This probably aids both understanding of the meaning and memorability, and certainly attention to a particular function provides a context for its use by students (for example, students can be encouraged to use the second conditional as in the example above by the teacher creating a 'situation' in which students give advice to each other). Some teaching materials produced during the 1970s gave the impression that all language was in some way 'marked' for functional use. To ensure that learners are not led into believing

Notes

that there is any necessary connection between language and the functional use to which it is put, learners can be encouraged to explore examples of language use to identify the functions expressed, and the range of linguistic devices which are used to achieve this.

Question 4

Written exercises may be used to test whether the learners have understood and are able to use the items which have been taught. They can also be used to give practice in the use of the items so that the learners become more confident in this use.

Question 5

Responses to this question will depend on the beliefs and opinions of the participants. However, it is likely that attention to form and meaning of language items, and some form of practice in their use, will be thought to be indispensable.

Classroom-based Task 12

Approaches to teaching grammar

Aim   This Task provides you with a framework to enable you to learn more about the ways in which some of your students respond to different approaches to learning grammar.

TASK

This Task involves you consciously using a variety of approaches to teaching grammar in your classes.

1   With a selected class, over a period of twelve or fifteen lessons, ensure that on at least one occasion you teach grammar in each of the following ways:
   a) Employing a 'strict' PPP model using a 'situational presentation'.
   b) Guiding students to work out the meaning of the grammar through prompting them to analyse its use in a text.
   c) Through setting up a task which requires the use of the grammar and then 'feeding' it to the learners while they are in the process of carrying out the task.

2   EITHER:
Ask the students to keep a diary of their learning in which they record:
   a) What they did in the lesson.
   b) What they feel they learnt in the lesson.
   c) How much they liked different parts of the lesson.
Ask them to comment specifically on these lessons in their diaries at the end of the lessons themselves or, possibly, at home subsequently.

   (Some groups of learners may respond to the idea of keeping a diary with more enthusiasm than others. With some groups of learners, the idea of keeping a learning diary may be more attractive if it is presented as an opportunity to write something regularly which will be corrected by the teacher.)

   OR:
Use a questionnaire after each of these 'grammar lessons'.

285

Questions might focus on affective factors.
Example Circle the appropriate number:
I felt frustrated   1   2   3   4   5   relaxed and confident in this lesson.

Questions might focus on cognitive factors.
Example Below is a series of questions, some of which are followed by three possible answers. Circle the answer which most closely describes your response to the question. Write a short answer to the other question.

The aim of this lesson was that you should develop the ability to use X to express Y.

1 Were you aware of this?   *very aware   a little aware   not aware*

2 Did you achieve this?   *very much   a little   not at all*

3 Are you clear what the grammar of this structure is?
   very clear   a little clear   not clear
   How would you describe this grammar?

4 Are you clear what this structure means?   *very clear   a little clear   not clear*
   How would you describe the meaning?

3   Whether a diary or a series of questionnaires is used, choose five or six students (representing a range of abilities within the class), and after each lesson compare their responses to the lessons.

Classroom-based Task 12

Approaches to teaching grammar

Notes

This Task is intended to be used after the Discussion Tasks in this chapter.

Suggestions for procedure

This Task needs to be planned some time in advance since it involves teaching a series of lessons. If questionnaires are used, participants can collaborate on preparing these. They can also collaborate on planning the three lessons.

Three or four participants can be asked to carry out the Task, and to report back to the whole group on their findings at a determined time in the future.

General discussion and possible outcomes

There is a history of evaluating different 'methods' by using tests to ascertain how much learners have learnt. An example of this on a very large scale is the Pennsylvania Project (Smith, 1970).

Such approaches to evaluation are thought to be flawed for a number of reasons. In the first place, it is impossible to 'match' groups exactly. It is also impossible to be certain that differences observed are due to the method itself rather than to characteristics of the teachers who embrace the methods, and moreover it is never possible to be sure that the tests, themselves, are absolutely valid.

For these reasons, this Task does not involve the use of tests to evaluate different approaches to teaching grammar. Instead, it looks at how students in a particular group respond to different approaches. The questionnaire which is suggested does not focus on 'success' of learning in any objective sense, but rather on the attitudes and perceptions of the learners.

287

Notes

If there appears to be some measure of uniformity in the way learners respond in this Task, it may be tempting to generalise on this basis. It is important, however, to consider the factors which may have affected the reactions of the learners. These may include:

1 The unconsciously projected attitude of the teacher (enthusiasm or confidence, or lack of these).
2 The level of the learners.
3 The approaches the learners are used to in their language learning.
4 The approaches which may conform more closely with the general educational traditions of the culture of the learners.

PART C   Resources bank

The *Resources bank* provides materials which participants may use in carrying out some of the Tasks in this book. Where a Task requires the use of a Resource (or a Resource is suggested as an alternative to materials provided by the trainer or by participants themselves), this is made clear in the Task and in the notes which accompany it. (The Resources may all be photocopied for use by participants.)

The *Resources bank* is divided into three sections:

Section 1   Compositions written by learners of English
(Resources 1–5)

Section 2   Schemes of work and lesson plans
(Resources 6–9)

Section 3   Extracts from published materials
(Resources 10–14)

Section 1   Compositions written by learners of English

Resource 1

I have recently seen one good film. It's the name doesn't remember me.

It is the very funny comedy, it talks a middle age woman a little bit bored and dissatisfied by her life. After a ~~xxxx~~ behaviour very normal in her life, suddenly, she decided to go with one friend of her, but without her husband, in Greece for holiday.

After she falls in love with a man Greek. The man had a restaurant and a boarding in a village pittoresque and she started to works for him and did not return to England to her husband.

So after a lots of up and downs her husband decided to go to Greece for pick her and bring her back in England.

Actually I couldn't understand all words in film, and also the accent sometimes was difficult to me, but I could to understand the over all story and some things very funny.

This film really enjoyed me.

Resource 2

I have rent a room very nice "Duchess Room" in Fitzroy Hotel and there will be a bottle of champagne wanting for us and a "Jacuggi" for two. An in the evening we will go to a restaurant very nice and we will be dren very nice. The reason to all this, is. When we went on oure honny mone to the Europe, we slept oure first neigt in London, and it was a very bad notel and room very bad. Then I maybe have some teather tickets and then we will meet with my familie. On another day we have invitet my familie out on a restaurant. So we are going to sleep 2 neigts in my familie's house and 2 neigts on Hotel.

Resource 3

It was a cold and stormy night raining and the wind blew through the road when a very strong thunder screaming splited the sky. Was you could see everything a car was lit up over there in darkness on the road and it seemed there was someone to it! What was he doing? After, suddenly was you could see anything in the city now had fallen back in the darkness the car had disappearenced..!

A few minutes later screamed a second stranger thunder made visible someone with a long black hair beside the car. She was a woman she was alone.... probably was she waiting someone who helped her I thought. Firstly she shuted herself up in the car then I approached the car and knocked at the window.... she stared me... her eyes seemed asking help and being ~~strabo~~ dubtfull at the sometime... then trust in me, unknown man who opened door. A few seconds later she explained me she was whipped out her home from his husband. She decided wait the morning in the car!!

© Cambridge University Press 1993   Martin Parrott: *Tasks for Language Teachers*

Resource 4

I mentioned I didn't to like cinema but I like watching t.v. and I often do that. Last night I saw story about the police who had watch a house that belonged someone's girlfriend who escaped from a jail. They are expecting him he will come to there and visit his girlfriend and in that case they will be able to arrest him. But there happens something very interesting. One of the police gets to know with the girl and after a while they fall in love with each other but the girl doesn't know what is it going on and she descovers this when her ex boyfriend's comes to her. So police attacks to her house to arrest him. Now everything is fine to make a wedding celebrate ~~apsi~~ and they got married together. The story is finish. But don't take muy word and watch out this such a nice film.

4 thornton Lane
cHe/sea . LONDON
bs'

Dear Sir
First of all,
    Thanks for giving me good present.
y it arrived yesterday. when I opend
Jour present, I was surPrised because I
would to buy that before. How did You
Know my intent? I thought you heard
it from my friend who is ALi. anyway
when you have a moment. I want to
see you. I want to talkover aboute
my friend's Party. I'd like giwe
him my Present bute I don't
Know a suitable Presente. en Because
I'm for the fist ttime to give
presente to some one . also I
want to know ford place where
is SHooping area.
    please ring me as soon as posible
I'm looking tord hearing from you.
            Habib

© **Cambridge University Press 1993** Martin Parrott: *Tasks for Language Teachers*

Section 2　Schemes of work and lesson plans

Resource 6
SCHEME A

	MONDAY	TUESDAY	WEDNESDAY	THURSDAY	
Week five	REVISION brainstorm vocabulary ('work') PHONOLOGY match words - word stress SPEAKING p30 discuss super-stitions (prepared for HW) GRAMMAR HAVE as main verb & as auxiliary (HW - p88)	groups to compare HW OHP LISTENING tape about books sts identify covers VOCAB matching ex. p31 - 32 HW read Language Review p36 - 37	GRAMMAR revise Q forms (cards) ex. on p30 READING p31 - finish for HW (hand in tomorrow)	ACCORDING TO NEEDS SPEAKING presentations: – Juan Carlos – Concha	60 mins
Week six	LISTENING p33 + stress exercises SPEAKING/GRAMMAR re-tell (group) reported speech	REVISION language quiz (2 teams or 4?) ACCORDING TO NEEDS HW to listen to news in Spanish, but to make notes in English (bring tomorrow)	LISTENING -World Service News -places -names -numbers sts choose one item for intensive work HW read rest of Lang. Review	ACCORDING TO NEEDS SPEAKING presentations: – Maria Paz – Jorge	60 mins
Week seven	VOCAB/PHONOLOGY sort words into groups according to vowel æ / ɒ / ʌ / REVISION HW - review p34	GRAMMAR/SPEAKING role-play to practise past simple v. continuous – revise grammar – set up role-play (file No. 6) HOMEWORK Ex p45. Sts to find cartoons and bring in tomorrow	GRAMMAR/SPEAKING groups - one st tells story of cartoon - others to identify which one it is ACCORDING TO NEEDS	VOCABULARY p. 39 LISTENING p. 43	60 mins

Teacher: Jack
Material: *Headway Upper Intermediate*, Oxford University Press, 1987

L

Resource 7
SCHEME B

	MONDAY	TUESDAY	WEDNESDAY	THURSDAY	
Week five	p29 SUPERSTITIONS Discussion: – answer questions – look at pics – elicit more Qs – pre-teach vocab p30 Ex 2	p30-31 Reading & question formation Vocab p 32 Test all vocab learned since Monday week 4	p33 Listening HW Students write about a 'ghostly' experience	p34-35 Speaking & writing Homework - finish writing film reviews & study grammar on p36-37	60 mins
Week six	Balloon debate - characters from novels Record, play back & correct mistakes	p37 - 38 Grammar exs in class + discussion of News	Finish grammar in book Language laboratory	UNIT 5 p39 Discussion & vocab - ('Do they know any other means of transport?') Begin reading p41	60 mins
Week seven	Finish reading p41 Do vocab p41-42 NB Take in dictionaries	Speaking & listening p43 'Have any of them had any accidents?'	Grammar exs p44-45 + controlled practice p45 Revision ex p46	Trip to Transport Museum	60 mins

Teacher: Lindsay
Material: *Headway Upper Intermediate*, Oxford University Press, 1987

Resource 8

LESSON A

Class: Beginners	(c.50 hours). Eight men, seven women, all Chinese (not all from Taiwan). They are all professional people and they get on well together as a class. Most of them had actually studied some English at school or university, but were classed as 'beginners' when they came to the institute.
Time: 1hr	
Timetable 'fit':	The class is using <u>Opening Strategies</u>[1] as their coursebook and syllabus. At the moment we are on Unit 7 (introduction of present continuous & revision of present simple). They 'met' the present continuous for the first time in the last lesson but one.
Aims:	To encourage students to feel confident about their ability to understand and to speak English by setting a task within their capability. To provide students with the opportunity to develop their oral fluency. To focus students' attention on the form of the present simple (affirmative, interrogative & negative).
Assumed knowledge:	Use of present simple for routines. Ways of telling the time. Some familiarity with the British Royal Family.

Anticipated problems:	Confusion with present continuous (ask: 'Is this now or every day?' - if necessary write up the following on the board and get the students to explain the difference to each other in Chinese: 'Li speaks Chinese. She is speaking English.').
	    Reluctance to speak in the role play (give them as much time as they want to prepare and let them learn some 'chunks' off by heart if this helps their confidence).
	    'Foreign-ness' of the subject matter (but actually I find that Taiwanese students develop a passionate interest in British Royalty over a period of time).

Materials:	<u>Streamline Departures</u>[2] Unit 32 (Worksheet 1, tape, page of book, and worksheet 2)

[1] Abbs, B. & Freebairn, I. (1982). *Opening Strategies*, Longman.

[2] Hartley, B. & Viney, P. (1978). *Streamline English: Departures*, Oxford University Press.

297

Resource 8

Content: STAGE	PROCEDURE	AIMS
Pre-listening T - S S - T	1 Oral practice. T asks sts: 'What time do you wake up/get up/have breakfast/lunch/dinner/go to bed?' 'What do you do before/after lunch?'	To get sts talking To allow late sts to settle
T - S	2 Pre-teach <u>Duchess</u> (pictures of Royal Family & family tree).	To enable sts to predict her routine
S - S T - S	3 In groups of three sts predict answers to Qs on worksheet 1. T collates predictions on board.	To arouse interest & focus attention
Listening T - S S - S	1 T plays tape. Sts listen to confirm/reject predictions. Sts discuss answers in groups of three. Repeat if necessary.	Practice in listening for detail
S - S	2 Sts listen and fill in gaps (worksheet 2). Repeat as often as necessary. Read complete transcript for sts to check answers.	Practice in closer listening
Grammar S - S	1 In pairs, sts underline examples of simple present. T checks by walking round - OHT with correct underlinings.	Attention to form of simple present
T - S	2 T deals with any problems.	
Role play S - S	1 Divide class into two groups of interviewers & two groups of interviewees. Each group brainstorms & 'rehearses' Qs (interviewers) or answers.	Opportunity to use structure to talk about routines
S - S	2 Reorganise class into pairs: interviewer/interviewee.	Practice
S - S	3 Plenary - interviewers report back to class one aspect of interviewee's routine.	Further practice 'Rounding off'
Homework T - S	Ask students to write an interview with a member of their family (routines).	Consolidation

WORKSHEET 1

The Duchess

Guess the following:

1 She gets up at ....

2 She has lunch at ....

3 She has dinner at ....

4 She goes to bed at ....

5 In the morning she ....

6 In the afternoon she ....

WORKSHEET 2

Duchess: I .... letters and .... the
replies to my secretary.

Duchess: I .... at nine thirty, and I
.... at ten.

Duchess: Well, I .... at seven o'clock.

Duchess: At eleven I .... in the garden
with Philip.

(From Bernard Hartley and Peter Viney: *Streamline English: Departures*, Unit 32, Oxford University Press)

32 An interview

Robin Knight, the television reporter, is interviewing the Duchess of Wessex for the programme 'The English At Home'.

Robin Now, Duchess . . . tell us about an ordinary day in your life.

Duchess Well, I wake up at seven o'clock . . .

Robin Really? Do you get up then?

Duchess No, of course I don't get up at that time. I have breakfast in bed and I read 'The Times'.

Robin What time do you get up?

Duchess I get up at ten.

Robin What do you do then?

Duchess I read my letters and dictate the replies to my secretary.

Robin . . . and then?

Duchess At eleven I walk in the garden with Philip.

Robin Oh? Who's Philip?

Duchess Philip's my dog.

Robin What time do you have lunch?

Duchess I have lunch at twelve thirty.

Robin And after lunch?

Duchess Oh, I rest until six o'clock.

Robin . . . and at six? What do you do at six?

Duchess I dress for dinner. We have dinner at eight o'clock.

Robin What time do you go to bed?

Duchess Well, I have a bath at nine thirty, and I go to bed at ten.

Robin Thank you, Duchess . . . you certainly have a busy and interesting life!

Questions

Who's interviewing the Duchess of Wessex?
Does she wake up at eight o'clock?
Ask "What time?"
Does she have breakfast in the kitchen?
Ask "Where?"
Does she read 'Time' Magazine?
Ask "What?"
Does she read her letters?
Does she dictate the replies to her husband?

Does she walk in the garden with her secretary?
Ask "Who with?"
Does she have lunch at twelve?
Ask "What time?"
What does she do until six?
What does she do at six?
Does she have dinner at seven?
Ask "What time?"
Does she go to bed at nine thirty?
Ask "What time?"

Exercise

A *She reads* 'The Times'.
B *She doesn't read* 'Time' magazine.
C *Does she read* 'The Sun'?

A She walks with her dog.
B . . . with her secretary.
C . . . with her husband?

A She dresses for dinner.
B . . . breakfast.
C . . . lunch?

Resource 9
LESSON B

This is a one-hour class with a group of 20 adolescent Chileans in their second year of studying English (three hours per week). The teacher is also Chilean.	Overall aims: Practice in listening skills: - inferencing - picking out particular details

Procedure

Stage	Time	Aim	Teacher activity	Student activity	Material
1	15 mins	Relax group Revise vocab Sensitise sts to word stress	1 Get all sts to stand around Javier & Maria José's desk. R1 2 Give Javier and MJ a set of cards to match up. R2 3 Get all sts back to their own desks. R3 Give each pair a set of cards. R4 Monitor & help (?). R5 4 (When they have finished) show correct answers on OHT. R6 5 Hum word stress patterns and elicit corresponding vocab items. R7	Watch Javier & Maria José in order to understand what to do in pairs Sort cards Check answers Shout out words	10 sets of cards for matching vocabulary and word stress patterns: hotel ╳ O o open ╳ o O
2	5 mins	Change focus	Collect in homework and answer any questions. R8	Informal chatting (Spanish) – asking questions about HW	
3	c. 30 - 35 mins	To arouse interest in the tape; inferential skills - to encourage sts to piece together the situation Listening in greater detail	1 Tell sts they are going to listen to 3 people talking about their weekends. As soon as they can identify the people put up their hands. Play begining of tape. Repeat above until most sts have some answers. Plenary discussion of answers (in Spanish if necessary). 2 Let sts open their books (p.71) & read Qs, (Ex A) & speculate about the answers. Close books. R9 3 Play whole tape. 4 Monitor groups and help as necessary. R10 Stop students speaking Spanish. R11 (Ex A) Repeat 3 & 4 as necessary. R12 5 Get sts to look at Ex B on p.71 & try to answer from memory. Sts compare answers in groups & identify what they need to know to complete exercise. 6 Play tape again and as many times as necessary. R13	Listening Speaking Speaking Listening Speaking Speaking Listening and comparing answers	Coursebook p.71 (Ex A & B; tape)
If time:		Expand vocabulary Get used to dictionaries	1 Get students to work in groups of 3 on vocabulary exercise. R14 2 Elicit problems and go over correct answers. R15	Speaking/pooling knowledge & using dictionaries	Coursebook p.72 (top of page)
			Remind kids to bring letters from their parents agreeing to the 'English Excursion' R16		

The 'R's refer only to Discussion Task 8.

Section 3   Extracts from published materials

Resource 10

(From Gail Ellis and Barbara Sinclair: *Learning to Learn English*, pp. 6–9, Cambridge University Press)

1.2 What sort of language learner are you?

Try the following quiz. Tick (✓) your answers to the questions.

	Usually	Sometimes	(Almost) never	Don't know
1. Did/do you get good results in grammar tests?				
2. Do you have a good memory for new words?				
3. Do you hate making mistakes?				
4. In class, do you get irritated if mistakes are not corrected?				
5. Is your pronunciation better when you read aloud than when you have a conversation?				
6. Do you wish you had more time to think before speaking?				
7. Did/do you enjoy being in a class?				
8. Do you find it difficult to pick up more than two or three words of a new language when you are on holiday abroad?				
9. Do you like to learn new grammar rules, words, etc. by heart?				

How to calculate your score:

Score: 3 points for each *Usually*
      2 points for each *Sometimes*
      1 point for each *Almost never* or *never*
      0 points for each *Don't know*

Total score: [ ]

Now read the appropriate comments on pages 8–9.

1.2   What sort of language learner are you?

Score: 23-27 points Analytic?

You may feel it is very important to be as accurate as possible all the time. You probably prefer the sort of language learning where you need to think carefully: for example, when you are doing grammar exercises, working out the meanings of words, practising pronunciation, etc. This is very often the sort of language learning you do in class or when you are studying alone.

You may be able to improve your language learning. Look at the following suggestions.

Score: 14-22 A mixture?

You may find that you do not fall exactly into either of the categories marked *Analytic?* or *Relaxed?*. Many people are a mixture and learn in different ways at different times depending on the situation and what they are doing.

Suggestion

Look at the descriptions for *Analytic?* and *Relaxed?*. You may find that you are more similar to one than the other and this could help you to think about what areas of your learning you might improve. If you can't decide now, try to do this during your course.

Suggestions

You could improve your fluency by:
- *trying to speak more*
  For example, try talking to English-speaking friends, tourists, etc. as often as possible.
- *not worrying too much about your mistakes*
  Trying to be correct all the time is hard work and can stop you from communicating well. Although making mistakes is an important part of the learning process, don't always try to correct yourself immediately. Remember that the people you speak to won't be listening for your mistakes, but for what you are trying to say. After you have finished speaking, you can usually remember the mistakes you want to work on; this is a good time to make a note to yourself to do something about them.
- *depending on yourself*
  Outside the classroom you won't always have a dictionary or a teacher to help you, so don't be afraid to depend on yourself: you probably know more than you think.

Score: 0-8 points Not sure?

Your score does not mean that you are not a good language learner. Perhaps this is the first time you have thought about the way you learn. To know more about this can be very useful in helping you to become a more effective language learner.

Suggestion

You can find out some general information about learning languages by looking at the descriptions marked *Analytic?* and *Relaxed?*. During your course, try to become more aware of the ways you learn. This can help you decide which areas of your learning you might improve.

1.2 What sort of language learner are you?

Score: 9-13 points   Relaxed?

You seem to 'pick up' languages without really making too much effort and you usually enjoy communicating with people. You may sometimes feel, however, that you should be learning more grammar rules, but you probably don't enjoy this and quickly lose interest.

You may be able to improve your language learning. Look at the following suggestions.

Suggestions

- *try finding more time to learn*
  You may need to spend more time thinking about and practising things like grammar, pronunciation, etc. Try to organise a regular time for learning.
- *try being more self-critical*
  You probably need to correct yourself more. You may not worry or even notice when you make mistakes, but if you try to become more aware of the mistakes you make regularly, you may find it easier to do something about them.

Note: You may like to try this quiz again after you have done some more learning, to compare the results.

Resource 11

(From Michael Swan and Catherine Walter: *The New Cambridge English Course 2*, p. 50, Cambridge University Press)

16
Here is the news

1 🔊 The following sentences are taken from a news broadcast. There are mistakes in ten of the sentences. Listen to the broadcast and see how many you can find.

1. President and Mrs Martin of Outland have just arrived in Fantasia for a state visit, which is expected to last three weeks.
2. Dr Rask has known Mrs Martin since their student days at the University of Goroda.
3. Dr Rask has just left for an overseas fact-finding tour.
4. Dr Rask is President of 'Families against Hunger', and for the last six days he has been visiting Third World countries.
5. Demonstrations are continuing against the proposed dam on the Upper Fant river, and demonstrators have been marching through the centre of San Fantastico for several hours.
6. Traffic in Wesk Square has not been able to move since half past eight this morning, and motorists are advised to avoid the city centre.
7. Heavy snow has been falling steadily for the past four weeks.
8. The River Fant has just burst its banks in North Milltown, and most of the town centre is under water.
9. Vegetable prices in San Fantastico have been going up steadily for the last ten days.
10. The Minister for Consumer Affairs has just announced that price controls on vegetables and meat will come into effect next week.
11. The Fantasian grotnik has risen to its highest level against the Outland dollar since last July: the exchange rate is now 1.32 dollars to the grotnik.
12. The fire which has been burning in Grand North Station for the last three days is now under control.
13. Three more firemen have been taken to hospital.

(From Michael Swan and Catherine Walter: *The New Cambridge English Course 2 Teacher's Book*, p. 50, Cambridge University Press)

---

1 News broadcast: finding discrepancies
- Let students look briefly through the thirteen sentences. Don't explain too much vocabulary – students do not have to understand every word to do the exercise.
- Play the recording right through once without stopping, and ask students whether they noticed any differences between the spoken and printed versions.
- Then play it again section by section, pausing for students to note the differences.
- Let them compare notes in groups.

Answers to Exercise 1
1. The state visit is expected to last three *days*.
2. Dr Rask has known *President Martin* since their student days.
3. Dr Rask has just *returned* from an overseas fact-finding tour.
4. Dr Rask has been visiting Third World countries for the last six *weeks*.
5. Correct.
6. Traffic in Wesk Square has been *very slow*.
7. *Rain* has been falling.
8. *Parts* of the town centre are under water.
9. Correct.
10. There will be price controls on vegetables and *fruit*.
11. The exchange rate is now *1.23* dollars to the grotnik.
12. The fire is in Grand *South* Station.
13. Correct.

Tapescript for Exercise 1

FBC Radio 2. Here is the news for today, Wednesday 25th April, at eleven a.m.

President and Mrs Martin of Outland have just arrived in Fantasia for a state visit. This is the first official visit by an Outland head of state since the end of the War of Independence in 1954, and it is expected to last three days. The President and her husband were at the airport to welcome President and Mrs Martin, who are old friends of theirs: Mrs Rask and Mrs Martin first met at the 1960 Olympics, in which Mrs Rask won a silver medal for the high jump, and Mrs Martin represented Outland in the 100 metres. Dr Rask has known President Martin since their student days at the University of Goroda.

Dr Rask has just returned from an overseas fact-finding tour. For the last six weeks, he has been visiting Third World countries in his capacity as President of 'Families against Hunger'. Speaking at a press conference shortly after his return, Dr Rask said that increased aid to the Third World was an urgent priority.

Demonstrations are continuing against the proposed dam on the Upper Fant river, and demonstrators have been marching through the centre of San Fantastico for several hours. Traffic in Wesk Square has been very slow since half past eight this morning, and motorists are advised to avoid the city centre.

The heavy rain which has been falling steadily for the past four weeks has caused widespread flooding. The River Fant has just burst its banks in North Milltown, and parts of the town centre are under water. The bad weather has ruined many vegetable crops, and vegetable prices in San Fantastico have been going up steadily for the last ten days. The Minister for Consumer Affairs has just announced that price controls on vegetables and fruit will come into effect next week.

Foreign exchange. The Fantasian grotnik has risen to its highest level against the Outland dollar since last July. The exchange rate is now 1.23 dollars to the grotnik.

The fire which has been burning in Grand South Station for the last three days is now under control. The origin of the fire, which started in the station restaurant on Sunday, is still unknown. Three more firemen were overcome by smoke this morning, and have been taken to hospital.

And now the weather. Heavy rain will continue in most parts of the country, (fade).

Resource 12

(From Marion Geddes: *Fast Forward 3*, pp. 54–6, Oxford University Press)

Rural Schools

1 Dotted around the British Isles are several tiny rural primary schools with only one teacher and a few pupils. Below is a list of characteristics of small rural schools. Discuss each characteristic and decide whether it constitutes an advantage or a drawback. Add any others to the list that you can think of.

> **Characteristics of small rural schools**
> The children:
>   have a flexible timetable
>   get individual attention
>   enjoy few facilities, e.g. for sport, science etc.
>   live near the school
>   have few playmates of the same age and sex
>   have the world of nature on their school doorstep

2 Now read the article 'Small-Scale Schools'. As you read it:

1 label each school on the map of the British Isles below.
2 for each school, name the single most important advantage the pupils appear to have.

3 Would you like to have been a pupil in a small rural school? Why/Why not?

4 Would you like to be a teacher in one of the schools described in the article? Why/Why not?

Imagine being in a school with only two or three pupils. HELEN PICKLES reports

Mousonmere Beach, Herm.

Rhum

Shetland Islands

Orkney Islands

Outer Hebrides

Inner Hebrides

Channel Islands
Guernsey

Key:
x = rural school

HERM

'In cities it takes a long time to walk to school, but it only takes me 30 seconds,' claimed Sarah Osborne, 7. Her school-teacher has the longest journey – a 12-minute hike up the hill. And that's a long walk on an island only 1½ miles long by ½ mile wide. Herm Island (pop. 40), is one of the smallest Channel Islands: 'There aren't any roads to cross because there aren't any cars.' Pupils on small islands have definite advantages, said Ann Scholl, 5: 'At a big school they have a hall where they do games but here we go down to the beach.'

'We can easily go and see all the wild life,' agreed Gareth Murray, 10. 'Curlews, puffins and oystercatchers, for example, then we come back to school and write about them.'

Once a week, the six pupils go to a school on Guernsey and join a class of their own age group, but the best part is the boat journey there and back. Said 7-year-old Russell Swann: 'I like it when we come back and it's rough, but my teacher hates it.'

SUTHERLAND

If Mary Ann, 6, turns up at school just 5 seconds late, it's immediately noticed. When teacher Mrs Jolly asks the class a question she always looks at Mary

Ann. When you're the only pupil in the school there's not a great deal you can do.

Mary Ann Grant's father is a keeper on a remote Highland estate in Sutherland. There isn't a school nearby so the education authority decided to give her her own teacher and schoolroom. 'I thought it would be the easiest job I had ever done,' said Mrs Jolly, 'but that soon changed. I have to take the part of another pupil, really, and it can be very exhausting. We might be doing arithmetic and suddenly a bird appears at the window, so we start a discussion about that.' Mrs Jolly is also learning things from Mary Ann: 'She teaches me about the stags and also tells me some of the Highland folklore.'

RHUM

'There's only one classroom in our school because the room next door is used as the church.' Sandra Mackay, 10, has just five classmates at her school on the Hebridean island of Rhum. This whole island is a nature reserve so red deer, feral goats and grey seals are a common sight. The pupils know they're lucky but small schools have their drawbacks.

'I like this school, but I do miss other boys to play with,' said Peter Mackay, the only boy in the school. Sports are also a problem. 'We have to improvise a lot,' said teacher Miss McMullen. 'We play badminton in the community hall, but the ceiling's a bit low.'

'Sometimes we go out in Land-Rovers,' said Beth Johnson. 'There are no cars here, the roads are too stony. Recently we went to look at a "shieling" where the crofting women lived in the summer to look after the sheep.'

PAPA STOUR

On Papa Stour – just off Shetland – the days are much shorter in winter so, when it gets dark, the school lessons finish for the day. The timetable has to alter with the seasons because the island is so far north. The six pupils, aged 4 to 8, are each given separate work to do for most subjects. 'But the timetable is very flexible and tends to fit around TV and radio programmes,' said teacher Mrs Buggy. Her husband helps out by teaching art, and he is also the school cook specialising in pizzas.

What do the pupils miss most on the island? 'Ice-cream!' they all cried. 'It has to come from the mainland and by the time it gets here it's melted.'

From *The Observer*

Resource 13

(From Penny Ur, *Discussions that Work*, p. 55, Cambridge University Press)

Resource 14

(From Brian Abbs and Ingrid Freebairn: *Building Strategies*, pp. 84–7, Longman)

Unit 12 Home again!

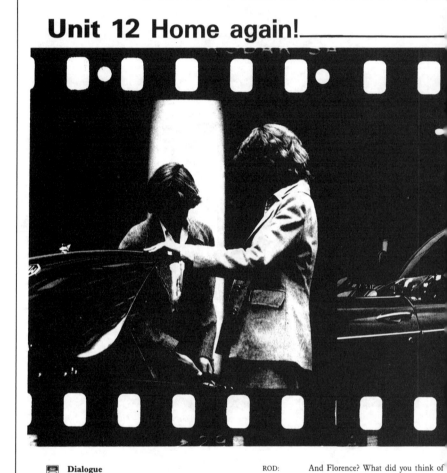

▣ Dialogue

ROD: Hello, Barbara! Welcome back! You look marvellous.

BARBARA: Rod! What a surprise! It's lovely to see you again.

ROD: Sorry I didn't telephone you before you left, but I didn't have time, in fact ...

BARBARA: Oh, that's all right. Forget it!

ROD: Well, how was Italy?

BARBARA: Fun, but tiring. Milan was interesting. It's bigger than I expected. Noisier and dirtier, too.

ROD: And Florence? What did you think of Florence?

BARBARA: Well, I've never been there before. I thought it was beautiful. More beau‍[tiful] than Paris, in fact. Have you ever bee‍[n] to Italy?

ROD: No, never. I'd really like to go to Rom‍[e] Well, the car's in the car park. Is this your luggage?

BARBARA: Yes, but the suitcase is very heavy.

ROD: Barbara! What's in it? Stones?

BARBARA: No, just twenty pairs of shoes! Oh, i‍[t's] nice to see you again, Rod!

84

314

Set 1 Apologies

> 1. Sorry I didn't telephone you, but I didn't have time.
>   Oh, that's all right. Forget it!

Apologise for	Explanations
a) not doing your homework	You forgot. didn't have time. lost your book.
b) missing the train	You didn't wake up in time. couldn't get a taxi. Your watch was slow. timetable was out of date.
c) not writing while you were away	You forgot. were very busy. lost the address.
d) not meeting your friend as you had arranged	You overslept. got the time of arrival wrong. had to help your parents.

Work in pairs. Make apologies to your partner, choosing different explanations. Your partner accepts your apology like this:
Sorry I didn't do my homework, but I forgot.
Oh, that's all right.

2. Roleplay these situations in pairs.
a) Apologise and explain to a friend why you didn't come to classes last week.
b) Apologise and explain to a friend why you didn't write or telephone him/her while you were away in London.
c) Apologise and explain to your employer why you arrived half an hour late for work this morning.

:
e did Rod meet Barbara?
didn't Rod telephone
ara before she left?
did he say when he
gised?
did Barbara think of Italy?
did she think of Milan?
Rod ever been to Italy?
e's Rod's car?
is Barbara's suitcase heavy?
rbara pleased to see Rod?

85

315

Resource 14

Unit 12
Set 2 Comparisons

> **1.** Milan is bigger than I expected. Noisier and
> dirtier, too.
> I think Florence is more beautiful than Paris.

FACTS ABOUT PLACES, PEOPLE AND THINGS

size		depth		width	
big	bigger	deep	deeper	narrow	narrower
large	larger			wide	wider
small	smaller				
thin	thinner				

temperature		height		length	
hot	hotter	tall	taller	long	longer
warm	warmer	high	higher	wide	wider
mild	milder	short	shorter		
cool	cooler				
cold	colder				

OPINIONS ABOUT PLACES, PEOPLE AND THINGS

dirty	dirtier	good	better	fast	faster
clean	cleaner	bad	worse	slow	slower
noisy	noisier	lively	livelier	fat	fatter
ugly	uglier	dull	duller		
		cheap	cheaper		

beautiful	more/less beautiful
interesting	more/less interesting
depressing	more/less depressing
expensive	more/less expensive
exciting	more/less exciting

Compare the features of countries like this:
China/large/Japan   China is larger than Japan.

1. England/small/France
2. London/big/Rome
3. Skyscrapers in New York/tall/buildings in London
4. The River Avon/short/the Thames
5. The Mississippi/long/the Nile
6. Mount Everest/high/Mont Blanc
7. The South of France/hot/the North
8. The Mediterranean/warm/the North Sea
9. The air at night/cool/the sea at night
10. Winters in Scandinavia/cold/the winters in Europe
11. English winters/mild/Scottish winters
12. The Aegean/warm/the Baltic

**2. Compare your country with any other country
you know well. Compare these features:**

population	roads	geographical features
climate	people	(mountains, rivers, lakes)
cities and towns	food	*anything else*
the standard of		

86 living

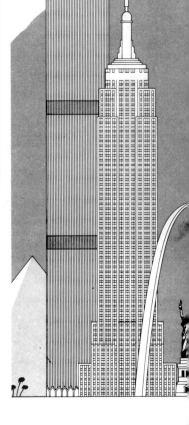

© Longman Group UK Ltd 1984

316

Unit 12

3. In pairs, read your comparisons to your partner. Your partner agrees, disagrees or responds like this:

Spain is larger than Portugal, isn't it?
Yes, that's true.
And the people in Portugal are livelier than the people in Spain.
Yes, I agree. *or* No, I don't agree. I think the people in Spain are livelier.
However, the food in Spain is less expensive than the food in Portugal.
Really? That's interesting. I didn't know that.

4. What comparisons would you make to a friend who can't decide between:

1. taking a boating holiday down the Rhine in Germany	AND	taking a walking holiday in the English Lake District?

(useful adjectives: *beautiful, warm, cold, cheap, relaxing*)

2. travelling by train through Europe	AND	travelling by car through Europe?

(cheap, fast, comfortable, relaxing)

3. wanting a career as a doctor	AND	wanting a career as a social worker?

(interesting, well-paid, rewarding)

4. joining a dance exercise (aerobics) class	AND	taking up jogging?

(energetic, sociable, difficult, fun, expensive, snobbish)

Make comparisons like this:
It's warmer in Germany than in the Lake District. And it's more beautiful too.
On the other hand, camping is less relaxing.

5. Test your knowledge!
1. Which is bigger, Concorde or a Boeing 747?
2. Which is older, the Pyramids or Stonehenge?
3. Which is taller, the Empire State Building or the World Trade Centre?
4. Which is more fattening, a quarter of a glass of whisky or a whole glass of milk?
5. Which is nearer the earth, Venus or Mars?
6. Which is less fattening, a glass of wine or a glass of beer?
7. Which runs faster, a cheetah or an antelope?
8. Which is larger, the Taj Mahal or St Peter's in the Vatican?

87

Bibliography

Abbs, B. & Freebairn, I. (1982). *Opening Strategies*. Longman.

Abbs, B. & Freebairn, I. (second edition 1984). *Building Strategies*. Longman.

Allwright, R. & Bailey, K. (1991). *Focus on the Language Classroom*. Cambridge University Press.

Bolitho, R. & Tomlinson, B. (1980). *Discover English*. Heinemann.

Brown, G. & Yule, G. (1983). *Teaching the Spoken Language*. Cambridge University Press.

Brumfit, C. & Mitchell, R. (1989). *ELT Documents 133. The Language Classroom as a Focus for Research*. Modern English Publications in association with the British Council.

Bygate, M. (1987). *Speaking*. Oxford University Press.

Byrne, D. (1987). *Techniques for Classroom Interaction*. Longman.

Byrne, D. (second edition 1988). *Teaching Writing Skills*. Longman.

Collie, J. & Slater, J. (1987). *Literature in the Language Classroom*. Cambridge University Press.

Davis, P. & Rinvolucri, M. (1988). *Dictation*. Cambridge University Press.

Dickinson, L. (1987). *Self-instruction in Language Learning*. Cambridge University Press.

Duff, T. (ed.) (1988). *Explorations in Teacher Training*. Longman.

Edge, J. (1989). *Mistakes and Correction*. Longman.

Ellis, M. & Ellis, P. (1985). *Counterpoint Coursebook – Beginners*. Nelson.

Ellis, G. & Sinclair, B. (1989). *Learning to Learn English*. Cambridge University Press.

Ellis, R. (1985). *Understanding Second Language Acquisition*. Oxford University Press.

Ellis, R. (1986). Activities and Procedures for Teacher Training. *ELT Journal*, **40**, 2.

Geddes, M. (1986). *Fast Forward 3*. Oxford University Press.

Gower, R. & Walters, S. (1983). *A Teaching Practice Book*. Heinemann.

Grabe, W. (1991). Current Developments in Second Language Research. *TESOL Quarterly*, **25**, 3.

Grellet, F. (1981). *Developing Reading Skills*. Cambridge University Press.

Hartley, B. & Viney, P. (1978). *Streamline English: Departures*. Oxford University Press.

Harmer, J. (second edition 1991). *The Practice of English Language Teaching*. Longman.

Hedge, T. (1985). *Using Readers in Language Teaching*. Macmillan.

Hedge, T. (1988). *Writing*. Oxford University Press.

International Teacher Training Institute London. (Eleventh edition 1991). RSA Diploma (DTEFLA) Distance Training Programme Course Materials.

Krashen, S. D. & Terrell, T. (1983). *The Natural Approach*. Pergamon.

Leech, G. (second edition 1987). *Meaning and the English Verb*. Longman.

Littlewood, W. (1984). *Foreign and Second Language Learning*. Cambridge University Press.

McLaughlin, B. (1987). *Theories of Second Language Learning*. Edward Arnold.

Maingay, P. (1988). Observation for Training, Development or Assessment? In T. Duff (ed.), *Explorations in Teacher Training*, Longman.

Malamah-Thomas, A. (1987). *Classroom Interaction*. Oxford University Press.

Norrish, J. (1983). *Language Learners and their Errors*. Macmillan.

Nunan, D. (1989). *Designing Tasks for the Communicative Classroom*. Cambridge University Press.

Nunan, D. (1989). *Understanding Language Classrooms*. Prentice Hall.

Nuttall, C. (1982). *Teaching Reading Skills in a Foreign Language*. Heinemann.

Pawley, A. & Syder, F. (1983). Two Puzzles for Linguistic Theory: Native-like Selection and Native-like Fluency. In J. C. Richards and R. W. Schmidt (eds.), *Language and Communication*. Longman.

Pincas, A. (1982). *Teaching English Writing*. Macmillan.

Prabhu, N. S. (1987). *Second Language Pedagogy*. Oxford University Press.

Richards, J. C. (1990). *The Language Teaching Matrix*. Cambridge University Press.

Richards, J. C. & Rodgers, T. S. (1986). *Approaches and Methods in Language Teaching*. Cambridge University Press.

Rixon, S. (1986). *Developing Listening Skills*. Macmillan.

Skehan, P. (1989). *Individual Differences in Second Language Learning*. Edward Arnold.

Smith, P. (1970). *A Comparison of the Cognitive and Audio-lingual Approaches to Foreign Language Instruction: The Pennsylvania Foreign Language Project*. Center for Curriculum Development.

Soars, J. & Soars, L. (1987). *Headway Upper Intermediate*. Oxford University Press.

Swan, M. & Walter, C. (1990). *The New Cambridge English Course Student's Book 2* and *Teacher's Book 2*. Cambridge University Press.

Underwood, M. (1987). *Effective Class Management*. Longman.

Underwood, M. (1989). *Teaching Listening*. Longman.

Ur, P. (1981). *Discussions that Work*. Cambridge University Press.

Ur, P. (1984). *Teaching Listening Comprehension*. Cambridge University Press.

Wallace, M. J. (1991). *Training Foreign Language Teachers*. Cambridge University Press.

Wajnryb, R. (1992). *Classroom Observation Tasks*. Cambridge University Press.

Wenden, A. & Rubin, J. (eds.) (1987). *Learner Strategies in Language Learning*. Prentice Hall.

Widdowson, H. G. (1990). *Aspects of Language Teaching*. Oxford University Press.

Wilkins, D. (1976). *Notional Syllabuses*. Oxford University Press.

Woodward, T. (1991). *Models and Metaphors in Language Teacher Training*. Cambridge University Press.

Index

Page numbers printed in bold refer to the Tasks in Part B of the book. Other page numbers refer to Part A or to the notes which accompany the Tasks in Part B.